THE LOST ALGONQUIN ROUND TABLE

HUMOR, FICTION, JOURNALISM, CRITICISM AND POETRY FROM AMERICA'S MOST FAMOUS LITERARY CIRCLE

EDITED BY
NAT BENCHLEY AND KEVIN C. FITZPATRICK

IUNIVERSE, INC.
NEW YORK   BLOOMINGTON

The Lost Algonquin Round Table
Humor, Fiction, Journalism, Criticism and Poetry
From America's Most Famous Literary Circle

iUniverse books may be ordered through booksellers or by contacting:

iUniverse
1663 Liberty Drive
Bloomington, IN 47403
www.iuniverse.com
1-800-Authors (1-800-288-4677)

Because of the dynamic nature of the Internet, any Web addresses or links contained in this book may have changed since publication and may no longer be valid.

ISBN: 978-1-4401-5151-4 (sc)
ISBN: 978-1-4401-5152-1 (dj)
ISBN: 978-1-4401-5153-8 (ebk)

Printed in the United States of America

iUniverse rev. date: 6/26/2009

My work on this book is dedicated to Tracy and Clayton and Christopher, whose father thought they should know why these people mattered ...

And to Kathy, who tolerates my diversions and even thinks some of them salutary.

—N. R. B.

To Christina, for her patience and unflagging support ...

And to my friends in the Dorothy Parker Society, may you continue to keep the spirit of the Jazz Age alive.

—Kevin C. Fitzpatrick

Acknowledgments

The editors gratefully acknowledge the following for their support and assistance:

A very low bow (rhymes with "how," not "know") of thanks to Jack Ziegler for his artistic ingenuity in creating an [sic] unique cover.

Anthony Adams

Christina Hensler Fitzpatrick

Valerie & Donald Fitzpatrick

Kate Pulitzer Freedberg

Nathaniel Freedberg

Marion Meade

Karolyn Milton

Abbey Potter

Darcie Posz

Stuart Y. Silverstein

The Algonquin Hotel

Men's Health

The New York Public Library

And, finally, Nat's gratitude to Kevin for propelling this project. May he keep the fires burning.

Contents

Foreword / Nat Benchley. xiii
The Myth of the Algonquin Round Table / George S. Kaufman 1

THE COLUMNISTS

The Power of the Press / Robert Benchley 3
Ruth vs. Roth / Heywood Broun. 4
Rustlings of Spring / Robert Benchley. 6
Buying a Farm / Heywood Broun 9
The New York Type / Dorothy Parker 15
Why I Am Not A Well-Dressed Man / Heywood Broun 18
From "The Diary of Our Own Samuel Pepys" / Franklin P. Adams 22

VICE

How I Lost My Fight With Nicotine / Heywood Broun 25
Reformers: A Hymn Of Hate / Dorothy Parker. 28
Bootleg / John V. A. Weaver 31
The Passing of the Thanatopsis / Alexander Woollcott. 35
It Was Originally the Thanatopsis Inside Straight and Pleasure Club /
    Franklin P. Adams. 42

VENUS & MARS

Men I'm Not Married To / Dorothy Parker. 47
Women I'm Not Married To / Franklin P. Adams 56
A Little Later / Marc Connelly 65
Saying It With Flowers / Franklin P. Adams. 66
Mame / John V. A. Weaver 69
The Art of Fascinating / Franklin P. Adams 72

THE CRITICS

Chaplin and Shakespeare, Eccentric Comedians / Robert Benchley 75
Second Thoughts on First Nights: John Barrymore / Alexander
    Woollcott. 79
The Silent Drama / Robert E. Sherwood. 82

The Theatre Program Reviewed / Robert Benchley 84
The Higher Education on the Screen / Robert Sherwood 87
Words and Music / Robert Benchley 92
The Blood Lust on Broadway / Robert E. Sherwood 94
The Actor's the Thing / Robert Benchley .95
The Cinema Primer / Robert E. Sherwood 97
French, English, American / Robert Benchley 99
From "It Seems To Me" / Heywood Broun 101
Jacob Ben-Ami in "Samson and Delilah" / Dorothy Parker 103
A Shelf of Recent Books / Ruth Hale. 107
Celluloid Psychology / Laurence Stallings 109
Second Thoughts on First Nights / Alexander Woollcott 115

MUSIC

The Indian Song Game / The Vicious Circle 119
Swing Music / Robert Benchley. 120
Crooning / Robert Benchley 122
Mr. Whiteman Experiments / Deems Taylor 124
The Other Side of Al Jolson / George S. Kaufman. 126

SHORT FICTION

Old Man Minick / Edna Ferber. 133
Manicure / Margaret Leech 154
Such A Pretty Little Picture / Dorothy Parker 166
The Cub Reporter / Frank Sullivan 176
Turn Out the Guard / Laurence Stallings. 179

VERSE

Women: A Hate Song / Dorothy Parker 199
The Gunman and the Debutante / Dorothy Parker 201
Song of the Open Country / Dorothy Parker 202
Love Song / Dorothy Parker 203
The Flapper / Dorothy Parker 204
Élégie Américaine / John V. A. Weaver .205
Carpe Diem / John V. A. Weaver. 207
When I'm All Through / John V. A. Weaver 208
A Tennis Player's Garden of Verses / Franklin P. Adams 209
Revised / Franklin P. Adams 210

A Wish / Franklin P. Adams. 210
Mr. Irving Berlin Rewrites "Paradise Lost" / Franklin P. Adams. . .211
Journalism / Franklin P. Adams. 212
Palm Beach / Franklin P. Adams 213
Precocity / Franklin P. Adams 214
To Dorothy Parker Campbell, And Alan / Franklin P. Adams 215

Not Really

The Courtship of Miles Standish, In the Manner of F. Scott Fitzgerald
   / Donald Ogden Steward 217
The Rapeseed Oil Letters / Robert Benchley 225
Style Hints for Meticulous Paupers / Frank Sullivan 226
Ivy Oration / Robert Benchley 229
Life's Calendar For December 1921 / Marc Connelly and George S.
   Kaufman. 234
The Iron Pipe Ad / Robert Benchley 238
Have You Tried the New Memory Courses? / Robert Benchley . . .239
My Invisible Cloak / Franklin P. Adams. 243
The Woolen Mitten Situation / Robert Benchley. 245

Biographical Sketches 251

A Note on the Text. 261

For Further Reading. 269

Web Sites 275

About the Editors & Cover Artist. 277

Nat Benchley

Foreword

So, why should we care about a pack of tipsy quipsters who frolicked ninety years ago, I hear you asking?

Why should we bother to read "lost" works of a gang of "vicious wits" long since dead?

What possible application can poems and essays and criticisms and columns from several generations ago have for us today?

And wasn't this "Algonquin Round Table" just a myth anyway? George S. Kaufman, one of the alleged founders, seems to think so (see "The Myth of the Algonquin Round Table").

Haven't they been collected and anthologized and analyzed and scrutinized and plagiarized to death? What new can there be?

Well, as it turns out, plenty. So, now will you stop asking all those questions, please?

Because, you see, the easy stuff, the highly witty, visible and memorable writings and quippings and eviscerations of the Round Table gang have been pored over for decades. (For those deficient in researching skills, we will provide some citations—or, as you youngsters call them, "links"—to some of these works later in this volume.) Their bon mots have been anthologized and paraphrased and bowdlerized since the Nineteen Twenties. Whether attributions are correct is by now absolutely a moot point, because the mere repetition has locked certain phrases and citations in history. There is no longer any point in trying to figure out who really said, "You can lead a horticulture, but you can't make her think." Because it is Dorothy Parker's for all time.

There are so many reiterations of the familiar stuff that stages overflow with plays and musicals rearranging the material in endless variations. (We, ourself, are guilty of one form of this. But we at least hope we have contributed something new to the lore. We do, after all, have a certain inside track on some of the participants.) Still, there continue to crop up new offerings almost monthly. If Kevin had a quarter for every one-woman play about Dorothy Parker he has been asked to read or see, well, he wouldn't be wearing cast-offs from St. Vincent DePaul, that's for sure. Even a cursory Internet search will turn up references to the individual members and the collective legend in just about every literate society. (One scholar even offered to write an exegesis on "The Wit of the Round Table as Foretold in the Elder Icelandic Edda," but we found his research fees too exorbitant.)

And the good stuff is truly good and memorable and quote-worthy. Why else would so many creative writers in so many different fields find it advantageous to quote bits (or steal entire passages) from this small gang of prolific poets, punsters, pundits and profligates?

But, still, the legend persists that their fame far eclipsed their merit. They became so famous for such a short, glorious, infamous period of time that some people think of them as comets who blazed across the sky and then evanesced without leaving a trace. And if all you have read or heard about them ranges [alphabetically] from FPA's "what this country needs is a good five-cent nickel" to Woollcott's "all the things I really like to do are either immoral, illegal or fattening," then you might believe that, too. So a large part of our *raison d'écrire* is to cut through the gin-soaked fog, dash around the flying quips and settle on some long-lost treasures of (mostly) greater length than a pun. (Where you might rate "The Indian Song Game" depends on whether you take them individually or as a collection.)

Despite all the carping that the attention paid to the collective wit of the Round Table was excessive and undeserved, one must (well, this one must, at least) admit that any group which can garner as many Pulitzer Prizes and Academy Awards as this must have done something right. Even if a lot of the meritorious writing was accomplished after they stopped meeting for lunch every day, you cannot imagine that talent suddenly flowed from an arid source. There must have been inherent intelligence there, even if it was glossed over during "the ten-year lunch." Which is why we wanted to go back and look at the unheralded writing.

Part of the problem is that there exists so much of their recorded writing that it takes dedicated (or foolish) editors and critics to sort through it, admit that it is not all gold and pull out the truly relevant.

It has been our pleasure to perform this task on your behalf.

One of the reasons we like some of the pieces included here is that many were written before the fame and acclaim, during a time of innocence and (dare I say it?) giddiness. Before the round table was The Round Table, and before the members' every move was chronicled in columns and diaries, they were writers, many struggling to make a living. They were writing about what interested them, not just what they might be paid to pay attention to. They were experimenting with form. They were stretching their literary muscles and trying to find a style. (At one point, after the fame and acclaim had intruded, Robert Benchley was asked to define his "style." He replied, "I don't know enough words to have a 'style.'" He was only half joking, even though generations of writers have since emulated his style.) And they weren't afraid to demonstrate their intelligence. I have been pleasantly surprised several times during the research to discover some wonderfully literate and thoughtful pieces containing no (or few) quips and some insightful analysis (see "Chaplin and Shakespeare, Eccentric Comedians"). Even I can be distracted from the depth of their education and erudition. Part of the reason for this is my grandfather's concerted efforts to hide his erudition in pursuit of his image as an idler: in his suite at the Royalton Hotel in New York, he used to read texts in German, but he kept them in the closet in between readings, so that no one would think him pretentious. Several of the others made similar efforts to downplay their intellect (some with unimagined success).

Another (unintentional) lesson to be learned from reading these wordsmiths and noticing their influence on contemporary writing is the viability of emulating, copying or even blatantly ripping off past masters. After so many millions of words have been written, it is exceedingly hard to be original. All artists look for inspiration in what has been created in their field. So it would behoove anyone striving for creative or original writing to study good, clean writing. Once that is mastered, then an innovative writer is free to take off and do it his or her own way. But just setting off to write ... stuff ... that may or may not hold together creates incomprehensible chaos. Even such masters of good writing as James Thurber and E. B. White—associates but not members of the Vicious Circle—admitted that they often found themselves half-way through a piece thinking it had been done, and better done, by some of their predecessors at *The New Yorker*.

It is very much in the same vein as good clowns, who must be physically adept before they can safely simulate total clumsiness. The really good ones, the Buster Keatons and the Bill Irwins, are agile and nimble before they appear clumsy and lead-footed.

My immediate paternal forebear always used to harp on me to read E. B. White. I wish I had listened to that advice a lot earlier. My father (no mean slouch at writing himself) was in awe of White's ability to derive the maximum impact from the minimum number of words. (I can still hear my father droning in my ears, "Forget adverbs!"—and he would sometimes append, "Unless you're writing Tom Swifties.") If the pieces collected here do not all rise to the level of White's brilliance (what does?), they at least share (or, in some cases, foretell) his affection for terseness and gentility of purpose. Reading these carefully crafted compositions just highlights the thinness of much of the unfiltered blather that passes as writing today. Many bloggers and other purveyors of words for public consumption would do very well to read some of these offerings and learn how much more effective fewer, better chosen words can be. There is little need to cut through clutter in these offerings: They have mostly been trimmed to the optimum length, with no fat to spare.

And, just to complete the möbius strip of good writers reading good writers, we may consider the connections between some of the masters (Twain, Leacock, Benchley, Kaufman, White, Thurber, Perelman, Gibbs, Angell, Newhart, Baker, Muir, Trillin, Allen, Keillor, Barry, Sedaris), all of whom admit to reading, studying and—in some rare cases—ripping off their predecessors. And all to great effect.

Don't get me wrong; this collection does not have to be studied. This is not a scholarly tome on which there will be a Very Important Test later on. But it is hoped (by the editors and their former teachers) that in reading these salutary writings, some of today's (active and/ or aspiring) writers may learn something beneficial, either through absorption, osmosis or, perhaps, photosynthesis.

One of the joys of putting together such a collection is in the research. With a singular purpose in mind, we have set out to read hundreds of pieces and poems and criticisms and fripperies, in order to offer you some new/old gems. Not every one of these will excite or exhilarate every reader. But we venture to guess that anyone who spends some quiet time leafing through and listening to the rhythms and euphonies herein will come away with a greater appreciation for the potential richness of our language.

And let us here and now lay to rest one rumor: This collection is not all humor—don't expect to laugh your way through. It is not a collection of their best quips and slashes (that book has been done). But, as we have tried to state, the members of the Algonquin Round Table were not always trying to be funny. Certainly not in the years around "the war to end all wars." Later on, some of them couldn't help themselves, they were expected to be funny. But during the years encompassed by most of these writings, they were setting some serious—and, occasionally, important—thoughts on paper.

Nor is this collection by any means intended to be definitive or all-inclusive. Quite the contrary. We would rather hope that this sampling might inspire readers to do their own digging and come up with more examples of the clean, concise writing which initially propelled this group into the public eye. There is also a boatload of biographies and autobiographies (of varying quality and accuracy) that may help stimulate an urge to read on.

One of the (many) reasons why modern attempts to recreate The Round Table (and there have been several that we know of) have failed is that the originals shared such a mutual affection that nothing had to be layered on or affected. They liked each other (for the most part), and they loved the English language. When they got together, they were, as Heywood Hale Broun said, "jolly innocents, slightly unsophisticated people who loved to play word games and clung together in a mixture of fear and love." They felt no pressure to perform for public consumption and thus were free to just enjoy their gatherings.

Even Edna Ferber, who actually disliked some of the other members (we won't get into name-calling here), said of the group of which she was a part, "Their standards were high, their vocabulary fluent, fresh, astringent, tough. Theirs was a tonic influence, one on the other, and all on the world of American letters. The people they could not and would not stand were the bores, hypocrites, sentimentalists and the socially pretentious. They were ruthless toward charlatans, toward the pompous and mentally dishonest. Casual, incisive, they had a terrible integrity about their work and a boundless ambition."

Some of them did a better job of hiding the ambition than others, but all of them were ultimately very successful in their chosen fields (and a few fields which chose them).

Marc Connelly should perhaps have the final word on the group's cohesion, for he was the final surviving member and the one who worked hardest at preserving the legacy. He had two (at least) memorable quotes about the group: when asked once to recall just when the Round Table as an active social entity ended, he thought for a moment and then replied, "I don't really know. That's rather like trying to remember falling asleep." And asked to quantify the group's fabled popularity, he said that it was simply that they all just loved each other very much.

At the time, even George Kaufman would have agreed.

Now, at the risk of injecting a personal note into the proceedings, we would like to make one observation. We spoke earlier of "tipsy quipsters." And, indeed, one of the prevailing images of the Round Table in the minds of many is of a gang of dipsomaniacs holding forth loudly from mid-Manhattan. Whatever the truth of their influence on American letters, the fact of their incredible productivity stands in stark contrast to their well-documented social activities. It is continually amazing to us when we consider the schedule maintained by this tight band of miscreants: lunch together, possible work, gather at Neysa McMein's salon, dine together, attend the theater, play poker, meet for a wee nightcap. Shake, shower and repeat.

In our own hale and foolish youth, we sometimes attempted a junior varsity version of that social life, even with considerably less consumption of potent potables. The public record is perfectly clear on our lack of success at equaling their productivity or their sociability. We stand in awe of their stamina and fortitude.

But mostly, we stand in awe of their creativity. So we hope that readers may approach these "lost" (and now they're found) works in the spirit in which they are offered: good reading; variegated; thought-provoking; smile-inducing; instructive examples of a time when the

English language was an important factor in our daily life. It is worth noting that most of the film reviews included herein were from the silent era: sound didn't intrude until 1927. It is still astounding to notice the number of plays produced and newspapers and magazines published during this time period. At the time of many of these creations, the nation's entertainment and diversion consisted of plays, magazines, newspapers and occasional radio broadcasts. Before explosions, visual trickery and human nudity became "entertainment," words were extremely relevant.

It is our hope that they can become so again.

Sharon/Share-Alike, CT

2009

George S. Kaufman

The Myth of
the Algonquin Round Table

It is about time, I think, that someone laid to rest the myth of the Algonquin Round Table. The legend persists that here was a tight little group of critics, playwrights, and novelists, all intent upon praising each other to the skies and rigidly damning the work of any upstart outsider. Just recently I read intimations to this effect in the columns of John Mason Brown and George Jean Nathan, among others. Perhaps there is some mild excuse in the case of Mr. Brown, for he rose to fame in the post-Algonquin days, and inherited the legend. But Mr. Nathan is old enough to know better. Older.

The truth is, of course, that the Round Table was made up of a motley and nondescript group of people who wanted to eat lunch, and that's about all. They had no power at all over the literature of the day, and it seems to me that the least thought on the part of their accusers would convince them of that fact. How in God's name could they wield any such power? How could any group wield such power in the critical world as it is made up today, and as it was made up then?

The Round Table members ate at the Algonquin because Frank Case was good enough to hold a table for them, and because it was fun. The jokes, as I recall, were rather good, but completely unimportant. I cannot recall that a serious literary note was ever injected, and anyone who tried to inject one would have had a piece of lemon chiffon pie crammed down his throat.

Perhaps one anecdote will suffice to show the high literary quality of those luncheons. There was among us, in those days, one John Peter Toohey, who was and is a theatrical press agent, and a good one. I believe that John had read several books at that time, but I am sure he will agree with me that he was not a literary giant. John's main luncheon interest was in the food—and the prices. Mr. Case asked

1

thirty-five cents for a slab of pie and about thirty cents for coffee, and John was Irish and a rebel, and he felt that this was too much.

So we hatched a little plan. With the connivance of Frank Case and his staff, a whole new menu was printed, on which the prices of everything were just about tripled. It was arranged that on the following Monday this menu should be solemnly handed to the lunchers at the Round Table. All of the waiters, of course, were carefully rehearsed in these shenanigans, and it need hardly be added that we had a record attendance that day.

I was about the third to arrive, but John was already there. He gave me a rather tight little nod, and his eye followed me eagerly as I took my seat. Then he reached over and tapped my arm. "You've got a little surprise in store for you," he whispered. "Just wait!" He followed me closely as I picked up the menu. "Well?" he inquired, leaning back to enjoy my outburst. But I took it rather calmly. "Things are going up all over town," I told him. "I suppose Frank just found it necessary to raise prices." "Raise prices!" he snorted. "Just wait till Alex gets here! He'll have something to say!"

But Woollcott also took it calmly, and so did the succeeding lunchers, although John, almost bursting, followed each one intently as he picked up the card. We all ordered as usual, but John, in protest, ordered only tea and toast, which, as I recall, came to two dollars and forty cents. Then he took charge of the plan of procedure. Frank Case must be brought to his senses. On the following day we were to scatter over the city—each was to lunch at a different hotel and each must bring back a menu to show Frank the absurdity of his prices. Marc Connelly was to go to the Ritz, Benchley was to go to the St. Regis, John himself to the Plaza, and so on.

On the following day, of course, John went to the Plaza—and the rest of us went to the Algonquin. John carried a Plaza menu back to Frank Case, and won his point—Frank broke down and admitted that his prices were too high.

And that, boys and girls, was the Algonquin Round Table. Just that and nothing more.

(1945)

Robert Benchley

The Power of the Press

The Police Commissioner of New York City explains the wave of crime in that city by blaming the newspapers. The newspapers, he says, are constantly printing accounts of robberies and murders, and these accounts simply encourage other criminals to come to New York and do the same. If the papers would stop giving all this publicity to crime, the crooks might forget that there was such a thing. As it is, they read about it in their newspapers every morning, and sooner or later have to go out and try it for themselves.

This is a terrible thought, but suggests a convenient alibi for other errant citizens. Thus we may read the following NEWS NOTES:

Benjamin W. Gleam, age forty-two, of 1946 Ruby Avenue, The Bronx, was arrested last night for appearing in the Late Byzantine Room of the Museum of Fine Arts clad only in a suit of medium-weight underwear. When questioned Gleam said that he had seen so many pictures in the newspaper advertisements of respectable men and women going about in their underwear, drinking tea, jumping hurdles and holding family reunions, that he simply couldn't stand it any longer, and had to try it for himself. "The newspapers did it," he is quoted as saying.

Mrs. Leonia M. Eggcup, who was arrested yesterday on the charge of bigamy, issued a statement to-day through her attorneys, Wine, Women and Song.

"I am charged with having eleven husbands, all living in various parts of the United States," reads the statement. "This charge is correct. But before I pay the extreme penalty, I want to have the public understand that I am not to blame. It is the fault of the press of this country. Day after day I read the list of marriages in my morning paper. Day after day I saw people after people getting married. Finally the thing got into my blood, and although I was married at the time, I felt that I simply had to be married again. Then, no sooner would I become settled in my new home, than the constant incitement to further matrimonial ventures would come through the columns of the daily press. I fell, it is true, but if there is any justice in this land, it will be the newspapers and not I who will suffer."

(1920)

Heywood Broun

Ruth vs. Roth

We picked up "Who's Who in America" yesterday to get some vital statistics about Babe Ruth, and found to our surprise that he was not in the book. Even as George Herman Ruth there is no mention of him. The nearest name we could find was: "Roth, Filibert, forestry expert; b. Württemberg, Germany, April 20, 1858; s. Paul Raphael and Amalie (Volz) R., early edn. in Württemberg—"

There is in our heart not an atom of malice against Prof. Roth (since September, 1903, he has been "prof. forestry, U. Mich."), and yet we question the justice of his admission to a list of national celebrities while Ruth stands without. We know, of course, that Prof. Roth is the author of "Forest Conditions in Wisconsin" and of "The Uses of Wood," but we wonder whether he has been able to describe in words uses of wood more sensational and vital than those which Ruth has shown in deeds. Hereby we challenge the editor of "Who's Who in America" to debate the affirmative side of the question: Resolved, That Prof. Roth's volume called "Timber Physics" has exerted a more profound influence in the life of America than Babe Ruth's 1921 home-run record.

The question is, of course, merely a continuation of the ancient controversy as to the relative importance of the theorist and the practitioner: should history prefer to honor the man who first developed

4

the hypothesis that the world was round or the other who went out and circumnavigated it? What do we owe to Ben Franklin and what to the lightning? Shall we celebrate Newton or the apple?

Personally, our sympathies go out to the performer rather than the fellow in the study or the laboratory. Many scientists staked their reputations on the fact that the world was round before Magellan set sail on the *Vittoria*. He did not lack written assurances that there was no truth in the old tale of a flat earth with dragons and monsters lurking just beyond the edges.

But suppose, in spite of all this, Magellan had gone on sailing, sailing until his ship did topple over into the void of dragons and big snakes. The professors would have been abashed. Undoubtedly they would try to laugh the misfortune off, and they might even have been good enough sports to say, "That's a fine joke on us." But at worst they could lose nothing but their reputations, which can be made over again. Magellan would not live to profit by his experience. Being one of those foreigners, he had no sense of humor, and if the dragons bit him as he fell, it is ten to one he could not even manage a smile.

By this time we have rather traveled away from Roth's "Timber Physics" and Ruth's home-run record, but we hope that you get what we mean. Without knowing the exact nature of "Timber Physics," we assume that the professor discusses the most efficient manner in which to bring about the greatest possible impact between any wooden substance and a given object. But mind you, he merely discusses it. If the professor chances to be wrong, even if he is wrong three times, nobody in the classroom is likely to shout, "You're out!"

The professor remains at bat during good behavior. He is not subject to any such vicissitudes as Ruth. Moreover, timber physics is to Mr. Roth a matter of cool and calm deliberation. No adversary seeks to fool him with speed or spitballs. "Hit it out" never rings in his ears. And after all, just what difference does it make if Mr. Roth errs in his timber physics? It merely means that a certain number of students leave Michigan knowing a little less than they should—and nobody expects anything else from students.

On the other hand, a miscalculation by Ruth in the uses of wood affects much more important matters. A strike-out on his part may bring about complete tragedy and the direst misfortune. There have been occasions, and we fear that there will still be occasions, when Ruth's bat will be the only thing which stands between us and the loss of the American League pennant. In times like these who cares about "Forest Conditions in Wisconsin"?

Coming to the final summing up for our side of the question at debate, we shall try to lift the whole affair above any mere Ruth versus Roth issue. It will be our endeavor to show that not only has Babe Ruth been a profound interest and influence in America, but that on the whole he has been a power for progress. Ruth has helped to make life a little more gallant. He has set before us an example of a man who tries each minute for all or nothing. When he is not knocking home runs he is generally striking out, and isn't there more glory in fanning in an effort to put the ball over the fence than in prolonging a little life by playing safe?

(1922)

Robert Benchley

Rustlings of Spring

In the current edition of the circus now at Madison Square Garden one is chiefly impressed by the dispirited behavior of the elephants. The combination of world conditions and the theatrical slump seems to have depressed them.

They dance, it is true, but not with the same snap and verve that used to mark their performance. "Doris," the *première danseuse* of the troupe, goes through the formal motions of the one-step, and although she is much better at it than her trainer, her mind is quite obviously not on her work. Love might perhaps be at the bottom of this individual abstraction, but certainly the entire group of what are known in the patois of the circus as "performing pachyderms," cannot have fallen in love all at once, and the air of detachment appears general. It simply must be listed among the emotional reactions indicative of the great unrest which is sweeping the world.

It is gratifying to note, however, that at the climax of one of the stupendous group formations, the top elephant unfurls the Stars and Stripes, thereby putting the whole troupe on record as one hundred per cent American. It would be a terrible thing if the performing pachyderm element in the country were to go red.

Aside from the elephants, the circus seems about the same. There is this year, however, no magnificent introductory pageant depicting the triumphal entry of Nebuchadnezzar into Tyre (I know he didn't), but the entire company marches around the arena once, which is about all you could ask. Neither is there any single smashing, nerve-racking feature in which a man on a bicycle drops from the top of a tower into a basin of water. The omission of these departments is doubtless due to the general return to normalcy counseled by our new President (his name has slipped me for the moment).

The chief performer, for whom the arena is cleared and the lights lowered, and in whose behalf the drummer rolls an awe-inspiring prelude, is "Mlle. Leitzel, Queen of Aerial Gymnasts, who will amaze you with her wonderful feats of strength and endurance. Suspended at dizzy heights, this Miniature Marvel of the Air breaks every law of gravity, casting her body over her own shoulders scores of times without pause!"

That's right. She does it. That is, she casts her body over her own shoulders scores of times without pause. Just how many of the laws of gravity this violates will have to be judged by someone who knows how many different laws of gravity there are. One is all that comes to mind just at this moment, and Mlle. Lleitzel avoids breaking the letter of this, whatever she does to its spirit, by always managing to keep a tight hold on something or other.

And, after all, when you have cast your body over your own shoulders scores of times without pause, what has been gained by it? You simply have cast your body over your shoulders scores of times without pause, and then you trip lightly to your dressing room. Of course, Mlle. Leitzel incidentally collects a substantial check from the P. T. Barnum estate, which must in part make up to her for the comparative futility of her calling in the great march of the world's progress.

Others of the more unimportant features are the wood-chopping contest and the living statuary. In the wood-chopping contest two men, evidently representing Harvard and Yale respectively, chop through the trunks of two large trees at what is probably high speed in tree-chopping circles. As a contest, however, it lacks a certain variety essential to keeping the spectators on their toes. And although Harvard's generalship and skillful chopping finally overcame the bull-dog grit and moral earnestness of Yale, there was a suspicion, as there always is in contests which are a part of a nightly program, that the choppers were really good friends after all and that the affair was fixed beforehand.

The living statuary has not changed much in all these decades, and the participants, grown white in the service, still give startlingly unreal representations of the more prominent seasons of the year. The group entitled "Spring" has been made doubly effective this time by the insertion of multi-colored electric lights in the vegetables and fruits; and according to the program the center group contains Miss Ena Claren, "known throughout Europe as the Perfect Venus." With all that Europe has on its mind today, this is no small distinction.

The way to go to the circus, however, is with someone who has seen perhaps one theatrical performance before in his life and that in the High School hall. In such company you gradually find yourselves marveling in unison that a man can even stand up on a moving horse's back and gasping at the very idea of a woman swinging in the most elementary maneuvers from a trapeze. The scales of sophistication are struck from your eyes and you see in the circus a gathering of men and women who are able to do things as a matter of course which you couldn't do if your life depended on it. And that's a rather salutary experience every once in a while. It keeps you in your place.

(1921)

Heywood Broun

Buying a Farm

Broun's column "It Seems To Me" had two regular characters: his son, Heywood Hale Broun (H. 3ʳᵈ) and the family dog, Michael. Broun eventually did purchase a farm, in rural Stamford, Connecticut.

It began as "a farm," but even before the catalogues arrived it was "the farm." Now we call it "our farm," although the land is still in Spain abutting on the castle. Chiefly, the place is for Michael. The backyard is much too small for him, and too formal. He regards the house with affection, no doubt, but with none of that respect which he has for the backyard. He is, as you might say, thoroughly yard-broken. When he puts his paws against the front door and barks for freedom he would be a harsh person indeed who would refuse to plan a plantation, a large one, for him. Of course, there was H. 3ʳᵈ to consider, also, but he seemed less restive. Things beyond the borders of a pram are so foreign.

By eliminating Maine, Ohio, and all farms priced at more than twenty thousand dollars, we succeeded at length in narrowing the field of selection to three. One, which has the attractive name of Farm No. 97, is in Connecticut. It has "good American neighbors on all sides." It is only half a mile to some village, not specified. Four of the ten acres are tillable and the rest in timber. Since there are at least 250 cords of wood bringing five to six dollars per cord, the author of the catalogue is entirely justified in the use of the phrase "ridiculously low" regarding the price of $1,500. The author of the catalogue goes on to say that "the owner is an aged widow," and we have gathered the impression that the author means to intimate that she is not quite competent. This would explain the ridiculously low price.

However, we wish to defend our motives in favoring Farm No. 97. It was not the opportunity to swindle a widow out of her homestead which tempted us, nor even the cordwood, but a single sentence almost at the bottom of the description. It read, "Aged owner, for quick sale, will include good mare that has paced a mile in 2:20." This would bring the village half a mile away within one minute and ten seconds, while the good American neighbors would be only seconds away.

E—— was the devil's advocate. "The description doesn't tell enough," she complained. "The 2:20 doesn't mean anything unless it says 'track fast, start good, won driving,' or something like that. And I'd like to know who held the watch. I think we ought to know what year it was that she made that mile in 2:20. Doesn't it say that the woman is an aged widow? Doesn't it stand to reason that she must have bought that fast mare some time in her forties, at least? Anyway, 2:20 isn't so very fast for a pacer. Dan Patch did it in less than two minutes."

In default of more definite information about the pacing mare, we turned to a farm called "Coin Money on a Bargain." This is an oyster farm, as it borders two thousand feet on the Patuxent River. The tillage, as the author says, "is loamy and fine for trucking." It is well fruited to apples and grapes. I drew, as I thought, a rather attractive picture of a scene before the big open fireplace in the modern four-room bungalow of "Coin Money on a Bargain." I pictured the group telling stories and roasting apples and stewing grapes and frying oysters over the embers. R—— interrupted to say that, without doubt, just as soon as H. 3rd began to crawl, he would fall into the river with the oysters.

"Yes," said E——, "and Michael would try and eat shells, and they'd disagree with him, like that coal he got hold of last night."

I mentioned the fact that oysters cost from thirty to fifty cents for a half dozen portion, and spoke of the manner in which the shellfish could be crowded along a 2,000-foot front.

"Yes," said E——, aggressively, "but how are you going to get them to market?"

There I had her. "You have forgotten the description," I remarked. "It says the farm is fine for trucking."

But eventually it was a place called Only Nine Hundred Dollars Down to which we turned our attention. It lay up north along the Hudson and a man named George F. Sweetser promised to show it off to purchasers.

In the newspaper advertisement it merely said "George F. Sweetser, Real Estate Agent." Only after his letter came did we realize the sort of man with whom we had to deal. The letter was much more communicative than the advertisement.

The left-hand half of the envelope read: "George F. Sweetser, Storm King on the Hudson, New York. Legalized expert judge of horses, cattle, poultry, fruits, etc.—pomologist and botanist—private scoring and mating poultry—starting judge of races—originator of Buff Brahmas—breeder of prize winning, standard bred poultry, cattle, etc.—superintendent of farm produce and grain at New York State Fair."

I was careful, therefore, to explain my business at the beginning. "I want to see a farm," I said.

"I'm certainly glad to see you coming out this way," said the pomologist. "We want new blood. We want active, hard-working young fellows around here. We got too many amateurs and old fogies. Would you believe it, a lot of fellows around here won't use green fertilizer, even when I tell them about it."

"No?" I said.

"They just want to stick in the old rut and do things the way their grandfathers did before there was a war. Do you know what it is that makes things grow?"

"Rain," I suggested, after a long pause.

"Yes, rain, of course," said the originator of Buff Brahmas, "but nitrogen, too. And where do we get nitrogen?"

"It comes from Chile, or Honduras, or some place down that way, doesn't it?" I hazarded.

"No, sir," said the starting judge of races. "Up here in Putnam County we get it right out of the air. That's what green fertilizer does— just brings it right out of the air."

And he reached up and clutched something, as if he was going to bring some down himself and show it to me. Instead, he let the gas drift away and pointed to a farm just across the road from the post-office.

"Do you see that farm over there?"

I nodded.

"Well, that man took my advice and he got 440 bushels of potatoes on two acres."

I tried to think just how far 440 bushels of potatoes might stretch if French-fried and placed end to end. It was beyond me.

"That's a lost of potatoes," I murmured.

"I'll say it is," answered Mr. Sweetser. "You know what potatoes were selling for last year?" he said aggressively.

"Not last year," I answered.

"Well, they were selling for $1.50 a bushel. I told that man over there to hold off a bit, but he didn't take my advice, and later on they sold for $2. It wasn't such a bad business, either at $1.50. Do you know how much 440 bushels at $1.50 are?"

I could do that one, and after awhile I said "$660."

"Yes, sir," said Mr. Sweetser. "And this farm I got for sale is eighty-five acres. Now, suppose you put all that in potatoes. How much could you get?"

"It would be a lot of money," I said, after a vain attempt to work it out in my head.

"Not that I'd advise you to put it all in potatoes. There's cows and corn and berries and pigs. This is lovely country for pigs. You certainly owe it to yourself to have pigs. If I was a young man I'd just do nothing but pigs. And there's alfalfa. You can cut that three times a year, and you get about five tons to the acre. There was a man on a place right next to mine that put four and a half acres into corn and he got $349.70 for it."

"How's the house?" I interrupted.

"Oh, don't you bother about the house," said Mr. Sweetser. "It's comfortable. That's what I'd call it—comfortable. And I allus say you're not buying houses; they don't count for nothing in the long run; you're buying land. Even if that was an elegant house, you'd want to fix it up some way to suit yourself, wouldn't you? I'd like to show you the place this afternoon. There's good corn, and I know you'd enjoy seeing the rye and the pigs. But, you see, I'm kinder pressed for time. I'm superintendent of a big place around here, and I got to look at that, and later on this afternoon I have to register the alien enemies—the women, you know—and to-night there's a meeting of the draft board. I guess I've told you enough, though, about what kind of land it is around here. Just look at this piece right here."

He led the way across the road.

"You wouldn't find finer soil than that if you was to drive all afternoon. Just look at it." And he kicked some of the rocks away so that I could get a closer view.

"Why, the crops alone and the timber ought to pay for this place in a couple of months. Why, I'd just love to buy it myself if I was a young fellow and wasn't so busy. If you come up this way again let me know when to expect you, because I've got to go up and superintend a fair next Thursday, and on Friday I'm judging chickens, and Saturday the school board meets."

It was at this point that fate took a hand in the affairs of the busy Mr. Sweetser for no sooner had we got into the car and started for home than a tire blew out.

I sat down under a tree to advise the real estate agent and watch him fix it. An old man from down the road also came over to watch. He was chewing a straw, and he wore a pair of suspenders called Sampson. I asked about the weather first, and he said, without much interest, that it had been too cool and too rainy. Then he took up the questioning.

"What part of the country are you from?" he inquired.

I said New York, and added New York City.

"Yes; I know," said the farmer. "I've been there. I saw the Hudson-Fulton celebration. I've seen about everything," he said, "I went to the San Francisco Exposition."

I nodded, and he went on: "Chicago was the first stop, and then through Kansas. Out of the window you could see wheat and corn all the way along. It was beautiful. And then by and by we came to the Rocky Mountains. They're mighty big mountains, and it took three engines to pull the train up. Sometimes on the curves you could almost touch the engine. Every now and then we'd go through a tunnel. Then we went down south into the big desert. There was nothing there but sagebrush. And they took us up to the Grand Canyon. Did you ever see it?" he asked.

I lied and said yes, but he went on: "The Grand Canyon's 123 miles long and twenty-five miles wide and one mile deep. I grabbed hold of a tree and looked over the edge, and down there at the bottom were all kinds of rocks, red and green and yellow, and there were horses' heads and horses' hoofs and barns and castles and haystacks and everything better than an artist could have done."

"I don't suppose you've seen any of these submarines around here," I interrupted, as a possible diversion.

"Oh, yes; I've seen them," he said; "not here, but out at the San Francisco Exposition. They had submarines and floating mines. They're big. They look like an old-fashioned white turnip, and they float under the water, and when a ship strikes one it blows up. An' they had a big buildin' out at the fair as big as that barn, and in the middle of it was a butter-making machine, and it could turn out more butter in an afternoon than I get off this place in a year. An' there was a Tower of Jewels 425 feet high, and it had 15,635 jewels on it from Persia. And they all shone in the sun. And they had flying machines, too. At night they put lights on 'em, and they went up in the air and turned somersaults over and over again. I wouldn't go up in one of 'em if you was to give me all that meadow land over there.

"After we left the fair we went up north through the spruce forests, and they tell me now that the government's sent 8,000 men up there to cut that spruce and put it into the flying machines, an' I suppose some of those trees I saw up in the air now turning somersaults.

"We didn't stop agin till we got to Detroit. That's where they make the Fords, Tin Lizzies, they call 'em around here. But I always say, What difference does it make what they call 'em if they can do the work? I always say one of 'em's as good as a horse—as good as two horses. An' then we came back here and I've stuck around for a spell 'cause I think I've seen most everything there is."

By that time the real estate agent had fixed the tire, and we drove away. The man with the Sampson suspenders was looking rather contemptuously at his flock of sheep. They would never get to San Francisco.

I can't remember now just why we didn't buy Only Nine Hundred Dollars Down but somehow or other the decision of the council went against it. Our attention at present is fastened on a place over in New Jersey called One Man Farm Equipped. This, like so many of the attractive bargains in the advertisements, belongs to a widow. As the paragraph in the newspapers has it "Widow left alone will sell farm for $1,000 spot cash." E— thinks that delay in the matter may be fatal because of the cheapness of the price. "How can we tell," is the burden of her plaint, "that they will leave her alone?"

(1919)

Dorothy Parker

The New York Type

"**W**ell, *you* know, many people say, when asked to oblige with a description of Mrs. Weldon. "She's the regular New York type. You *know*. She's just perfectly typical."

I have never come up to that point where I am quite clear as to what they mean when they so easily use that phrase, "the New York type." It would require, indeed, some record-breaking endurance arguing to convince me that there was any such thing. But, on a good, clear day, I can see something of their reason in choosing Mrs. Weldon as an example. She is true, with a little of the merciless faithfulness of a caricature, to the picture that other-towners hang in their mental galleries and call "Portrait of a Manhattan Matron."

Mrs. Weldon is somewhere in the late thirties; she does not say just where. Whatever her age, it is her pride not to look it; her pride, her sport and her career. Thirty times a day, at a humbly low estimate, she glances anxiously in a charming little mirror, applies powder, moistens an eyebrow, blends the delicate outlying pink mysteriously into the neighboring white, remoulds her lips nearer to her heart's desire. Four times a year, she has her hair freshly imprinted with what some master of irony has called a permanent wave.

Mrs. Weldon's fingernails are as precious to her as a small boy's hard-won collection of marbles is to him. At the cost of practically eternal vigilance, they are kept very long, carved to slightly cruel points, and lacquered an improbable red. Occasionally, being but flesh and therefore heiress to its ills, she breaks one of them. This is one of the few situations in life that she cannot meet with a clear head. She becomes, in her own phrase, simply furious.

She is tall and slim, and would be slimmer. Tell her of a new reducing diet, and you will find no more flattering audience.

Mrs. Weldon dresses expensively, with an adherence to the current style that allows no wandering away into realms of strange fabrics and curious colors and unknown dressmakers. The distinction of her dress lies in its sedulous lack of individuality. "Is it smart?" is the solemn test-question she asks of her soul, before she buys any article of apparel, even to a handkerchief.

"Smart" is her word of highest praise. She does not keep it for dress alone. Up to the perfection it signifies to her must come furniture, *objets d'art*, even flowers, before Mrs. Weldon will admit them to her apartment.

She is proud of her small apartment, in a smart, chaste white building, in a smart part of town—not the very smartest part, it is true, but still near it, and when does hope die? It is perhaps a little expensive, even for the earnings that Mr. Weldon amasses in some mysterious manner down in Wall Street. (Mrs. Weldon has never been able to understand just what it is that he does; there is something a little bit boastful in her laughing acknowledgement of her total lack of interest in stocks and things). It is expensive, she admits, but as she says, you have to live somewhere. And it is so convenient to the children's schools. Mrs. Weldon is particular that her children attend smart schools with other smartly-dressed children. She has never inquired into the curricula. But she takes, she says, a real interest in their school life. She never forgets to send their teachers handkerchiefs, note-paper or paper-cutters at Christmas, and when the children give plays, she almost always attends, as if symbolizing the triumph of motherhood over boredom.

There are two children, a boy named for his father, and a girl called after her mother. Mrs. Weldon was glad that her second child was a girl; it's such fun to dress girls, she says. And a girl, she points out, is so much company. The little girl has been, to date, great company for her nurse and her playmates. Her son Mrs. Weldon regards with much admiration, considerable bewilderment, and not a little fear. She is stricken with a mild sort of panic if left alone with him.

Mrs. Weldon complains, with wistful laughter, that she really never sees those kiddies of hers, any more, their days are so taken up. In consolation, possibly, she crams her own days to their brims. She is always busy. If she sees an unoccupied hour ahead of her, she rushes to the telephone, seeking anybody who will help her wrestle with solitude. Then she tells you that, honestly, she never seems to have a minute to herself, and sighs.

In the first place, there is shopping. There is always shopping. Then she must keep in constant touch with her friends, whom she still rather inaccurately calls "the girls." Then there is bridge—she plays shrewd, daring, superb bridge. There are luncheons and teas at smart restaurants, where, with any luck at all, a Vanderbilt or a Peggy Joyce may come in at any moment and just sit down and eat like anybody else. There are matinees—she must attend certain matinees, for Mr. Weldon cares only for musical comedy, and has a way of sleeping like a little, tired child at quieter entertainments. And then, of course, she must get her reading done.

Although she reads many current novels, she never reads biography, poetry, short stories, or history. She reads two fashion magazines a month, as faithfully as if by doctor's orders. She reads anywhere from two to five headlines in each day's paper, turns promptly to the society column and takes every word of it. Here, indeed, she proves herself the scholar. She has an enormous fund of information about the social. She knows dates and maiden names and who used to be married to whom.

She never attends concerts, recitals, lectures, exhibitions of sports or little theaters. Once or twice a season, she goes to the opera. She calls her friends up the next morning, to tell them who was there. She has never voted.

She is as deep as a dime, as profound as a work by Elinor Glyn, as receptive as a closed vault, as immediate as a topical song. She is, many people say, the perfect New York type.

I remember telling you, when we were talking a while ago, that I don't quite believe there is any such thing. I know that there are many Mrs. Weldons in New York; but there are many others also.

And if I were to meet her on a desert island, heaven forbid, I could not tell if she were from New York, Washington, Hartford, Philadelphia, Detroit, Chicago or any point West.

(1928)

Heywood Broun

Why I Am Not A Well-Dressed Man

Society is not to blame. The fault is my own. I had my chance. For more than a year I shared an office with a writer who conducted a column called "What The Well-Dressed Man Will Wear." It was generally assumed that this would be a great lesson to me, but at the end of the year the column conductor was fired and I looked precisely the same as at the beginning of the experiment.

I have always felt that it was his failure to influence me for the better which broke his heart.

Of course I did learn in time what I ought to wear, but the responsibility of always doing the right thing was too much for me. A well-dressed man can hardly have time enough to be anything else. And there isn't any sense to it. In male attire elegance seems to have become a synonym for discomfort.

No man has ever been born into the world who does not itch a little in evening clothes. Train a lad from infancy and a high collar will still harass his chin.

Take that advertisement which reads "How Did Your Garters Look This Morning?" My inclination is to answer "Terrible" and then, after a moment's pause for effect, to add "What of it!" I don't think I'm really what you would call garter-conscious. Without stopping to look I couldn't even tell you what color they are.

Sometimes I go for months without ever giving my garters a thought. There are just two kinds of garters—good and bad. Good garters are the ones which keep your socks up and bad garters are those that don't. Black, white, red, yellow and brown are equal in my sight. There is no reason to draw a color line. No garter which does its work faithfully and quietly will ever be discriminated against by me. I have somewhat the same feeling about socks. They should know their place. Male hosiery ought to be seen and not heard. The latest style which provides for black and white checks makes no appeal. My ankles are my own business. I have no desire whatsoever to invite comment. If a person wants to express himself let him look higher. A little recklessness becomes a necktie, but the ankles of men were designed by nature for mere utility and it is ridiculous to try and impart to them any quality of estheticism or entertainment.

Still it isn't quite fair for me to act like a martyr in regard to all this. More than mere devotion to a principle has reduced me to my present estate. Once a group of male relatives decided that something ought to be done about me. They felt that the whole family was being brought into disrepute and so they got together and raised a purse for me to carry to the best tailor in town. Nothing was left to my discretion. I began to feel like an artist's model as the tailor and all his collaborating experts circled around me.

There passed a weary time. Again and again I had to go to the shop while an expert in freehand drawing chalked designs on my back which looked for all the world like a chart of the movement of the ball in the first half of a Yale-Harvard football game. But work as they would they could not prevent a fumble.

Twelve hours after I left the shop in my new suit the Spring rains began, and now those clothes look exactly like all the rest which were unpremeditated garments supplied at a reasonable figure to anybody who was prepared to go up two flights.

Somehow or other clothes just won't cling to me.

I suppose I must have a form, but it is one which no self-respecting suit cares to follow. This secession and recession is most evident in waistcoats. A vest of mine may begin by extending almost to the knee and in a week's time it will have climbed and climbed hand over hand until I could wear it as a fascinator.

My job as a journalist requires me to crawl around on my hands and knees only upon special occasions and yet before a month is out I have to tack when walking against head winds.

Evolution had manifested certain intentions in regard to the human toe, but along comes the boot-maker and attempts to exercise the veto power.

The maker of feet and the maker of shoes have never talked things over and agreed on any cooperative plan.

Above size twelve I find there is very scant opportunity for selection in shoe shops. Only those models which provide great open spaces are available for me. The assumption seems to be that in such sizes grace of line is not of the moment. We in the thirteen class are so many lumberjacks to the shoe manufacturer. Against that I make no complaint except that these Brobdingnagian brogans make me a marked man. When I walk into restaurant or cabaret the waiters form a hollow square and prepare to sell their lives dearly. Flasks are hidden. The orchestra ceases to play and the proprietor very ostentatiously begins to put up the shutters. I am invariably identified by the very sound of my tread as one who has pounded many pavements and has just been snatched off my beat for plain clothes duty in the apprehension of Volstead violators.

Though I may seem to smile at much of this my heart has been close enough to breaking many a time. In several fields of literary and dramatic criticism my opinion is outlawed. Once upon a time, I was bold enough to object to plays and stories about life in the smart Long Island set with a dogmatic, "This is not faithful to the people of whom the author is writing. They don't behave in such fashion."

I had my downfall and rebuke and I am no longer venturesome. The play which aroused my ire concerned week-end frivolity in Great Neck. Now I had spent a Sunday in Great Neck and I felt competent to criticize. I did not remember having observed anybody kissing the housemaid or sitting down to discuss immortality with the butler. And so I sneered at the play and said that the authoress quite obviously was writing of a society with which she was altogether unfamiliar.

She had her revenge. There was a first night just a week later and as I started up the aisle I observed a woman in the back of the house intently regarding my shoes. She kept staring at them until I felt that I too must look. To my discomfort I found that they were somewhat below my best standard. As it happened the roads over which I traveled that month had been muddy for several weeks. As I passed the woman playwright she lifted her eyes from the muddy boots and gave me a contemptuous smile of triumph. It was an expressive smile which seemed to say, "What can a man who wears shoes like that know about the nature of society life in Great Neck, Long Island?" There was no answer.

A year or so ago I was much encouraged to read in the newspapers that the King of Spain had started the fashion of wearing a soft shirt and attached collar with a dinner coat. I had been doing it for some time, but now that he was helping in the movement I felt that we might get somewhere. Unfortunately he dropped out of the fight after a single summer. They had cabinet meetings in Spain and dissuaded him. Apparently the feeling was that this was the entering wedge of radicalism. The prime minister feared that a king who was attempting to get a little ease around the neck might go further and decide that a crown wasn't very comfortable either. And so Alphonso quit and left me to carry on the fight alone.

Generally speaking I think that "a sweet disorder in the dress" ought not to be a matter of plan. It should just happen that way. If a man is going to take thought and pains he might as well go the whole distance and wear checkered socks and look to his garters.

While it is true that I have never been able to achieve the better sartorial effects it is not so that I am among those who affect bohemian attire. My clothes may be poor things but they are my own. I am not their slave, to be sure, but neither are they mine. Once I knew a village poet of whom a cruel observer said, "I wonder who he gets to wear his collars for the first three days."

I am not in that class. I am what I am without premeditation. Never have I planned to look any way in particular. And taking thought about clothes seems to me a little contemptible. Beau Brummell is not worth emulation.

Let us look instead to the fireman—some fireman who has just been wakened by an alarm. He does not stop to cogitate what sort of tie will go well with his socks. There is no period of concentration on the problem of a suitable handkerchief. No indeed, his only concern is to get on enough clothes and get them on quickly. The community demands nothing more of him.

It would be a much better world if the same dispensation applied to all men. And if the world will not grant us this freedom let's go and take it anyway.

(1920)

Franklin P. Adams

From "The Diary of Our Own Samuel Pepys"

Saturday, January 3, 1920

To J. Toohey's in the evening, and played at cards until late, and won a small sum, albeit H. Ross taunted me with my inability to win, saying he could play better than I, albeit he lost what it would have taken him six months in the army to get.

Monday, January 12, 1920

R. Benchley tells me he hath resigned his position with "Vanity Fair" because they have discharged Mistress Dorothy Parker, which I am sorry for ... To the opera house and heard "Martha," a tuneful score, and E. Caruso and Miss Mabel Garrison sang well, but the story of the opera is a second-rate affair.

Sunday, October 1, 1922

A. Samuels told a story of a Maine rustic whose wife was frequently taken with fits, and he would be summoned from his labour in the fields when they came on, but, by the time he reached the house, she would be recovered. But, one day, when he was at his ploughing, a fellow called to him, crying, Come to the house quick, your wife is in a bad way, I think she is dying. And when the rustic came to the house, he found his wife lying dead on the floor. Well, quoth he, that's more like it.

Monday, December 4, 1922

But the only thing I ever wrote of enduring verse was "Tinker to Evers to Chance," and I am the only one who remembers who wrote it save Mr. Theophilus Niles, who said, the day I wrote it, You will be known as the man who wrote the great poem, and I said, Tut, or some such honest deprecation forasmuch as I knew it even then for the trivial piece it was, and not even original with me, I taking the refrain from the box score of the baseball game.

Thursday, April 23, 1925

… so uptown and met Nell Wylie the poet, and said, "Guess whose birthday this is," and she said, "Yours?" and I said, "No, but you're getting warm." "Shakespeare's" she said. Which was the prettiest compliment I had had all day.

Sunday, November 8, 1925

I did sit next to Miss Mary Lewis, a fine, fair girl from Arkansas, who hath been chosen to sing at the Opera House, and we talked of this and that, and of expressions of gratitude for success, in the sincerity of which I disbelieve, and she agreed with me—that it is only yourself you have to thank for success as well as for failure. Which was the honestest utterance ever I had heard from a young woman with new fame, for most of them think they ought to say they owe it all to this or that person, for his kindness, when the truth is that the shoe is on the other foot. Lord! People do say to me, how kind you were to George Kaufman when he started and where would he be without you? Which is very bosh, forasmuch as he helped me more than I him, and I was far more grateful to him for sending me his quips and poems than he could have been that I printed them.

Saturday, April 24, 1926

So in my petrol-waggon to the courts, and trying to enter Harlem River Terrace—which was being paved, thank Heaven—I was stopped by a man who said, "Use your brains," but I told him it was my day off; but what he meant was that I might not drive over the road, but he was overchurlish about it, methought.

Monday, October 9, 1939

To the early train and to the city, and thence to Brooklyn, and when I emerged from the subway I did not ask how to get to Bedford Avenue and the first man I asked said that he did not know, he himself being an alien in that borough. So to a jalopperie and bought the modernest motor-car ever I owned, of the year 1932, and so to the office to work, and so A. Greene brings the car to me, and instructs me how to drive it, which I did learn at once, and so drove home, and the cheers that greeted me were worth the few shillings I had paid for the contraption.

Tuesday, October 10, 1939

I could not wake this morning until late, but my boys tell me they were out a little after six to inspect my new toy.

VICE

Heywood Broun

How I Lost My Fight With Nicotine

Every now and then we think very seriously about swearing off smoking. Tobacco doesn't bother us particularly, but we find matches bad for the nerves. The strain of always having a box on hand is terrific. Our job makes it necessary for us to carry a pencil, and when a person has to be constantly on the alert to be provided with matches, cigarettes and a pencil, the responsibility is too heavy.

We aren't always on the alert. All too often we find that we haven't any matches. Then we must walk almost fifty feet to the city room and borrow one. We try to scatter our requests among the various members of the staff, but it is not possible to avoid repeating. One match may not be so much, but in the course of time obligations develop. There must be men around this office to whom we are indebted to the extent of an entire box. And being dependent on the bounty of others makes us uncomfortable.

Accordingly, we practically decided yesterday afternoon that we would smoke no more. Just before the resolution was completely nailed down in our mind, along came the mail with a copy of the No-Tobacco Educator. Having read this journal of reform, we have decided to smoke more furiously than ever before. Our desire to curtail our responsibilities is still acute, but we have decided to amend our resolution and swear off matches.

We cite a few of the things in the No-Tobacco Educator which have moved us to develop our bad habit of smoking and make a vice of it.

"What would happen," writes the Rev. G. A. Allison, "if every individual who spends 10 cents a day for tobacco would send a religious paper to twenty homes instead?"

This swept away any financial worries we may have had about tobacco and reminded us that even if we cut off the daily 10-cent drain, we might easily spend the money for something much more foolish.

On another page of the same magazine we find: "No normal person likes tobacco. And when a man says he likes tobacco, he is either abnormal or he is a liar."

That inspirited us tremendously. Truthfully, we do like tobacco very much, so it must be that we are abnormal. Of late we had begun to fear that we were not. When the man in "The Good Old Days" remarked, "You told me you'd sell the place for a song, so of course you'll take my notes," we were shocked to discover ourselves joining in the burst of merriment which swept the theatre. And when the barkeeper closed up the dear old saloon, the last night before Prohibition, and turned off the light in the torch held by the miniature Statue of Liberty, we held back the tears with difficulty.

Yes, we began to worry that we were moving toward normality so fast that another week might find us sobbing in the front row at "Abie's Irish Rose." But now we know that our liking for tobacco is a saving grace. We are not as other men, and every time we light a cigaret pride will surge over us as we realize that, though appearances may be against us, we are actually abnormal.

But perhaps the most persuasive propaganda for smoking in the entire tract is contained in an article called "Almost Persuaded," which is as follows:

" 'You say you smoke thirty cigarets a day?'

" 'Yes, on an average.'

" 'And you don't think they hurt you?'

" 'Not in the least. I blame my hard work.'

"The physician shook his head and smiled, but evidently he was vexed. He reached across a table and took a leech from a glass jar.

" 'Let me show you something,' he said. 'Bare your arm.'

"The smoker bared his pale arm, and the doctor laid the black leech upon it. The hungry leech soon fell to work. Its body began to swell. Then all of a sudden a kind of shudder convulsed it and it fell to the floor, dead.

" 'That's what your blood did to that leech,' said the physician. He took up the little corpse between his finger and thumb. 'Look at it,' he said. 'Quite dead, you see. You poisoned it.'

" 'I guess it wasn't a healthy leech in the first place,' said the smoker sullenly.

" 'You think it wasn't healthy? Well, we'll try another.' And the physician took out two other leeches and placed them on the young man's arm.

" 'If these die,' said the patient, 'I'll swear off—or I'll cut my allowance down to ten.'

"Even as he spoke, the smaller leech quivered and dropped off, dead. A moment later, the larger one fell beside it.

" 'This is ghastly,' said the young man; 'I'm worse than a pestilence to these leeches.'

" 'This is caused by the poisonous chemicals of tobacco in your blood,' said the medical man. 'All users of tobacco have this condition.'

" 'Doctor,' said the young man thoughtfully, 'I half believe you're right.' "

And that was a curious reaction upon the part of the young man. Ours was just the opposite, but then you know we are abnormal. If the choice is between leeches and cigarets, we have no desire to be the pride and support of any leech. If one got on our arm we would be in favor of his dying just as soon as possible. There even comes to us the happy thought that by increasing our allowance of tobacco we may accumulate a large enough store of poisonous chemicals in the blood to be a pestilence to all passing mosquitoes.

The No-Tobacco Educator also offers what seems to us convincing evidence that a good many abstainers are not quite bright. On the cover of the magazine is an article by the Rev. George W. Thumm, Malden, W. Va., called "A Little Child Shall Lead."

"A few years ago," begins Mr. Thumm, "I kept a store and was selling tobacco. On Sunday I taught a class of small boys in a Sunday school. Teaching a temperance lesson one Sunday, I told the boys the results of using alcoholic drinks and explained to them how sinful it would be for them to blight their lives with tobacco.

"A seven-year-old boy said, 'If it is wrong for us to use tobacco, is it not wrong for you to sell it?' At this question I was astonished. For a moment I stood speechless."

If Mr. Thumm had only kept his head clear with cigarets, he would have seen this question coming from the very beginning and would have had sense enough to give up his Sunday school class before any seven-year-old child could show him up in that fashion.

(1921)

Dorothy Parker

Reformers: A Hymn Of Hate

I hate Reformers;
They raise my blood pressure.

There are the Prohibitionists;
The Fathers of Bootlegging.
They made us what we are today—
I hope they're satisfied.
They can prove that the Johnstown flood,
And the blizzard of 1888,
And the destruction of Pompeii
Were all due to alcohol.
They have it figured out
That anyone who would give a gin daisy a friendly look
Is just wasting time out of jail,
And anyone who would stay under the same roof
With a bottle of Scotch
Is right in line for a cozy seat in the electric chair.

They fixed things all up pretty for us;
Now that they have dried up the country,
You can hardly get a drink unless you go in and order one.
They are in a nasty state over this light wines and beer idea;
They say that lips that touch liquor
Shall never touch wine.
They swear that the Eighteenth Amendment
Shall be improved upon

Over their dead bodies—
Fair enough!
Then there are the Suppressors of Vice;
The Boys Who Made the Name of Cabell a Household Word.
Their aim is to keep art and letters in their place;
If they see a book
Which does not come right out and say
That the doctor brings babies in his little black bag,
Or find a painting of a young lady
Showing her without her rubbers,
They call out the militia.
They have a mean eye for dirt;
They can find it
In a copy of "What Katy Did at School,"
Or a snapshot of Aunt Bessie bathing at Sandy Creck,
Or a picture postcard of Moonlight in Bryant Park.
They are always running around suppressing things,
Beginning with their desires.
They get a lot of excitement out of life,—
They are constantly discovering
The New Rabelais
Or the Twentieth Century Hogarth.
Their leader is regarded
As the representative of Comstock here on earth.
How does that song of Tosti's go?—
"Good-bye, Sumner, good-bye, good-bye."

There are the Movie Censors,
The motion picture is still in its infancy,—

They are the boys who keep it there.
If the film shows a party of clubmen tossing off ginger ale,
Or a young bride dreaming over tiny garments,
Or Douglas Fairbanks kissing Mary Pickford's hand,
They cut out the scene
And burn it in the public square.
They fix up all the historical events
So that their own mothers wouldn't know them.
They make Du Barry Mrs. Louis Fifteenth,
And show that Anthony and Cleopatra were like brother and sister,
And announce Salome's engagement to John the Baptist,
So that the audiences won't go and get ideas in their heads.
They insist that Sherlock Holmes is made to say,
"Quick, Watson, the crochet needle!"
And the state pays them for it.
They say they are going to take the sin out of cinema
If they perish in the attempt,—
I wish to God they would!

And then there are the All-American Crabs;
The Brave Little Band that is Against Everything.
They have got up the idea
That things are not what they were when Grandma was a girl.
They say that they don't know what we're coming to,
As if they had just written the line.
They are always running a temperature
Over the modern dances,
Or the new skirts,
Or the goings-on of the younger set.
They can barely hold themselves in
When they think of the menace of the drama;
They seem to be going ahead under the idea
That everything but the Passion Play
Was written by Avery Hopwood.
They will never feel really themselves
Until every theatre in the country is razed.
They are forever signing petitions
Urging that cigarette-smokers should be deported,

And that all places of amusement should be closed on Sunday
And kept closed all week.
They take everything personally;
They go about shaking their heads,
And sighing, "It's all wrong, it's all wrong,"—
They said it.

I hate Reformers;
They raise my blood pressure.

(1922)

John V. A. Weaver

Bootleg

(With a graceful bow to Don Marquis)

You heard me! How many times I got to tell you?
Them is my words: you leave that girl alone.
Leave her alone, you hear? Leave her alone!
You think I'll have my son foolin' around
A little snippy rat that's all stuck-up,
And thinks my son's not good enough for her?
"Yeh," that's what Bill says, "Yeh, it's like I say;
Ellen is got swell friends up on the Drive;
I'm sorry she had to break a date with Fred.
But still, you know, the world is changed a lot,
And we changed with it. You're about the same,
But me—well, I been gettin' right along,
And honest, Jack, you see the sense yourself—
Why should I let my daughter marry a clerk?"

Can you believe it? Why, I damn near fainted.
His daughter too good for the likes of us!
Of course I got so mad I couldn't see!
Of course I pasted him square in the eye!

31

And if I catch him sayin' things about me
I'll knock his stuck-up head off! And I tell you,
If you go near the dirty oilcan's place,
And crawl around that snippy brat of his,
I'll kick you out into the street to stay.
You hear that? Right out in the street you go!
The nerve! The dirty, lousy, low-down crook!
A Bootleg gettin' stuck-up over money!
The world is crazy, that's all there is to it!
Crazy, I tell you! All turned upside-down!

Listen. It's fifteen years I know this Bill.
Them good old days, most every afternoon
On the way home from the lumber yards I'd drop in
And get a beer, and gas around a while.
That was my second home, I useta say,
And Bill's Place was a home you could be proud of.
Say. The old woman never kep' a floor
As clean as Bill's was. And the brass spittoons
And rail-you could of shaved lookin' in one.
And all the glasses polished! And the tables
So neat! And over at the free-lunch counter,
Charlie the coon with a apron white like chalk,
Dishin' out hot-dogs, and them Boston Beans,
And Sad'dy nights a great big hot roast ham,
Or roast beef simply yellin' to be et,
And washed down with a seidel of old Schlitz!

Oh, say, that sure was fun, and don't forget it.
Old Ed, and Tom, and Baldy Frank McGee,
And the two Bentleys, we was all the reg'lars.
It was our meetin'-place. And there we stood,
And Lord! The rows about the government,
And arguin! and all about the country,
How it was goin' to the dogs. And maybe
Somebody'd start a song, and old Pop Dikes
Would have to quit the checker-game in the corner
That him and Fat Connell was always playin',

And never gettin' through. I never seen
No bums come in and stay for more'n a minute;
Bill didn't like to have no drunks around;
He made 'em hit the air. Well, some of us,
Of course, might get just a wee mite too much
Under the belt, but who did that ever hurt?
At least we knowed the licker wasn't poison.
And when somebody would get very lit
Bill was right there to try and make him stop;
I can't see how it ever hurt us any.

And Bill! He was some barkeep! One swell guy!
A pleasant word for everybody, always,
Straight as a string, and just the whole world's friend.
I never saw a guy was liked so much.
He hardly took a drink, just a cigar,
And oncet a while a pony, say, of lager.
And my, the way that bird could tell a story!
Why, many a time I laughed until I cried.
And if it happened I was out of dough,
Bill was right there to make a little loan.
Generous, that was Bill, and one good pal.
A great old place it was, that place of Bill's.
Them was the happy days!-them was the days.

I never will forget that good-bye party
The night that Prohibition was wished on us.
You bet it wasn't any rough-house then.
We all stood 'round the bar, solemn and quiet,
And couldn't hardly think of what to say.
Bill—it was funny what had happened to him.
He didn't crack a smile the whole blame night.
He just would shake his head, and bite his lips,
And gosh, the way his eyes was shootin' fire.
The last thing that he said before I left,
"By God, I'll get back at 'em, you just wait!
I'm closing here. But don't you fret—I'll get 'em—
The dirty, pussy-footin' lousy skunks!"

I had to go home early. And the next day
I seen the wagons comin' to take the bar
And all the furniture. I felt like cryin'.

Well, you know what this prohibition is.

Bill goes away, and stays about three months.
And then one day I meets him on the street.
"Well, Jack," he says, You want some real good gin?"
"Just what I need," I says. "All right," he says,
"You come down to the house at nine o'clock.
I'll fix you up. I'll give you half a case
Four Bucks a bottle.."... "Four a bottle!" I says,
Thinkin' he must be kiddin'. "Sure," he says,
"I got to make my profit. There's the risk.
This is good stuff. I made it by myself.
I guarantee that it won't make you sick."
"I'm sick already, just from hearin' the price.
No thanks. Not now," I says. He says all right,
But when I want some, just remember him.

And so, of course, later I did want some,
And had to pay that much, and even more;
But hell, what can you do? So long's you're sure
The stuff ain't goin' to burn your insides out,
You got to pay the price. And all the friends
That Bill had useta have is customers,
And all get stung the same. And dozens more.
Them old days Bill was one fine friend for sure,
Happy and nice and straight and generous.

And now to think he high-brows you and me!
A great big house he's got, and a new Packard,
And di'monds for his wife, that scrubbed the floors
Back in the days when he was only barkeep.
That's what this Prohibition done for him,
And what's it do for me, I'd like to know?

It makes a crook of me, the same as him,
Only I'm losin' money, and he gets it.
Why, say, I catch myself all of the time
Laughin' about this Prohibition law,
And figgerin' new ways how I could break it.
And that's the way it is with everybody.
We get to see that one law is a joke,
And think it's smart to bust it all to pieces.
And pretty soon there's all the other laws,
And how're you goin' to keep from think' likewise
About a thing like stealin', and all that?
No wonder that we got these here now crime waves!
No wonder everybody is a crook!

But that ain't what I'm sayin' to you now!
You leave that stuck-up little Jane alone!
They's plenty of girls that's pretty in the world—
You leave that dirty oilcan's daughter be.
Ten years ago she used to run around
And rush the can for me and other folks.
Now she's a real swell lady! Damn her eyes,
And Bill's, and them there pussy-footin' fish!
The world is, crazy! And I'm goin' nuts!
High-tonin' me! You hear me? If I catch you
Foolin' around that girl, I kick you out,
So fast you won't know what has ever hit you!

A bootleg's daughter! Hell!

(1922)

Alexander Woollcott

The Passing of the Thanatopsis

The Thanatopsis—less frequently but more accurately known as the
Young Men's Upper West Side Thanatopsis and Inside Straight

Club—is no more. At least, I suppose it isn't. Three of its most reliable members—Heywood Broun, Marc Connelly and I—handed in our resignations in the Fall of 1923, and it seems hardly probable that the remaining ten or twelve members are still forlornly holding the meeting every Saturday evening.

We resigned because poker (with just three final rounds of jackpots, everybody up, at nine o'clock in the morning) is a preposterous waste of time. That's what we say—a waste of time. The persistent rumors that we resigned from pique at our losses are unworthy of those who circulate them. It just happens to be true that Mr. Connelly (as always) and Mr. Broun and myself, for a change, did suffer some rather severe misfortunes; but, as we always say, it all evens up in the course of a year. To be sure, George Osborne said the same thing to Dobbin as long ago as the pre-Waterloo chapters of "Vanity Fair," but it's still as true as ever. Just about.

No, our objection to poker is that it's a waste of time. Just what we will do with the time thus saved has not yet been definitely decided. Broun is doubtless writing a few novels, or planning to. I remember his first announcing his contract to write "The Boy Grew Older." I might (and, in fact, will) add that it was at a birthday dinner of mine when he explained that it was to be done in a few months. That careful craftsman, Alice Duer Miller, knowing how much other work he had on hand, protested that he would not have time. "Well," muttered Broun doggedly, "I'm not very busy Friday afternoons."

Connelly, I imagine, has reverted to rum at the Players' Club (the game, not the potion), and I spend the quiet evenings alone with my books.

It was more than the mere waste of time that led to our resignation from the Thanatopsis Club. Some of the finer fibered members had been feeling for some time that, beneath its surface jollity and camaraderie, there was brewing a distinct animosity. We had all been very good friends at the start, and most of us were still speaking. But hardly a member had been adroitly called home when he was several hundred dollars ahead, who was not sped on his way by the hearty hope of all his pals that he would fall down and break his neck. Indeed, the only brother who enjoyed the unbroken good will of the fraternity was Brother Marc Connelly, whose charming, childlike and quite incurable curiosity as to what the other guy might be holding made him an invariable loser. In fact, there were many weeks when his royalty checks from "Merton of the Movies" and "To the Ladies" were laughingly divided every Saturday evening among his cronies of the Thanatopsis, who voted him a jolly good fellow, you may be sure.

Other jolly good fellows, at one time or another, have been Jerome Kern, who is a *good* composer; Robert E. Sherwood, the bitter movie critic who, unfortunately, became extremely married; Montague Glass, cautious but dependable; John V. A. Weaver, who lost in one perfectly delightful afternoon the entire royalties of "In American" for the preceding six months, and so had to sort of eat around for some time; Donald Ogden Stewart, who, at poker, is even funnier than in his books; and, bless his heart, Prince Antoine Bibesco, the engaging Minister at Washington from Roumania. Another was the permanent Infant Phenomenon of American letters, F. Scott Fitzgerald, whose jollity, it is true, was somewhat complicated by his passion for pausing in the midst of his deal to do some of the cutest card tricks you ever saw.

In all honesty, I cannot keep up a pretense that all the casual visitors to the Thanatopsis were jolly good fellows. As I recall, William Slavens McNutt proved hopeless when regarded as a victim. And E. Haldeman-Julius, that snappy publisher out Kansas way, who is always breaking out like a rash in the magazines with his positively last, final offer to send you, postpaid, an entire set of Oscar Wilde for five cents— Haldeman-Julius left none of his profits with his hosts.

Nor did the only two women who have ever been tolerated in the game prove to be either so jolly or so good as we could have wished. Indeed, both Neysa McMein and Mrs. Raoul Fleischmann (known to the Middle Western press as "Quincy's talented daughter" and "Quincy's untalented daughter," respectively) —both of these fair visitors played shrewdly, pocketed their winnings, and refused ever to sit in the game again on the grounds that the stakes were too high.

Then there was that least jolly fellow of them all—a certain rich man who was brought in one night by a sponsor, who explained that he would be almost too easy. Next day we looked the fellow up in Dun and Bradstreet, which gave his fortune at $60,000,000. We wrote that excellent bureau a little note.

"Dear Sir," we said, "He now has $60,000,210."

The passing of Prince Bibesco caused a mild hilarity in the Thanatopsis. His seeming unawareness of what was going on led to the friendliest welcome being accorded him. With a delicate accent that is simply unproducible in type, he would inquire in the midst of a painful pot, "Does the—what do you call them? I forget. Oh, yes—does a sequence excel in competition with three facials?"

"He probably means," someone would explain gruffly, "does a straight beat three kings?"

But when it began to dawn on the guileless Thanatopsis that the Prince knew full well what a straight would beat, and that, as a matter of fact, he was beaming at the time on a brave but busted flush, a dark suspicion was born among the members that Balkan diplomacy was lifting its ugly head in their innocent revels. It was found, to be sure, that one could get even with the prince by referring to his game as "funny without being Bulgar," or by pretending to confuse Roumania with Serbia. But on one occasion he achieved a feat in poker so excruciating that these minor reprisals were felt too inadequate. Then there was Herbert Bayard Swope, the thunderous editor of the *World*, inspired to an immortal dismissal.

"Boy," he cried to the nearest flunky, "boy, the prince's hat and cuffs!"

But, as I have said, it gradually became apparent that poker was undermining the amiability of even the most equable members; that its acid was corroding the oldest friendships. For instance, this must have dawned on Henry Wise Miller one evening. (Mr. Miller is the only member of the Thanatopsis who is in trade, being literary only by marriage. He represents Alice Duer Miller at the meetings, for her only game is cribbage, and she is no whiz at that). One evening, Brother Miller stepped outside to spank his automobile, or whatever it is that motorists do to their cars when they step outside to look at them. Even as he stepped, on this occasion, he cried for help. There, half way down the street, a gang of larcenous thugs was struggling with the locked machine.

"Ah, moi!" cried Miller in his admirable French. Now if, on that evening, he had been a jolly good fellow—but his brothers just looked at the preposterous, hoarded mass of chips from which he had been thriftily investing as the game waned. They looked at it and grinned.

"Ah, moi!" The voice of Miller sounded fainter and fainter down the block.

"I open it," said F.P.A. "I open it at $13.50."

The same suspicion of unfriendliness must have dawned, too, on the usually successful and not at all jolly Heywood Broun that Fall when, after losing $250 one night at the Thanatopsis, he went into the country for a rest and, amid somewhat complicated pastoral scenes, next night lost $850 more. Thus one weekend had cost him a sum which, if properly invested, would, in time, have provided two much needed years at Hamilton College for H. 3rd.

Yet, when he came plaintively back to town and told his story to the brethren, they did not say, "Heywood, draw on me for anything you may need." They did not say, "Tough luck, old fellow," nor silently press his hand in the quiet way of strong men. Not they. They did, in fact, none of these things. Without exception, his pals almost died laughing.

The aforesaid suspicion certainly ate into the heart of John Peter Toohey, the author of "Every Fresh Hour," who gave the Thanatopsis its name and is usually addressed as "Our dear founder." One night he arrived late at the game, explaining with difficulty that he had had the hiccoughs for forty-eight hours and might die if anyone held three aces on him. Everyone laughed heartily and there was only immense good humor when, from time to time, our founder would withdraw to the hall and do something to himself that seemed to help for awhile. But finally he grew desperate.

"I have heard," he said, "that a last resort is to stand on your head. I am afraid that I shall have to ask two of you gentlemen to hold my feet." But this intrinsically entertaining appeal came at a time when the game was growing haggard and when the winners, at the slightest interruption, would seize the chance to slip off home to the wife and kiddies—the dirty crooks. "I am afraid—," our founder began again, but no one was listening.

At last, when the game did dissolve, two brothers agreed to drop Toohey at the Presbyterian Hospital on their way home, inasmuch as they would be passing it anyway. But, by this time, he was so discouraged about the human race that a nervous panic seized him when he found it would be necessary to wake the night nurse. Indeed, he was so alarmed at the way she would take his interruption of her slumbers that when she did come drowsily down, the hiccoughs had been scared out of him, and have not recurred since.

Those of us who have now withdrawn from this corroding atmosphere cannot be missing so very much after all. The famous banter of the Thanatopsis, the wit that was supposed to glance dazzlingly off its stacks of chips, has been grossly exaggerated and, under present conditions, must, I think, be pretty forlorn.

To be sure, George S. Kaufman has been known to lift the general average by occasional contributions, as when he upset the club's gravity one evening by observing casually that he was descended from old Sir Roderick Kaufman, who went on the crusades. Fourteen eyebrows rose in well bred surprise, and Kaufman added, hastily, "as a spy."

But, for the most part, the Thanatopsis jokes have become routine; and I, for one, shall not greatly miss hearing Kaufman, every time he holds an ace and a nine, say he is going to make an ace-nine bet. Or every time he has a two in the hole and a three is dealt him, hearing him complain bitterly that he is being tray-deuced.

I was amused enough when, one night I forgot bring a promised liqueur to the game, Mr. Broun offered to go back to my house for it. He would always, he said, be glad to walk a mile for a kümmel. But I grew rather tired of his little joke about the port he always served on rainy nights. It was a second rate rabbinical beverage; but, as Broun used to say, with a fatuous delight in his own (I suppose it was his own) wit, "Any port in a storm."

I shall not miss the singing. There was the song that escaped into the outer world through the medium of F.P.A.'s column. It ran something like this:

> "Oh, Mr. Connelly, oh, Mr. Connelly,
> I'll wager thirty dollars on this hand;
> I think its pretty fair,
> Perhaps I have a pair;

Have you got thirty bucks at your command?"

"Oh, Mr. Broun, oh, Mr. Broun,
I'll call you, for I think you are a loon.
As upon your hand I gaze,
I see just a pair of trays."
What have you got, Mr. Connelly?"
"A pair of sevens, Mr. Broun."

Far more inspiring, to be sure, both musically and lyrically, was the club's own anthem, a stirring chant, sung standing by every member except the one who had just made a fool call. The melody was that of the Bosun's song in "Pinafore," and the magnificent refrain was:

"He remains a God damned fool."

No, the delights of the Thanatopsis were not sufficient to outweigh its evils. Thus, a club that was formed on the Butte Montmartre during the war, passes into history. It was started there by Harold W. Ross, a buck private who was editor of the *Stars and Stripes* and who, at Nini's little hole-in-the-wall near the Place du Tertre, used to show a good time to the sundry lieutenants who would come up to Paris for a week's leave and who, sometimes, departed despondently for their outfits the second day. (Ask one of them who is now in the faculty at Johns Hopkins.) Back in New York, this game gradually took form as the weekly Thanatopsis. Now that, too, has passed. Or at least, I suppose it has. Though, immediately on hearing me use the word "pass," some officious zany may have opened it.

(1924)

Franklin P. Adams

It Was Originally the Thanatopsis Inside Straight and Pleasure Club

This article was written by F.P.A. for Harold Ross. The New Yorker rejected it. This is the first time it has been published.

There was a day, in January 1935, when this paragraph appeared in a magazine called *The Stage:*

> "Miss Lillian Hellman, who has yellow hair, brown eyes, and talks as well as she writes, by the way, is one of the few women who have played in sessions of the Thanatopsis Inside Straight Club, of which Heywood Broun, F.P. Adams, Alexander Woollcott, the Marx Brothers, Russel Crouse and Herbert Swope, have made one of Broadway's noisiest legends."

A lie. Miss Hellman never sat in at a session of the Thanatopsis Club; she never saw a Thanatopsis Club in session even as a *kibitzer*. A kibitzer, as you know, is a spectator who doesn't buy chips, but who frequently gives advice to the players, something like a senator during a war. Also, Harpo is the only Marx who played.

For when the Thanatopsis Club, not yet so christened, was organized, Miss Hellman, bless her yellow hair and brown eyes, was in rompers, and probably didn't know one deck from another. It held its first real session in the West Eleventh Street apartment of Harold W. Ross and John T. Winterich, a pair of recently demobilized private soldiers, who had done time on the *Stars and Stripes*, that now almost legendary weekly newspaper issued from February 1918 until May 1919. Sergeant Alexander Woollcott also was a member of that staff of army geniuses. It was the sergeant and I whose Thursday duty it was, during my tenure on the only paper I ever requested to be discharged from, to make up the *Stars and Stripes*. The paper was set by the entirely French compositors who set the Paris edition of the London *Daily Mail*. They followed copy, as the typographical phrase goes, because, knowing no English, they could not choose but set. So one night, when Paris was in darkness, on account of Big Bertha and air raids, Woollcott and I wondered what would happen if we wrote for a seven-column streamer (it was a seven-column paper), "PERSHING IS A BIG STIFF." Then we were to run away and hide for the duration of the war. But we lost our nerve. We were a pair of soldiers, and army life had robbed us of initiative and individuality. For Woollcott, it may be said, that he got at least all of his individuality back. It should teach us all never to become discouraged.

So when the cruel war was over, there was a feeling that the poker game, as played at Mimi's in Montmartre, by Ross, Woollcott, Winterich and Walter Duranty, should be kept alive. And on that night in 1919, there was a game at Ross and Winterich's apartment. There were the hosts, Broun, Woollcott and I. It was a table-stakes game, with $10 stacks. After that there was, usually on Saturday night, a weekly game, always at the house of one of the players. Presently the game was augmented by Robert E. Sherwood, John Peter Toohey, George S. Kaufman and Raoul Fleischmann. Toohey had so many games at his house that he became know as our Dear Founder. It was the next year—because of the Thanatopsis Club in Sinclair Lewis' "Main Street"—that I began referring in the paper to the Thanatopsis Inside Straight and Pleasure Club. Later, as avarice reared its hideous head, the Pleasure was elided and it was known, until some of its members became a trifle insolvent, about 1931, as the Thanatopsis Literary and Inside Straight Club. In its peak days, when innocent merriment was all we thought of, we were the jolliest lads in town. In the early '20s the personnel of the game changed. There were Henry Wise Miller, Harpo Marx, Irving Berlin and Gerald Brooks, a patron of the arts. Among those who stood it—or were allowed to play with us once or twice— were Charlie Chaplin, William C. de Mille, Don Marquis, Donald Ogden Stewart, Michael Arlen, Jerome D. Kern, Ring Lardner, Jed Harris, Sam Harris and Laurence Stallings. Stallings played frequently, and so did Charles G. Norris.

We had our own clichés. None of our members ever referred to three sevens as "21" or three tens as "thirty miles" or as "Judge Duffy." Or to four kings as "two pairs … of kings." But if Broun—most of these were his—had a deuce as his hole card and a three showing, he would say that he had been "trey-deuced." A four and a deuce exhibited his "fourty-twoed." If a queen was the high card, and the dealer said, "The queen bets," somebody would say, "Gentlemen, Good Queen Bets!" Jacks 'n' Eights was known as the suburban hand, while a trey full of eights—pronounced eats—was the cafeteria hand. And one riotous evening when somebody signified his intention to remain out of the dealt hand by saying, "Droppo, the Monk," we had in quick succession: "Checko, the Slovak," "Zeno, the Stoic," "Quito, the capital of Ecuador," "Zero, the Cipher," "Nero, the Emperor," "Hello, the Greeting," "Below, the Belt" and "Will o', the Wisp." There were doubtless others, but comical as they seemed during a game, I know how they read and how unfunny they sounded at 3 a.m., when the resistance was low, especially for losers.

The stakes grew higher as the years grew more golden for us all; we ended with $300 stacks and bought from one another when a player was down to $50, so that sometimes a man could make a single bet of $500. But the Thanatopsis struck a reef, and sank with few survivors—Brooks, Kaufman, Swope, Fleischmann and Marx.

So Broun and I gravitated to another game—a less exciting, more relaxing game—during which I no longer had to worry whether my children would cry for bread. This was a limit game, a round of stud, and two rounds of draw—$2 bets, and raises in multiples of same. No wild cards, no variations from the five-card game. The club quaintly is called the Hoyle Club. The usual players are Broun, Howard S. Benedict, Russel Crouse, Percy Waram, Dashiell Hammett, Arthur Kober, and at times visitors from the cinema colony.

The comicalities, real and fancied, in this minor league game, are dissimilar to the old Thanatopsis wheezes, though Comrade Broun is still loyal to the identical jests that he fashioned in 1919 and 1920. It still is, of drink, "Any port in a storm," and of soup or punch spoons, "the ladles, God bless 'em!" The Hoyle Club goes in for verse; its laureate, whose bays are undisputed, is Theron Bamberger, who rhymes every called hand with a couplet. Such as:

> *A pair of deuces?*
> *The pot is youses.*

> *A pair of fours?*
> *The pot is yores.*

And so on, with fives, "the pot derives," meaning nothing, though sixes, "the pot affixes" is better. As was:

> *A pair of sevens*
> *The pot replevins.*

Mr. Bamberger, though no hand seemed to stump him, seldom improved on replevins, and for a few weeks the game was held at the Replevins Club. When a horse named Replevin was running at Bowie, each member of the Hoyle Club lost a pant or two on that unspeedy galloper.

Now here is where Lillian Hellman comes in. For now and then, for an hour or two, she *has* kibitzed at the Hoyle Club games. And when a member has been telephoning, or is out of the game temporarily for some other reason, Miss Hellman has played the absent member's hand. But we are anti-feminist in the poker games. Women not only are slow, but they also slow up the game by failing to remember the value of the chips and the size of the bet. And even when they kibitz, they second-guess. Your true kibitzer is the too-late adviser. He says to the winner, who called, "Why didn't you raise him?" And to the loser, "You shouldn't have called."

(1935)

Dorothy Parker

Men I'm Not Married To

No matter where my route may lie,
No matter whither I repair,
In brief—no matter how or why
Or when I go, the boys are there.
On lane and byways, street and square,
On alley, path and avenue,
They seem to spring up everywhere
The men I am not married to.

I watch them as they pass me by;
At each in wonderment I stare,
And, "but for heaven's grace," I cry,
"There goes the guy whose name I'd wear!"
They represent no species rare,
They walk and talk as others do;
They're fair to see—but only fair—
The men I am not married to.

I'm sure that to a mother's eye
Is each potentially a bear.
But though at home they rank ace-high,
No chance of heart could I declare.
Yet worry silvers not their hair;
They deck them not with sprigs of rue.
It's curious how they do not care—
The men I am not married to.

L'Envoi

In fact, if they'd a chance to share
Their lot with me, a lifetime through,
They'd doubtless tender me the air—
The men I am not married to.

FREDDIE

"Oh boy!" people say of Freddie. "You just ought to meet him some time! He's a riot! That's what he is—more fun than a goat!"

Other, and more imaginative, souls play whimsically with the idea, and say that he is more fun than a barrel of monkeys. Still others go at the thing from a different angle, and refer to him as being as funny as a crutch. But I always feel, myself, that they stole the line from Freddie. Satire—that is his dish.

And there you have, really, one of Freddie's greatest crosses. People steal his stuff right and left. He will say something one day, and the next it will be as good as all over the city. Time after time I have gone to him and told him that I have heard lots of vaudeville acts using his comedy, but he just puts on the most killing expression, and says, "Oh, say not suchly!" in that way of his. And, of course, it gets me laughing so that I can't say another word about it.

That is the way that he always is, just laughing it off when he is told that people are using his best lines without even so much as a word of acknowledgment. I never hear any one say, "There is such a thing as being too good-natured" but that I think of Freddie.

You never knew any one like him on a party. Things will be dragging along, the way they do at the beginning of the evening, with the early arrivals sitting around asking one another have they been to anything good at the theatre lately, and is it any wonder there is so much sickness around with the weather so changeable. The party will be just about plucking at the coverlet when in will breeze Freddie, and from that moment on the evening is little short of a whirlwind. Often and often

I have heard him called the life of the party, and I have always felt that there is not the least bit of exaggeration in the expression.

What I envy about Freddie is that poise of his. He can come right into a room full of strangers, and be just as much at home as if he had gone through grammar school with them. He smashes the ice all to nothing the moment he is introduced to the other guests by pretending to misunderstand their names, and calling them something entirely different, keeping a perfectly straight face all the time as if he never realized there was anything wrong. A great many people say he puts them in mind of Buster Keaton that way.

He is never at a loss for a screaming crack. If the hostess asks him to have a chair Freddie comes right back at her with, "No, thanks; we have chairs at home." If the host offers him a cigar he will say just like a flash, "What's the matter with it?" If one of the men borrow a cigarette and a light from him Freddie will say in that dry voice of his, "Do you want the coupons too?" Of course his wit is pretty fairly caustic, but no one ever seems to take offense at it. I suppose there is everything in the way he says things.

And he is practically a whole vaudeville show himself. He is never without a new story of what Pat said to Mike as they were walking down the street, or how Abie tried to cheat Ikie, or what old Aunt Jemima answered when she was asked why she had married for the fifth time. Freddie does them in dialect, and I have often thought it is a wonder that we don't all split our sides. And never a selection that every member of the family couldn't listen to, either—just healthy fun.

Then he has a repertory of song numbers, too. He gives them without accompaniment, and every song has a virtually unlimited number of verses, after each one of which Freddie goes conscientiously through the chorus. There is one awfully clever one, a big favorite of his, with the chorus rendered a different way each time—showing how they sang it when grandma was a girl, how they sing it in gay Paree and how a cabaret performer would do it. Then there are several along the general lines of Casey Jones, two or three about negroes who specialized on the banjo, and a few in which the lyric of the chorus consists of the syllables "ha, ha, ha." The idea is that the audience will get laughing along with the singer.

If there is a piano in the house Freddie can tear things even wider open. There may be many more accomplished musicians, but nobody can touch him as far as being ready to oblige goes. There is never any of this hanging back waiting to be coaxed or protesting that he hasn't touched a key in months. He just sits right down and does all the specialties for you. He is particularly good at doing "Dixie" with one hand and "Home, Sweet Home" with the other, and Josef Hofmann himself can't tie Freddie when it comes to giving an imitation of a fife-and-drum corps approaching, passing, and fading away in the distance.

But it is when the refreshments are served that Freddie reaches the top of his form. He always insists on helping pass plates and glasses, and when he gets a big armful of them he pretends to stumble. It is as good as a play to see the hostesses' face. Then he tucks his napkin into his collar, and sits there just as solemnly as if he thought that were the thing to do; or perhaps he will vary that one by folding the napkin into a little square and putting it carefully in his pocket, as if he thought it was a handkerchief. You just ought to see him making believe that he has swallowed an olive pit. And the remarks he makes about the food—I do wish I could remember how they go. He is funniest, though, it seems to me, when he is pretending that the lemonade is intoxicating, and that he feels its effects pretty strongly. When you have seen him do this it will be small surprise to you that Freddie is in such demand for social functions.

But Freddie is not one of those humorists who perform only when out in society. All day long he is bubbling over with fun. And the beauty of it is that he is not a mere theorist, as a joker; practical—that's Freddie all over.

If he isn't sending long telegrams, collect, to his friends, then he is sending them packages of useless groceries, C.O.D. A telephone is just so much meat to him. I don't believe anyone will ever know how much fun Freddie and his friends get out of Freddie's calling them up and making them guess who he is. When he really wants to extend himself he calls up in the middle of the night, and says that he is the wire tester. He uses that one only on special occasions, though. It is pretty elaborate for everyday use.

But day in and day out, you can depend upon it that he is putting over some uproarious trick with a dribble glass or a loaded cigar or a pencil with a rubber point; and you can feel completely sure that no matter where he is or how unexpectedly you may come across him, Freddie will be right there with a funny line or a comparatively new story for you. That is what people marvel over when they are talking about him—how he is always just the same.

It is right there, really, that they put their finger on the big trouble with him.

But you just ought to meet Freddie sometime. He's a riot, that's what he is—more fun than a circus.

MORTIMER

Mortimer had his photograph taken in his dress suit.

RAYMOND

So long as you keep him well inland Raymond will never give you any trouble. But when he gets down to the seashore he affects a bathing suit fitted with little sleeves. On wading into the sea ankle-deep he leans over and carefully applies handfuls of water to his wrists and forehead.

CHARLIE

It's curious, but no one seems to able to recall what Charlie used to talk about before the country went what may be called, with screaming effect, dry. Of course there must have been a lot of unsatisfactory weather even then, and I don't doubt that he slipped in a word or two when the talk got around to the insanity of the then-current styles of women's dress. But though I may have taken up the thing in a serious way, and have gone about among his friends making inquiries, I cannot seem to find that he could ever have got any farther than that in the line of conversation. In fact, he must have been one of those strong silent men in the old days.

Those who have not seen him for several years would be in a position to be knocked flat with a feather if they could see what a regular little chatterbox Charlie has become. Say what you will about prohibition— and who has a better right?—you would have to admit, if you knew Charlie, that it has been the making of him as a conversationalist.

He never requires his audience to do any feeding for him. It needs no careful leading around of the subject, no tactful questions, no well-timed allusions, to get him nicely loosened up. All you have to do is say good evening to him, ask him how everybody over at his house is getting along, and give him a chair—though this last is not essential— and silver-tongued Charlie is good for three hours straight on where he is getting it, how much he has to pay for it, and what the chances are of his getting hold of a couple of cases of genuine pinch-bottle, along around the middle of next week. I have known him to hold entire dinner parties spellbound, from cocktails to finger bowls, with his monologue.

Now I would be well down among the last when it came to wanting to give you the impression that Charlie has been picked for the All-American alcoholic team. Despite the wetness of his conversation he is just a nice, normal, conscientious drinker, willing to take it or let it alone, in the order named. I don't say he would not be able to get along without it, but neither do I say that he doesn't get along perfectly splendidly with it. I don't think I ever saw anyone who could get as much fun as Charlie can out of splitting the Eighteenth Amendment with a friend.

There is a glamour of vicarious romance with him. You gather from his conversation that he comes into daily contact with any number of picturesque people. He tells about a friend of his who owns three untouched bottles of the last absinth to come into the country; or a lawyer he knows, one of those grateful clients sent him cases of Champagne in addition to his fee; or a man he met who had to move to the country in order to have room for his Scotch.

Charlie has no end of anecdotes about the interesting women he meets, too. There is one girl he often dwells on, who, if you only give her time, can get you little bottles of chartreuse, each containing an individual drink. Another gifted young woman friend of his is the inventor of a cocktail in which you mix a spoonful of orange marmalade. Yet another is the justly proud owner of a pet marmoset which becomes the prince of good fellows as soon as you have fed him a couple of teaspoonfuls of gin.

It is the next best thing to knowing these people yourself to hear Charlie tell about them. He just makes them live.

It is wonderful how Charlie's circle of acquaintances has widened during the last two years; there is nothing so broadening as prohibition. Among his new friends he numbers a conductor on a train that runs down from Montreal, and a young man who owns his own truck, and a group of chaps who work in drug stores, and I don't know how many proprietors of homey little restaurants in the basement of brownstone houses.

Some of them have turned out to be but fair-weather friends, unfortunately. There was one young man, who Charlie had looked upon practically as a brother, who went particularly bad on him. It seems he had taken a pretty solemn oath to supply Charlie, as a personal favor, with a case of real Gordon, which he said he was able to get through his high social connections on the other side. When what the young man called a nominal sum was paid, and the case was delivered, its bottles were found to contain a nameless liquor, though those of Charlie's friends who gave it a fair trial suggested Storm King as a good name for the brand. Charlie had never laid eyes on the young man from that day to this. He is still unable to talk about it without a break in his voice. As he says—and quite rightly, too—it was the principle of the thing.

But for the most part his new friends are just the truest pals a man ever had. In more time than it takes to tell it, Charlie will keep you right abreast with them—sketch in for you how they are, and what they are doing, and what their last words to him were.

But Charlie can be the best of listeners, too. Just tell him about any little formula you may have picked up for making it at home, and you will find the most sympatheic of audiences, and one who will even go to the flattering length of taking notes of your discourse. Relate to him tales of unusual places where you have heard that you can get it or of grotesque sums that you have been told have been exchanged for it, and he will hang on your every word, leading you on, asking intelligent questions, encouraging you by references to like experiences of his own.

But don't let yourself get too carried away with success and attempt to branch out into other topics. For you will lose Charlie in a minute if you try it.

But that, now I think of it, would probably be the very idea you would have in mind.

LLOYD

Lloyd wears washable neckties.

HENRY

You would really be surprised at the number of things that Henry knows just a shade more about than anybody else does. Naturally he can't help realizing this about himself, but you mustn't think for a minute that he has let it spoil him. On the contrary, as the French so well put it. He has no end of patience with others, and he is always willing to oversee what they are doing, and to offer them counsel. When it comes to giving his time and his energy there is nobody who could not admit that Henry is generous. To a fault, I have even heard people go so far as to say.

If, for instance, Henry happens to drop in while four of his friends are struggling along through a game of bridge he does not cut in and take a hand, thereby showing up their playing in comparison to his. No, Henry draws up a chair and sits looking on with a kindly smile. Of course, now and then he cannot restrain a look of pain or an exclamation of surprise or even a burst of laughter as he listens to the bidding, but he never interferes. Frequently, after a card has been played, he will lean over and in a good-humored way tell the player what he should have done instead, and how he might just as well throw his hand down then and there, but he always refuses to take any more active part in the game. Occasionally, when a uniquely poisonous play is made, I have seen Henry thrust his chair aside and pace about in speechless excitement, but for the most part he is admirably self-controlled. He always leaves with a few cheery words for his players, urging them to keep at it and not let themselves get discouraged.

And that is the way Henry is about everything. He will stroll over to a tennis court, and stand on the side lines, at what I am sure must be great personal inconvenience, calling words of advice and suggestion for sets at a stretch. I have even known him to follow his friends all the way around a golf course, offering constructive criticism on their form as he goes. I tell you, in this day and generation, you don't find many people who will go as far out of their way for their friends as Henry does. And I am far from being the only one who says so, too.

I have often thought that Henry must be the boy who got up the idea of leaving the world a little better than he found it. Yet he never crashes in on his friends' affairs. Only after the thing is done does he point out to you how it could have been done just a dash better. After you have signed the lease for the new apartment Henry tells you where you could have got one cheaper and sunnier; after you are all tied up with the new firm Henry explains to you where you made your big mistake in leaving the old one.

It is never any news to me when I hear people telling Henry that he knows more about more things than anybody they ever saw in their lives.

And I don't remember ever having heard Henry give them any argument on that one.

JOE

After Joe had two cocktails he wanted to go up and bat for the trap drummer. After he had three he began to get personal about the unattractive shade of the necktie worn by the strange man at the next table.

OLIVER

Oliver had a way of dragging his mouth to one side, by means of an inserted forefinger, explaining to you, meanwhile, in necessarily obscure tones, the work which his dentist had just accomplished on his generously displayed back teeth.

ALBERT

Albert sprinkled powdered sugar on his sliced tomatoes.

(1922)

Franklin P. Adams

Women I'm Not Married To

Frank Adams wrote this in response to Parker's take on the male animal. The pair released it as a slim book in 1922. His original dedication read, "To Mrs. Franklin P. Adams. But for whom this book might not have been written, but for whom it was." Ironically, F.P.A. would leave her two years later.

"Whene'er I take my walks"—you know
The rest—"abroad," I always meet
Elaine or Maude or Anne or Flo,
Belinda, Blanche, or Marguerite;
And Melancholy, bittersweet,
Sets seal upon me when I view—
Coldly, and from a judgment seat—
The women I'm not married to.

Not mine the sighs for Long Ago;
Not mine to mourn the obsolete;

With Burns and Shelley, Keats and Poe
I have no yearning to compete.
No Dead Sea pickled pears I eat;
I never touch a drop of rue;
I toast, and drink my pleasure neat,
The women I'm not married to!

Fate with her celebrated blow
Frequently knocks me off my feet;
And Life her dice box chucks a throw
That usually has me beat.
Yet although Love has tried to treat
Me rough, award the kid his due.
Look at the list, though incomplete:
The women I'm not married to.

L'Envoi

My dears whom gracefully I greet,
Gaze at these lucky ladies who
Are of—to make this thing concrete
The women I'm not married to.

ELAINE

There have been more beautiful girls than Elaine, for I have read about them, and I have utter faith in the printed word. And I expect my public, a few of whom are—just a second—more than two and a quarter million weekly, to put the same credence in my printed word. When I said there have been more beautiful girls than Elaine I lied. There haven't been. She was a darb. Blue were her eyes as the fairy flax, her eyebrows were like curved snowdrifts, her neck was like a swan, her face it was the fairest that e'er the sun shone on, she walked in beauty like the night, her lips were like the cherries ripe that sunny walls of Boreas screen, her teeth were like a flock of sheep with fleeces newly washed clean, her hair was like the curling mist that shades the mountain side at e'en, and oh, she danced in such a way no sun upon an Easter day was half so fine a sight! If I may interrupt the poets, I should say she was one pip. She was, I might add, kind of pretty.

Enchantment was hers, and fairyland her exclusive province. I would walk down a commonplace street with her, and it would become the primrose path, and a one way path at that, with nobody but us on it. If I said it was a nice day—and if I told her that once I told her a hundred times—she would say, "Isn't it? My very words to Isabel when I telephoned her this morning!" So we had, I said to myself, a lot in common.

And after a conversation like that I would go home and lie awake and think, "If two persons can be in such harmony about the weather, a fundamental thing, a thing that prehistoric religions actually were based upon, what possible discord ever could be between us? For I have known families to be rent by disagreements as to meteorological conditions.

"Isn't this," my sister used to say, "a nice day?"

"No," my reply used to be; "it's a dreadful day. It's blowy, and it's going to rain." And I would warn my mother that my sister Amy, or that child, was likely to grow up into a liar.

But, as I have tried to hint, beauty was Elaine's, and when she spoke of the weather I used to feel sorry for everybody who had lived in the olden times, from yesterday back to the afternoon Adam told Eve that no matter how hot it was they always got a breeze, before there was weather at all.

It wasn't only weather. We used to agree on other things. Once when she met a schoolgirl friend in Hyde Park whom she hadn't seen since a year ago, out in Lake View, she said that it was a small world after all, and I told her she never said a truer word. And about golf—she didn't think, she said one day, that it was as strenuous as tennis, but it certainly took you out in the open air—well, that was how I felt about it, too. So you see it wasn't just the weather, though at that time I thought that would be enough.

Well, one day we were walking along, and she looked at me and said, "I wonder if you'd like me so much if I weren't pretty."

It came over me that I shouldn't.

"No," I said, "I should say not."

"That's the first honest thing you ever said to me," she said.

"No, it isn't," I said.

"It is, too," was her rejoinder.

"It's nothing of the kind," I said.

"Yes, it!" she said, her petulant temper getting the better of her.

So we parted on that, and I often think how lucky I am to have escaped from Elaine's distrust of honesty, and from her violent and passionate temper.

MAUDE

Maude and I might have been happy together. She was not the kind you couldn't be candid with. She used to say she admired honesty and sincerity above all other traits. And she was deeply interested in me, which was natural enough, as I had no reservations, no reticences from her. I believed that when you cared about a girl it was wrong to have secrets from her.

And that was her policy, too, though now and then she carried it too far. One day I telephoned her and asked her what she had been doing that morning.

"I've been reading the most fascinating book," she said.

"What book?" I asked politely.

"I can't remember the title," she said, "but it's about a man in love with a girl, and he—"

"Who wrote it?" I interrupted.

"Wait a minute," said Maude. I waited four minutes. "Sorry to have kept you waiting," she said. "I mislaid the book. I thought I left it in my room and I looked all around for it, and the I asked Hulda if she'd seen it, and she said no, though I asked her that the other day about something else, and she said no, and later I found out that she had seen it and put it in a drawer, so I went to the library and the book wasn't there, and then I went back to my room and looked again, and

I was just coming back to tell you I couldn't find it when here it is, guess where, right on the telephone stand. Who wrote it? Hutchison is the author. A.M.S.—no wait a minute—A.S.M. Hutchinson, not Hutchison. There's an 'n' in it. Two 'n's' really. But I mean an 'n' between the 'I' and the 's.' I mean it's Hut-chin-son, and not Hut-chi-son. But what's the difference who writes a book as long as it's a good book?"

There may have been more, but I was reasonably certain that the author's name was Hutchinson, so I hung up the receiver, though the way I felt at the time was that hanging was too good for it.

I had dinner with her that night at a restaurant.

"Coffee?" asked the waiter.

"No," I said. And to her: "Coffee keeps me awake. If I took a cup now I wouldn't close an eye all night. Some folks can drink it and not notice it, but take me; I'm funny that way, and if I took a cup now I wouldn't close an eye all night. Some can, and some can't. I like it, but it doesn't like me. Ha, ha! I wouldn't close an eye all night, and if I don't get my sleep—and a good eight hours at that—I'm not fit for a thing all the next day. It's a pretty important thing, sleep; and—"

It was important to Maude, self-centered thing that she was. Here was I confiding to her something I never had told another soul, and she wasn't merely dozing; she was asleep. I rattled a knife against a plate, and she awoke.

It was a good thing I found out about her in time.

ANNE

In winter, when the ground was white,
I thought that Anne would be all right;
In summer, quite the other way,
I knew she'd never be O.K.

She liked to go to the theatre, but what she went for was to be amused, as there was enough sadness in real life without going to the theatre for it. She told me that I was just a great big boy; that all men, in fact, were just little boys grown up. I took her to a movie show, and she read most of the captions to me, slowly; and when she read them to herself her lips moved. She never took a drink in days of old when booze was sold and barrooms held their sway—that is my line, not Anne's—but now she takes a cocktail when one is offered, saying, "This may be my last chance." Women, she told me, didn't like her much, but she didn't care, as she was, she always said, a man's woman. Just the same, folks said, she told me, that she was wonderful in a sick room.

And so, what with the movies and one thing and another the winter passed. She was glad I was a tennis player, and we'd have some exciting sets in the summer. No, she said games. I should have known then, but I was thinking of her hair and how cool it was to stroke.

Well, one May afternoon there we were on the tennis court. It belonged to a friend of hers, and it hadn't been rolled recently, nor marked, though you could tell that here a base line and there a service line once had been.

I asked her which court she wanted and she said it didn't matter; she played equally rottenly on both sides. Nor was that, I found it, overstating things. She served, and called 'Ready?" before each service. When she sent a ball far outside she called "Home run!" or "Just out!" And if I served a double fault she said either "Two bad" or "Thank you." When the score was deuce she called it "Juice!" And when I beat her 6-0—as you could have done, or you, or even you—she said she was off her game, that it was a lot closer than the score indicated, that she'd beat me before the summer was over, that didn't the net seem terribly low or something, and that I wasn't used to playing with women or I wouldn't hit the ball so hard all the time.

Little remains to be told. Anne is now the wife of a golfing banker. Wednesday night I met her at a party.

"Golf?" she echoed. "Oh, yes. That is, I don't play it; I play at it. Tennis is really my game, but I haven't had a racket in my hand in two years. We must have some of our games again. I nearly beat you last time, remember."

FLO

I hadn't seen Flo since she was about fourteen, so when I got a letter asking me to call I said I'd go. She was pretty, but the older I get the fewer girls I see that aren't.

Of course I ought to have known. The letter was addressed with a "For" preceding my name, instead of "City" or the name of the town, Flo had written "Local." Even a professional detective should have known then.

It was just her refined vocabulary that sent me reeling into the night. She wondered where I "resided" and how long I'd been "located" there; she had "purchased" something; she said "gowned" when she meant "dressed"; she had "gotten" tired, she said, of affectation. She said she had "retired" early the night before, and she spoke of a "boot-limber."

And as I was leaving she said, "Don't remain away so long this time. Er—you know—hath no fury like a woman scorned."

BELINDA

I remember Belinda. She was arguing with another young woman about the car fare. "Let me pay," said Belinda; and she paid.

"There," I mused, "is a perfect woman, nobly planned."

I met her shortly after that, and she came through many a test. Once I saw her go up to an elevated railroad station, hand in a nickel, and not say, "One, please." Once I asked her about what day it was, and she said "Wednesday" without adding "All day." She spoke once of a cultivated taste without adding "like olives," and once said "That's another story" without adding "as Kipling says." And once—that was the day I nearly begged her to be mine—when she said that something had been grossly exaggerated she failed to giggle "like the report of Mark Twain's death."

So you see Belinda had points. She had a dog that wasn't more intelligent than most human beings; she wasn't forever saying that there was no reason why a man and a woman shouldn't be just good pals; she didn't put me at ease, the way others did, by looking at me for three minutes and then saying that good looks didn't matter much in a man, after all; she didn't, when you gave her something, take it and say coyly, "For me?" as who should say, "You dear thoughtful thing, when you might have brought it for John D. Rockefeller," And she didn't say that she couldn't draw a straight line or that she had no card sense or that she couldn't write a decent letter.

She could write a decent letter. She did. Lots of them. To me, too. She wrote the best letters I ever read. They were intelligent, humorous, and—why shouldn't I tell the truth?—ardent. Fervid is nearer. Candescent is not far off. And that is how I lost her.

"P.S." she wrote. "Burn this letter, and all of them."

A few weeks later Belinda said, "At the rate I write you, my letters must fill a large drawer by this time."

"Why," I said, "I burn them. They're all burned."

"I never want to see you again as long as I live," she said. "Good-by."

And my good-by was the last communication between me and Belinda.

BLANCHE

Blanche is a girl
I'd hate to wed,
Because of a lot
Of things she said.

"Excuse my French"
When she says "Gee-whiz!"
On the telephone:
"Guess who this is."

You ask her did
She like the show
Or book, she'll say,
"Well, yes and no."

For the "kiddie" she
Buys a "comfy" "nighty";
She says "My bestest,"
And "All rightie."
"If I had no humor, I'd simply die,"
Says Blanche … I know
That that's a lie.

She wouldn't marry;
"Oh, heaven forbid!
"Men are such brutes!"
You said it, kid.

MARGUERITE

Marguerite was an agreer. She strove, and not without success, to please. She hated an argument, one reason perhaps being—I found this out later—that she couldn't put forth on any subject. But I had theories, in the days of Marguerite, and I wanted to know whether she was in sympathy with them. One of my theories was that a lot of domestic infelicity could be avoided if a husband didn't keep his business affairs to himself, if he made a confidante, a possible assistant, of his wife. I had contempt for the women whose boast it was that Fred never brings business into the house.

So I used to talk to Marguerite about that theory. When we were married wouldn't it be better to discuss the affairs of the business day at home with her? Certainly. Because simply talking about them was something, and maybe she could even help. Yes, that was what a wife was for. Why should a man keep his thoughts bottled up just because his wife wasn't in his office with him? No reason at all; I agree with you perfectly.

About politics: Wasn't this man Harding doing a good job, and weren't things looking pretty good, everything considered? He certainly is and they certainly are, was Marguerite's adroit summing up.

Well, I had theories about books and child labor and pictures and clam chowder and Harry Leon Wilson's stuff and music and the younger generation and cord tires and things like that, and she'd agree with everything I said.

Then one night, as in a vision, something came to me. I had a theory that it would be terrible to have somebody around all the time who agreed with you about everything. Marguerite agreed.

I had another theory. Don't you agree, I put it, that we shouldn't get along at all well? And never had she agreed more quickly. I thought she really put her heart into it.

And we never should have hit it off, either.

(1922)

Marc Connelly

A Little Later

He:	*She:*
I'm very sure of her;	I know that he is true;
It is myself I doubt.	The one I doubt is I.
I don't mean to infer	What is a girl to do
That I'm a gadabout.	When others make her sigh?
I love her very much;	What if another man
But when another maid	My dreaming heart should wake?
Appears she seems to touch	I don't believe I can
My heart, and I'm afraid.	Have made a great mistake.
Some day it may occur	Is youth an avenue
When I'm not looking out.	And love a passer-by?
I'm very sure of her;	I know that he is true;
It is myself I doubt.	The one doubt is I.

(1920)

Franklin P. Adams

Saying It With Flowers

I am not of the patronizing sort that doesn't read—or affects not to read—the boxing news, the Gossip of Filmland, the Frank Crane stuff, the syndicated "How to Keep Well" articles. I read them all and they do me good, for I take them seriously. In fact, I owe my clean-limbed young Americanism chiefly to my adherence to advice that I read a few years ago in "The Life of Jess Willard." Mr. Willard advised me—I always think the author is looking straight at me—to do certain exercises daily, and every day since the morning I read that counsel I have done those strengthening exercises. Somebody told me, a few days after I began to emulate Mr. Willard, that Mr. Willard didn't write those pieces at all, but that they were written by Mr. George Creel. It was like telling me there was no Santa Claus. I think I cried a little, but I kept right on with the exercises, and now anybody that says a word against George Creel has me, with five or six years of unremitting training, to fight.

I take, as I said, the printed word seriously. A dealer myself in the printed word, it never occurs to me that anyone might read my own carefully chiseled phrases and say, "Yes, but is it true?" or, "Oh, well, I doubt it," or even, "What of it?"

I am like Ernest in the old George Ade fable, who had been Kicked in the Head by a Mule when young and Believed everything he Read in the Sunday Papers.

And so this evening—my passion for truth makes me refrain from saying "the other day," because it wasn't the other day, though it will be when this appears—I read, among other things on the woman's page (and what I started out to say was that I am not of the patronizing sort that pretends not to read the woman's page) an "article," as they call them, by Dorothy Dix. It was entitled, "Do Women Want to Be Petted?" and, with my habit of answering every question, rhetorical or not, that is put to me, I said, "No," and added, with a revealing candor that I use in meditation, "At any rate, not by me."

Well, I read this piece of Miss Dix's, which told of the sufferings and sacrifices of the average married woman. "The only thing that can repay her," I read, as I stood in the warm, well-lighted Subway train, speeding along through the night, after a jolly day spent in the joys of literary composition in a room full of reporter-pounded typewriters and thrillingly noisy telegraph instruments, "is the tenderness of her husband. His kisses, warm with love, and not a chill peck of duty on the cheek, his murmured words of endearment, are the magic coin that settles the long score that a woman charges up against matrimony, and that makes her rich in happiness."

"The woman" —by this time the train had got to Fourteenth Street, and the crowd of eager, merry home goers, ardent to arrive at their joyous apartments, made reading difficult—"who has looked from the lovely gown and soft furs in a show window to her own shabby frock, and know that she could afford nothing better because the children had to have shoes and the coal was nearly out; the woman who has wrestled with pots and pans and the wash tub all day, while the baby howled and the other children fought, until her nerves were raw—will she be soothed by her husband's treating her as an equal when he comes home at night, and conversing with her about the Federal Reserve bank and the railroad situation? I trow not."

"But if," —and this took me from Seventy-Second Street to Cathedral Parkway—"he puts his arms around her, and pats her on the shoulder, and says, 'There, there, now,' and tells her she is the dearest, bravest, most wonderful little woman in the world, and he just wishes he had the money to doll her up and show people that his little wifekins has got any of those living pictures backed off the screen, why, somehow, the tiredness goes out of her back, and the envy out of her soul, and the sun's come again in her heaven, and she is ready to go down on her knees and thank God for giving her such a husband, even if he isn't a money maker."

I emerged from the Subway, and soft and glowing with the romance Miss Dix had suffused me with, I stopped at a florist's.

"How much," I asked, "are those violets?"

"Two dollars," he said, as who should say, "And what a privilege to buy them at any price!"

"I send them?"

"No," I said.

He wrapped them with the contemptuous air florists have for men who carry their offerings with them. They, I take it, are the transient trade. Your real wooer, it came over me in a flash, never brings his flowers.

I entered the house with the airy tread of youth, adventurous and confident. The Little Woman, as I call her in my lighter moments, was seated at her desk writing checks—struggling, I mused, with the problem of inelastic currency.

"See," I said, pointing with modest triumph to the violets.

"Where did you get them?" she asked.

"At Papakopolo's," I said.

"Well," she said—and I have no doubt she was right—"if you paid more than a dollar you got stuck. You always let a florist give you anything. Go and put them in the icebox."

"There, there, now," I said, quoting Miss Dix. "You are the dearest, bravest, most wonderful little woman in the world. I just wish I had the money to doll her up and show people that my little wifekins has got any of those living pictures backed off the screen."

"Since when," asked the Little Woman—and she is the bravest, as Miss Dix says, L.W. in the world—"since when have living pictures gone into the movies, and is that where you go in the afternoon when I call the office at three and they say you've left for the day? No wonder you never make any money ... Do you know why Wabash Preferred "A" and those other railroad stocks don't go up? It's partly because of the full-crew law and partly because of the Federal Reserve Board."

Well, she had me there. I don't know much about the Federal Reserve, and my whole interest in the railroad situation is in whether a train I am on or am waiting for is on time or late.

I get about a good deal, looking for what my admirers call Material for my Little Articles, and I meet lots of people. If I ever meet Miss Dix, I am going to introduce her to the Little Woman.

(1919)

John V. A. Weaver

Mame

I s'pose I was a dumb-bell. That's what Mame said,
Least wise she didn't say it in them words,
But "dumb-bell"—that was what she meant, all right,
And all because I couldn't understand her.

But what can you do with a girl that wants to set
Out on a rock and watch the waves come up,
Right in plain daylight? And you're talkin' to her,
And all at oncet she says, "Can't you keep quiet?
Can't you see the waves is whisperin' secrets at me?" ...
—If she wouldn't of been so wonderful to look at,
And so darn sweet the few times that she *was* sweet,
I wouldn't never fooled with her at all.
But that's the funny thing. The more I seen her,
And the more she went off into—you know—fits
Like she was miles away, the more I wanted her ...

Here's one trick I put up with from this Mame.
One time at ten p.m. she comes to the house,
Says, "Get your heavy coat, we're goin' ridin'."
"Ridin'," I says. "Say, Mame, what's eatin' you?
A blizzard's outside, and the worst this year."
"Shut up. Come on," she says, and drags me out.
We rides two hours in a open hansom, —
I guess it was one that Noah had in the ark—
The snow just stingin' and beatin' on our face,

And all because Mame never done it before,
And seen the cab, and wanted to. She said
It was a real adventure. … I got chilblains …

What can you do when you take a girl to dinner,
And she goes and orders—heck—of all things—snails!
And when I ast her to a real good show,
She makes me change it to some darn grand oprer,
And won't set downstairs, but she has to stay
Up in the Peanut Gallery, with the Dagoes.

I sure did stand a lot! … She was bad enough
In the city; but when she got out to the country
She sure complete went wild. If she seen a field
Where they was grass and flowers, she takes a run
And jumps and rolls aroun'; and not just her,
She makes me do it, too. I was so shamed,
It wasn't right, us bein' so old, you might say. …

And one time towards evenin' we was walkin',
And comes to a little crick. The fish was jumpin'
And right away she says, "I want to fish!"
We couldn't fish, I argues, there wasn't no poles
Nor hooks, nor lines nor nothin'. She says, "Hush.
I got a pin. You bend it on a rock,
I'll get a line, all right. Go on and bend it."
Whiles I was turned aroun', I hears a rip,
She hands me a long piece of her underskirt,
Honest, it made blush. She breaks a stick off,
And catches a grasshopper, and she fishes.
And what do you think? She catched a fish, at that,
A thing about two inches long. And say,
I thought it was a whale, the fuss she made.

She was so happy, I didn't know what to think,
And afterwards we laid down on a haystack,
And she was watchin' the stars, and sorter hummin',
So sweet I got a notion it was me

That she was singin' about, and I tried to kiss her.
That sure was one bum guess. She turns all white,
And says, "All right, you had to ruin it.
I might of knew." And then we went back home,
Her starin' straight ahead, and sayin' nothin' …

And then, the next day, she was fine again.

I couldn't tell what she was ever thinkin'.
Things went on that way, me bein' her dog,
You might say, tryin' to bust away, and yet
All the time comin' back. So then, one day,
I swore I'd have a showdown. I was through
With all this foolin'. Either I was right
Or either wrong, and I was goin' to find out.

I ast her to eat lunch with me at Schlogel's.
I gets there first, all set up and excited,
And in a minute here she comes, all fixed up,
Prettier'n a little red wagon. We sets down,
And "That's a nice new suit. How good you look,"
Says Mame, and so I'm feelin' fine, right off,
And she is wonderful, laughin' and talkin'
So's I can't hardly wait to say my spiel.

I orders, and the waiter beats it. Then
I clears my throat, and looks at her, and starts,
"Mame, I got somethin' that I want to ast you—
Mame—" And I starts to lean 'way over to her,
And finds my pants is ruined.
What do you think?
Some boob has stuck a great big wad of gum
Right to the chair, and I was settin' in it!

You know, I got so mad I couldn't think.
I clean forgets all I was tryin' to say,
And hollers "Damn it!" … There was my new suit
All ruined with that gum. Mame busts out laughin'

And when she laughs I m gettin' all the sorer.

Then she gets sore, too. "What's a little thing
Like that," she says. "You ack just like a kid!"
Maybe I did, but who's the guy that wouldn't?
I calls the manager, and bawls him out
Like any guy would do.

               And suddenly
Mame she gets right up, and she sorter smiles
And says, "Good-bye. And this is real good-bye.
Charley, you'll never learn to really live
Unless you get so little hurts don't matter.
Life is too big to let a thing like gum
Mean such a lot to you." … And out she sails.
I calls her up next day. She tells me no,
She found that her and me can't hit it off.

"Here's the whole truth: You drag me down," she says.
"You don't know how to dream, and never won't.
That's all. Good-bye."

                          (1922)

Franklin P. Adams

The Art of Fascinating

"Which of these two men," the advertisement demands, "has learned the secret of fifteen minutes a day?" The advertisement is P.F. Collier & Son Company's.

Gaze on the picture. A beautiful young woman is seated, between two men, at a table. Coffee has been served; and, though nobody is smoking, indications are that a pleasant time is being had. But, soft! Not by all. Beaming upon the young man to her right with a warm approval that another spark would make into candescent admiration and worship, the young woman, her lips slightly parted, sits; the young man at her right obviously is talking to her; the young man at her left, with what we take to be an envious look, observes his rival. He appears to be biting his nails, registering his jealousy. He looks not unlike the old pictures we used to see in the patent medicine advertisement labeled, we believe, General Debility. So much for the picture.

"Here," continues the advertisement, "are two men, equally good looking, equally well dressed. You see such men at every social gathering. One of them can talk of nothing beyond the mere day's news. The other brings to every subject a wealth of side-light and illustration that makes him listened to eagerly. He talks like a man who has traveled widely, though his only travels are a businessman's trips. He knows something of history and biography, of the work of great scientists, and the writings of philosophers, poets, and dramatists."

"The answer," the advertisement goes on—but you know what it says. You know that it says you may have this man's Success for the asking; that if you became a bookworm that burrowed fifteen whole minutes a day in your books—the Five-Foot Shelf, to be precise— Beauty would beam upon you, too; you, too, would be a Masterful Man, a Conquering Hero.

Remote be it from us to throw doubt upon the effect of an advertisement. Why, some of our best friends are advertisers, and we wouldn't offend one of them for the solar system with Betelgeuse thrown in. But candor compels the admission that our answer to the question quoted in the first sentence of this piece was wrong. In a word, we thought the discomfited looking man was the bookworm. To us he looked as though he were thinking, "How is it possible for the girl to listen to that incessant, egotistic piffle? She appears interested. Is she? I've seen 'em pretend to be fascinated by what men are saying, when all the time their little brains—if any—were thinking of something else. I wish I could get away and get back to my Five-Foot Shelf. This is a sad evening. Won't he ever stop?"

What the advertisement wants you to think he is saying is, "A murrain on his fatal gift of fascination! Him with his fine words and his book learning! I wish I had not squandered my time. How lightly, yet how confidently, he mentions Cavour, Columbus, Darwin, Epictetus,

Emerson, Euripides! And next week, curse his acquisitiveness, he will have read up to F, perhaps G!"

And also, according to the advertisement, the Cultured (self) young man is speaking of just such things; and Beauty, enraptured, marvels that one head, handsome though it may be, can hold all that knowledge.

But our interpretation of the picture is this: It looks to us, as has been said, as if the disgruntled young man were the tome-hound. And, despairing of leading the talk to matters of history and biography, etc., he is listening to the handsome young man say to the Fairest of Her Sex, "And I said to him, 'Say, Mr. Swope, who do you think you're talkin' to?' And I took my hat and walked out and left him flat. I'm as good as he is … Say, what do you say to going over to Montmartre or the Palais Royal and having a couple of dances or six?"

"I'd love to," says Beauty, "if Mr.—now—Gazish will excuse us."

"Oh," the bookworm—according to our interpretation, not to Collier's—would say, "Certainly. Sure. That's all right. I ought to be going home anyway."

That's what would have happened. We know. As Frank Bacon might say, we were a bookworm ourself once.

(circa 1922)

Robert Benchley

Chaplin and Shakespeare, Eccentric Comedians

The comic supplements and Charles Peabody Chaplin are fair game these days for anyone who wants to register his disgust at horseplay and whitewash as comedy accessories. Any right minded person will grow purple with disapproval when confronted with a comic strip showing the Gazink Boys impaling their grandparents on a picket and will shake his head gravely when brought face to face with the undeniably popular endorsement of a movie featuring a swinging door, custard pie, and a padded policeman. Such things indicate a fatty degeneration of the national sense of humor, say the esthetes. And so they do.

But let no one complain of the slapstick unadvisedly. Let him think well what he must sacrifice if he would be consistent in his scorn of the kick-and-ouch school of satire. It does not mean simply giving up the Funny Section of his paper, or leaving the theatre when "Keystone" is flashed on the screen. The man who would shut "komedy" out from his life altogether must be prepared to abandon what may be one of his most cherished poses, an attitude which gives him standing in his community and stamps him as a patron of the arts. He must look out for his laughs at Shakespeare. For it is from the Bard of Avon, if I may be allowed the nickname, that much of our low-brow merriment of to-day springs.

A gentleman sat in front of me at "The Merry Wives of Windsor" last week who could barely contain himself when Bardolf landed a strong left on Falstaff's stomach, thereby causing him to bellow and blow out a mouthful of suds from the pot of sack he was drinking. It was simply too delicious a bit of fun for the gentleman to bear, and he clapped his knee and looked at his companion as if to say, "After all, where can you find such genuine humor as in Shakespeare?" Had he asked me the question, I should have told him that he could find the same thing two blocks down, where there was a reel in motion showing a waiter with a make-up something less offensive than Bardolf's who, at that very moment, was executing the very same blow on the stomach of a policeman who was drinking a mug of beer, and with exactly the same delightful results. And yet it wouldn't take a very sporting man to bet that the gentleman in front of me would leave the moving-picture house in disgust at such an exhibition of crassness.

Now, of course, there are no stage directions in "The Merry Wives of Windsor" which say: *Bardolf strikes Falstaff in stomach, causing him to blow suds.* That is the work of the producer who knows what the public wants. Likewise the various slappings and bumpings and trippings which mark the entrance and exits of the low comedy characters. One can imagine the director of a Shakespearean production standing down in the pit at a rehearsal and saying:

"Now, you two page-boys over there by the door. Don't stand there doing nothing. Hit each other! First Page-boy bite Second Page-boy and Second Page-boy pull First Page-boy's nose! Kick him! That's right! Throw beer at him! Fine! Now, remember that!"

Any jury would acquit Shakespeare of this part of the performance, but no manager would dare to insert anything like Falstaff's laundry monologue, which Shakespeare undoubtedly admitted was "a little thing of my own." If those in the audience who applauded almost every line of that speech as delivered by Mr. Wise were to hear the same lines from a team of soft-shoe dancers as patter-talk they would each one write a letter to their favorite paper the next morning signed "The Fifth of Five Generations of American Patriots."

There is the apologist who says that Shakespeare wrote for his age. So do the writers of the Komedy Reels, for ages four to eight, inclusive. And yet there must have been some mild old gentlemen of Shakespeare's time who shook their heads at Falstaff's business and said to each other "Good, my coz, but this is yawpish stuff. An I were the Master Justice the author might spout his low-brow lines i' the cooler."

Such critics probably professed to find the real humor to their taste in Chaucer.

Far be it from an unpretentious piece like this to say that Launcelot Gobbo is not funny. Equally far to say that he is funny. But, those who can scream at his twitting of his blind father ought at least to be able to get a giggle from a comic strip in which Winifred Weenix pulls the crutches out from under her blind aunt. If one is funny, the other is. You don't have to look up the notes in the back of the Rolfe edition to find that out.

Let us say that you are at a moving-picture show. You don't often go, but it is interesting once in a while, especially the educational films and the news weeklies. And then, too, the audience is so fascinating to watch. Before you are aware of it a Vogue Komedy is announced and you are caught like a rat in a trap. It deals with a fat plumber who has arranged a clandestine meeting with the wife of an exceedingly jealous waiter. Just as the fat plumber has taken the buxom wife on his knee a sound of crashing glass is heard, announcing the advent of the furious waiter-husband. After sufficient rolling of the eyes and trembling of the knees to convince the most backward intelligences in the audience that the fat man is terrified, he is hustled into a clothes-hamper and the janitor is called to carry it to the laundry. Enter jealous husband, who pulls down five pictures and smashes a bust of Longfellow in his attempts to prove his wife faithless: Close-up of the clothes-hamper going down the dumb-waiter.

The next scene is laid in the laundry and is full of punch. Zip! Comes the hamper down a chute, and, Splash! into a tank, from which the fat plumber emerges, in due course, dripping and blowing. Great facial expression and continual applause.

You edge your way out, filled with a great sadness. As you turn for one last disgusted look before making for the exit you see the fat plumber again, dressed up as an old woman, being kicked and whipped and mauled about the scene by the infuriated waiter.

After such an exhibition, the cool air seems so refreshing that you would like to walk all the way home, but you must hurry, for you have to dress and go out that evening to "The Merry Wives of Windsor," a treat to which you are looking forward with genuine pleasure, for you are always sure of a good laugh at Falstaff's antics, especially in the clothes-hamper scene in Mistress Ford's house, and at the inimitable jollity when Ford beats Falstaff, who is disguised as Mother Prat. It would not be fair to say that this scene is similar to that in the movies which was so offensive, for in the Shakespearean production Ford enlivens the comedy of the thing by calling the old lady a witch, hag, baggage, polecat and ronyon. The Board of Censors would never let that "ronyon" get by in the movies.

On the other hand, and also with the other foot, what a chance there would be for our Mr. Chaplin in "Henry the Fourth"! Cast as Pistol in the scene in the Boar's Head Tavern, with Doll Tearsheet as a foil and an assortment of tables, chairs, pots of sack and a sword or two, and he would have the entire English department of any university flat on their backs with laughter—provided they didn't know who he was.

If some company could only combine Shakespeare and Chaplin, with the ingenuity of the modern Shakespearean producer and the comedy accessories of the modern film corporation in the way of rubber hose, mortar and fish ponds, what a reel could be made! A laugh from start to finish!

Scene: A street in Venice.

Enter Embroglio with a seltzer bottle. Bumps into Crashius, knocking him into a tub of whitewash.

Embroglio: How now, Crashius!

Crashius: How now, yourself! (*Kicks him into a high dudgeon.*)

Em.: Bring you good news from Glandular?

Cr.: Good news, f' faith! (*Pushes him into the wall of a castle, which falls and buries him.*)

Em.: (*From the ruins*): B'r Lady, an were my skull much further driven, a wag might call it well a kidney-bean. But, stay, good Crashius, from whence to whither fare you with that custard pasty?

Cr.: No further than your worship's bridge-work. (*Throws it at Embroglio's mouth. Hits it.*)

Em. (*Blowing custard*): A pox on such a spiteful act.

(*Enter Townspeople, Hautboys, Alarrums, and Torches, pushing Fire Extinguisher.*)

Cr.: Hence, home, you rough-necks. Is Venice then a sleeping-coach? That privacy's disturbed at will?

Townspeople, etc. (*Shouting*): We want Universal Military Service!

(*Turn hose on Embrogio and Crashius. Terribly slow curtain.*)

This is just a rough sketch, of course. A much finer thing could be done with time and more hose. But the essentials are there. Lovers of Chaplin would be satisfied. Lovers of Shakespeare's extra low comedy could not help but be enchanted. And between the two classes you could easily fill the house.

(1917)

Alexander Woollcott

Second Thoughts on First Nights: John Barrymore in "Richard III"

We went again to "Richard III" the other night and sat enthralled until the simultaneous fall of Crookback Dick and the final curtain. Then the Girl in the Next Flat sighed deeply, rose as though still under the bemused spell of the play, and for the first time in her usually orderly life, gravely put her hat on backward, a true tribute to a great experience in the theatre.

This "Richard III" provides so rich and satisfying an evening, like a sudden dish or rare and enrapturing meat served to one who had been dieting overmuch on hearts of lettuce and very thin sandwiches. It is such a bully good show it will give a pleasantly tingling shock to all those who still go to Shakespeare conscientiously, like earnest Chautauquans filling pathetic notebooks with words of wisdom let fall by passing lecturers, a fine jolt for all those who take their Shakespeare with wry face and a sense of rectitude, as one takes calomel.

The performance in the central role is easily the highest point reached in the precipitous and electrifying ascent of John Barrymore to his present commanding position in the English-speaking theatre—the ascent which began unexpectedly four years ago when, turning deliberately and quietly from all the trivial, purposeless and vapid stuff that had absorbed his wandering attention for a dozen wasted years, he announced tacitly, by his very appearance in "Justice," that he was about claim his inheritance, about to enter upon the enjoyment and the responsibility of his great estate. Whereupon there was a delightful clucking from the fond nurse, from Old Nelly in the dairy, from the apple-cheeked wife of the lodgekeeper, bobbing curtseys in the lane, from all the old women of the theatre that he, the young master—bless 'is 'eart, and we that knowed 'im when 'e was a young rascal up to all manner o' tricks—that the wandering soul and hope of a great house had decided to come home at last. Indeed, this old woman, in particular, waddled to a typewriter, and with an expression which must have been quite Sybilline in its frenzy, pounded out the following sentiment on "Justice" for *The Times*:

> "It is interesting not only as a fine and moving play, extraordinarily well staged, but as a heartening evidence of the eternal renewal of the theatre, when that old gentlemen next door writes a long and lachrymose essay to prove that the last of the great Shakespearean players has made his final exit from the stage under his very window. At the time there may be dancing to the music of the hurdy-gurdies a mite of a girl destined in her day to be the greatest Juliet of them all."

It is his work in "Richard III" which makes it seem certain that Barrymore has come home to stay. It was always within the possibilities that a disrespectful hearing of "Justice" would send him back to pot-boiling revivals of "Uncle Sam," "The Fortune Hunter" and "Believe Me, Nanthippe." Then with "Peter Ibbetson" came another danger point—the peril of laughter. That glamorous and delightful play called upon the lackadaisical comedian to come before us very grave and beautiful and romantic and lovelorn, and if, as the agonizing first night of the Du Maurier play, someone out front had guffawed at the very thought it is quite likely that the career of John Barrymore would have ended then and there—altogether likely that he would have grinned his own appreciation of the situation, winked and played the rest of the romance with his tongue in his cheek. Since then the danger of a relapse has been improbable. After "Richard," it is unthinkable.

The ascent from "Justice" has been marked by a corresponding change in the equipment and the very appearance of this actor. It was in "Peter Ibbetson" that old friends discovered, with a start, how fine to look upon he was and that he was actually taller than they had thought. He had, apparently, added cubits to his stature—possibly by no more miraculous intervention than the inspiration to stand up straight. Now he has acquired, out of space, a voice. His voice three years ago was dry and monotonous, his speech slovenly and sometimes common. All that is largely changed. He entered upon the Shakespearean task with a patiently acquired voice, one rich, full and flexible. This is really the advance of which he may be proudest.

Always in the earlier adventures he struck high notes, moments of beauty and imaginative creation which were unattainable by other actors of our time and were chiefly responsible for an enthusiasm for him that has since spread from a cult to a popular opinion. But always, at the same time, there were visible flaws and weaknesses, lapses of control, spasms of effusiveness that overstepped the modesty of nature. The merest tyro across the footlights could recognize and carp at them. In "Richard," for the first time, the high level is maintained throughout. It is all wool and a mile wide.

The comparison of the two Barrymore brothers has been a prevailing indoor game, though it is really better played in the open, with mats or soft, spongy turf. Gradually this seems to be giving way to a comparison between John Barrymore and Richard Mansfield, and to a notion that he comes nearest to filling the vacancy left by Mansfield's death. The nature as well as the quality of his work marks him for it. He can hardly have Mansfield's place, however, nor deserve to have it, until he has carried the best he has to offer outside this pleasant and preposterous city of ours.

(1920)

Robert E. Sherwood

The Silent Drama

"Prof. Einstein"

On the principle that they all get into the movies sooner or later it is not surprising that Dr. Einstein should attempt to expound his well-known theory on the screen.

The Einstein Relativity film, which is now being subjected to the critical scrutiny of our erudite public, is a series of animated diagrams which demonstrate that various things are relative. They go no further into this abstruse subject, which is fortunate—because, as it stands, the film pulled this ignorant reviewer several fathoms beyond his depth.

In fact, after seeing this strange picture, I am convinced that I don't belong to that select jury of twelve good men and true who really understand what the Einstein Theory is all about. And if you ask me, I don't believe that they know so darned much about it themselves.

"Adam and Eva"

I have much less difficulty in understanding Marion Davies. Her claims to fame (if any) are so obvious that even the dullest eye cannot fail to perceive them.

In "Adam and Eva," her latest vehicle, Miss Davies wears the usual priceless costumes, engages in the usual Venetian fête and performs the usual amount of girlish romping.

It is a pretty fair picture, as those things go. The plot, which drags a family of wealthy parasites from their palaces and drops them into agricultural labor, presents many opportunities for good farce; and such adroit comedians as T. Roy Barnes, Tom Lewis and William Norris make the most of these opportunities.

"Adam and Eva" is both neat and gaudy.

"Driven"

The old superstition that a photoplay's value is gauged by the cost of its production received a severe jolt in "Tol'able David," and it has now been almost completely upset by "Driven."

Although "Driven" is one of those Universal Jewels, which usually run up into seven figures, it is apparently the most inexpensive production that has been made since the old days, when feature pictures occupied as much as half a reel. In spite of this grievous handicap, it is extraordinarily good.

Like "Tol'able David," it is a homely tale of Southern mountain folk. There are no flashy costumes in the picture—not even an ordinary business suit; there are no mob scenes; there are no dream episodes, in which the characters are transported back to a previous incarnation in ancient Babylon; strangest of all, there are only two studio sets, and these are anything but elaborate.

There is one thing in "Driven" which most of the more pretentious pictures lack, and that is vital, human drama. For which rare quality, let us all be duly thankful.

I doff my hat to Charles Brabin, who directed "Driven." He has proved that a motion picture can be independent of the producer's bank roll.

"Othello"

The German production of "Othello" is a keen disappointment. With two such worthy actors as Emil Jannings and Werner Krauss, one has every reason to expect great things of this film.

One can expect in vain. Mr. Jannings is excellent as the tragic Moor, but Mr. Krauss, in the despicable rôle of Iago, gives an imitation of Sam Bernard playing the rich Mr. Hoggenheimer in "The Girl from Kay's."

Moreover, there are far more sub-titles than there are pictures. Most of them are quotations from Shakespeare, to be sure; but personally, if I have to read "Othello," I had much rather do it at home.

"Down to the Sea in Ships"

Elmer Clifton, a former acolyte in the Griffith temple, has branched out for himself and produced a marvelous picture of the old New Bedford whaling days, "Down to the Sea in Ships."

A whale is an unruly beast, and it is not the sort of animal that would pay much attention to directorial commands, shouted through a megaphone. Because of his size, no doubt, he is an independent fellow, with small regard for accepted movie traditions. Nevertheless, Mr. Clifton has handled his whales in masterly fashion, and when he asks them to do tricks, they comply obediently.

"Down to the Sea in Ships" combines historic significance, educational value, and beauty with sturdy drama. It is realistic and thrilling.

Mr. Clifton has successfully reflected a heroic phase of American history, and he has also proved that the whale has a home life just like anybody else.

(1923)

Robert Benchley

The Theatre Program Reviewed

"The Bonehead" may or may not be at the Fulton Theatre when this appears. It was announced a day or two after its opening that the producer was sailing for England shortly to arrange for its production there. This announcement usually means much the same thing as the announcement of a defeated political candidate who states that he is about to demand a recount, or that of a suspected assemblyman who gives it out that he will insist on a thorough investigation of the charges made against him.

Whether or not "The Bonehead" is still running matters very little, however, in the sweep of the world's affairs. Probably nothing could matter less.

No one should have been deceived in "The Bonehead." It was clear from the start that it was going to be about Greenwich Village, free love and free verse; so you knew right away that it was going to be dull. A burlesque cannot be burlesqued.

This much having been decided during the first ten minutes, there remained nothing else to do but to look at the program. And, as a review of "The Bonehead" would be of practically no historic or documentary value (and as it was the sole offering of that notable week), the program is really all there is to talk about.

And a most fascinating program it was, too. Did you know, for instance, that London is leaning toward the shorter garments, the blunter lapels, the natural sleeve-head which is neither square nor puffed, the skirt which drapes and ripples but does not flare? No, I thought not. And how do you ever expect to know things like that if, when you go to the theatre, you pay all of your attention to the acting?

Had "The Bonehead" been a different sort of play, I might never have had it brought home to me that I could get a knitted waistcoat for golf which, because of its being a five-buttoned affair with a waist-seam and two lower flapped pockets, is snug and yet, at the same time, so elastic withal that it will follow my every posture like my shadow.

(At this point I was interrupted by someone on the stage making a joke about Flatbush. I counted four more Flatbush jokes at intervals when I was turning the pages of the program. I have no idea how many more I missed.)

But to return to our review.

A certain racy international flavor is given to the program by the insertion of French phrases in an advertisement. The following appeal, for instance, is delicate and yet irresistible:

"Madame, Mademoiselle, le secret de vôtre beauté et de vôtre grâce, n'est-il pas l'usage de ma poudre?"

Then, in order that no one may go wrong and read something into the French which is not there, a literal translation into clear and idiomatic English is furnished directly beneath, and what is our surprise to learn that all that it means is this:

"*Translation:* Madame, Mademoiselle, the secret of your beauty and charm, is it not my face-powder?"

Surely a fair enough question and deserving of a fair answer. And surely two minutes well spent reading the native language of Voltaire (and of Victor Hugo, too, for that matter). One feels refreshed, as on returning from a stroll in the Bois.

The annoyance is therefore doubly poignant at this juncture to hear Mr. Nicander, who is playing the title rôle in "The Bonehead," pronouncing "Epicurean" with the accent on the "cure." He is telling someone in a loud voice that he is an Epi*cure*an. Someone ought to speak to him about that. At any rate, he ought to use a lower voice. How do they expect anyone in the audience to read if the people on the stage are going to run about talking stridently and mispronouncing words?

A discussion of economics follows on the next page. I learn here that, although it is commonly believed that high quality means high prices, such is not the case in buying flowers at our shop. No, indeed. Our flowers (believe it or not) are the finest, most beautiful and longest lasting, AND are most moderately priced. Thus, in so many words, is another popular superstition demolished, although I personally have never been under any particular delusion that high prices had anything to do with high quality. Isn't that a rather old-fashioned idea?

(That sounds like John Daly Murphy's voice on the stage. John Daly Murphy here, and in a part like this! My, my! It only goes to show that you never can tell.)

The theatre management announces reassuringly at the top of the page that it takes only three minutes to empty the house "under normal conditions with every seat occupied." It seems a bit optimistic to speak of every seat being occupied at the Fulton as representing normal conditions. But, of course, that is none of my business. And I can say this much for "The Bonehead": Two Bolshevists are introduced into the play, and neither of them has long hair or whiskers, and they both wear clean white collars. Furthermore, the bomb which they carry looks like a bomb, and not like a medicine-ball with a spluttering fuse. For these original departures from convention due recognition should be given.

But, after all, the program's the thing! I would especially recommend to all audiences a careful perusal of the advertisement for cough-drops. Don't miss it!

(1920)

Robert E. Sherwood

The Higher Education on the Screen

The cinema is rapidly replacing the school as a medium of education for the young. School teachers and professors everywhere have been forced to admit that their youthful charges are learning a great deal more about life in the motion-picture palaces than they ever can in the class-rooms; and the resultant degree of precocity and sophistication in the young idea is cause for both amazement and alarm.

In fact, the day is actually at hand when the silver screen will supplant the blackboard. The present system of education has been weighed in the balance and found wanting—and not only the kindergartens and schools, but the universities as well, are doomed.

What will be the viewpoint, the attitude, of the average child of a few years hence—a child trained mentally by the cinema? How will this one differ from us, who had to content ourselves with the meager supply of information furnished in the old fashioned and soon-to-be-obsolete institutions of learning?

Geography

First, let us consider the study of geography. At an age corresponding to ours when we were just about capable of grasping the fact that Quito is the capital of Peru, the child of the future will have an adequate working knowledge of conditions in the Bad Lands of Montana, the Limehouse wharves in London, and the downtown districts of Shanghai. He will be perfectly acquainted with the habits and habitat of the Apaches—both Parisian and Arizonian—and will know things about the points of east of Suez that Kipling never dreamed of. He will never have to open the pages of Rand-McNally, and will not be bothered with such details as the outline of continents or the tide tables in their relation to the lunar orbit; but every film trained child will be glad, upon examination, to disclose the following facts of geographic interest:

1. Africa is a vast expanse of passion bounded by Alla Nazimova and Theda Bara.

2. A forest is something which catches fire in Reel 4.

3. The Grand Canyon is that ditch which Douglas Fairbanks jumps across.

4. A desert island is a spot of land which yachts run into and which generally turns out to be inhabited by Norma Talmadge.

5. The Pacific Ocean is a body of water six paces due west of the Mack Sennett Bathing Girls.

And so forth.

Sociology

Nor will the question of social values be neglected. The seething spirit of unrest—a spirit both of mutual distrust and jealousy which breeds the germ of revolution—will be killed in its infancy by the provisions of a mutual meeting ground for people in all stations of life. The man in the street will condescend to fraternize with the man in the drawing room because, having seen him in the pictures, he knows all there is to know about him. For instance, every child who behaves himself and watches the screen closely will know:

That a rich man is (9 times out of 10) a rascal bent upon the wooing of Pearl White.

That he may be identified by his immaculate sartorial equipment, which includes a belted waistcoat, a Glen-Urquhart plaid cap and cloth-topped shoes.

That he lounges about in exclusive clubs which are heavily upholstered in the neo-Selznick style, and drinks rows upon rows of whiskeys straight.

That he shakes dice and the shimmy, and misleads parlor-maids when not otherwise engaged.

Whereas:

A poor man is invariably noble.

That he, in his turn, may be identified by the fact that his shirt is always open, disclosing a corrugated neck and a liberal expanse of knotted chest, which he thumps periodically.

That he likes nothing better than to murder his rivals "with his two hands."

That, even if he "ain't long on book l'arnin'," he's "true blue."

History will, of course, receive a certain degree of attention. From now on, contemporary events will be so effectively mirrored in motion pictures that future generations will have a living record of that which has gone before, instead of the uninteresting and inaccurate volumes which we, in our simple way, have had to muddle through with. The little scholars of the future will be able to check up on the various shortcomings of their predecessors in a manner hitherto undreamed of.

History of the War

The World War will be chiefly notable throughout the years to come because it is the first great historical event to be chronicled by means of the motion picture camera. The War has already received much valuable publicity on the screen, and there is no doubt but that it will furnish a well nigh inexhaustible source of entertainments and diversion for our descendants in the peaceful days of the future.

What a comfort for the man who has been Over There to know that his great-great-grandchildren will be privileged to see all the war photoplays which have descended upon us since "that mighty grey horde swept into Belgium" in August 1914! Perhaps the man who has been Over There will wonder what impression this same great-great-grandchild will receive of his forefather's share in the famous victory; we hazard the opinion that the impressions (if the child has faithfully followed all the war films) will be something like this:

What did my great-great-grand-daddy do in the Great War? He:

(1) Captured a village, practically single-handed, just in time to save an exquisite French girl from an unspeakable fate.

(2) Lay wounded in the heart of No-Man's-Land until rescued by a Red Cross dog.

(3) Received the Légion d'Honneur and a kiss from Marshal Foch—a part posed by a corpulent old man with a walrus mustache and a Sam Browne belt over his left shoulder; and finally he

(4) Returned home to find that he had been given up for lost by everyone except *her*—who had never wavered for so much as an instant.

There were many obstacles which blocked the path of the camera-man in Northern France, where many of the leading battles took place. The light was so poor (due to constant overdoses of high explosive) as to preclude the possibility of any effective photography, the result being that the scenes had to be reproduced in California, some six thousand miles away. Motion picture promoters hope that the next war be staged in a more suitable location than the last one; and this hope is shared, to a certain extent, by the inhabitants of Northern France.

Literature

Literature will not be quite submerged as a study, but it will receive the subordinate place that it deserves and will be offered only in supremely condensed form. The subtitles in photoplays will provide ample reading matter for the young and will serve to fulfill the mission in which such stalwart *literateurs* as Hans Anderson and Peter Grimm have utterly failed. The average romance could be told in a few sentences—punctuated, of course, with the real action of the screen—somewhat as follows:

"Pure and unsmirched as the driven lily, Myra Figgis was the only glint of sunshine which penetrated the dark shadows of Hell-bent Alley."

"Arnold Stanchworthy, social vulture, cast doubtful eyes upon the little sunflower of the slums."

"And so — —"

"Years sped past in their relentless flight."

"Jim Muldoon was a man who UNDERSTOOD."

" 'You cur.' "

" 'Jim! Oh, Jim! You've killed him.' "

"Down through the ages, pure as the sunset, comes the eternal message of LOVE —deathless, undying—without end."

"Next week—The screen version of Ibsen's 'Ghosts' with Roscoe (Fatty) Arbuckle."

The Millennium

The result of this is obvious—the mind will mature far earlier than the body and the physical will become subservient to the intellectual. This approximates the ideal state.

Could we but see and talk with some of these prodigies of the future, we would gain a faint conception of the narrowness of our own minds in this primitive age. Think of it!—a nine-year-old child of today is incapable of writing anything less puerile than "The Young Visiters," for instance. Tomorrow after the cinema has replaced the school, our ladies will be composing unexpurgated versions of "The Thousand and One Nights."

Then, indeed, will we be able to open up the floodgates and let the millennium rush in.

(1920)

Robert Benchley

Words and Music

Our attitude toward musical comedy is gradually becoming one of numbed resignation. In the first flush of a reviewer's youth (which, judging from most reviews, is between sixty-eight and seventy), we elbowed our way into a new musical show expecting to get several good laughs, one or two tunes that we could whistle, and perhaps a little carnal stimulation. Then, as we got none of these, we went out and told our neighbor that it was a terrible show.

Years of such disappointment have mellowed us. We now expect nothing, and consequently unless we are made violently ill by a musical comedy we nod pleasantly and say "Not bad, not bad!" After all, that is very little to ask.

Most of the comedy in "Lady Butterfly" does not pass even this elementary test. There are dozens of funny men rushing on, talking very fast, waving their arms, kicking each other, and rushing off again. With the exception of Lionel Pape, who sits quietly cracking walnuts, they are terrible. Whether they would be so terrible if they didn't have to repeat things like "*Bon marché, pomme de terre,*" it is hard to judge, but let us say that it is the fault of the lines, no one of which is under eighteen years of age. The jokes about Coué may be young in years but they seem older. We have now reached the stage where, when we hear a character make a beginning on "every day and in every way," we start strangling. The man who established the tradition that a musical comedy joke should be timely has a great deal to answer for. Will Rogers is the only living person who can get away with timely material and he changes his every day. Furthermore, his remarks are only frosted with timeliness, for underneath most of them lies a quality which makes them good for all time, as, for example, his warning that we musn't get into another war now because we haven't any slogan. If any wiser, more discerning satire for the ages than that has been produced in the last ten years, we haven't heard it.

It is only fair to say that we were not constantly in need of medical care at "Lady Butterfly." The piece has been effectively staged by Ned Wayburn; there is quite a lot of good dancing; once every hour or two something fairly funny is said, and, as there are always in any audience ten or a dozen people who have never heard the jokes before and who will laugh at anything, there is a general merriment abroad which makes the thing seem to be going with a bang. Furthermore, there is the breezy presence of Allen Kearns and Marjorie Gateson, which helps. There you have both sides of the case. Make your own decision.

The Winter Garden has been all done over, so that now it resembles the interior of a large gold tooth. It's grand!

The new show there is perhaps a little better than usual. This must not be taken as hysteria on our part. All we say is that it is perhaps a little better than usual. There is one good tune, and a couple of comedians (Jack Pearl and Lou Holtz) who occasionally pass the nausea test (imagine our chagrin when we discovered ourself laughing at Lou Holtz); Benny Leonard (himself) who is graceful and pleasant enough to let himself be punched in the face and walked on by the comedian; Marie Dressler and, of all people, Cyril Scott. The addition of Cyril Scott and Gilda Leary to the cast hints at an unaccountable scheme on the part of the Shuberts to tone up a Winter Garden show with some legitimate acting. The disadvantage to Miss Leary and Mr. Scott can hardly be offset by their refining influence on the show.

We will say one thing nice. After all the comic prize-fights that have been done (especially Bobby Clark's in his burlesque days), Messrs. Pearl and Leonard succeed in making theirs surprisingly fresh. And Marie Dressler in the Between-the-Acts skit offers some well-deserved dirty cracks at certain types of audience pest, most of whom laugh heartily at the scene while crawling over the feet of their neighbors on the way back to their seats.

(1923)

Robert E. Sherwood

The Blood Lust on Broadway

It has been said that the animal who tastes human blood will never be satisfied with anything else.

This has been demonstrated in a most decisive way during the current New York theatrical season. In fact, the death rate among actors on Broadway has become equivalent to the death rate among steers in Chicago—and the slaughter is conducted in almost as gruesome and cold-blooded a way. This is not due to a natural post-bellum reaction among the playwrights, who haven't any more German spies to shoot at sunrise, nor is it the work of vindictive managers infuriated by the results of the actors' strike. It is, rather, the outcome of the insatiable desire on the part of the theatre-goers themselves, for the sight of murder and the taste of blood.

The crime wave did not really get well under way until the end of June when "At 9:45" opened at the Playhouse, followed, in rapid succession, by "The Crimson Alibi," at the Broadhurst, and "A Voice in the Dark" at the Republic. These three productions were billed as mystery plays, but there was little or no mystery clouding the reasons for their success; they were all cast in the same mould, and all started the evening with a good, rousing murder. This put the audience in an amiable and receptive frame of mind—and the subsequent ramifications of the plot mattered little.

With these three substantial hits as concrete evidence of how the wind blows, the season has degenerated into a veritable orgy of bloodshed, and the list of dead far exceeds the list of injured. Alfred Lunt, in the title rôle of "Clarence," gets off with a bullet in the liver; but every other wound which has been inflicted thus far in the theatrical season has proved pleasantly fatal. In the first act of "The Storm," Jaques Fachard (played by Max Mitzel) succumbs to the popular demand for murder; and the supreme moment in "Déclassée" is furnished when Ethel Barrymore, as Lady Helen Haden, is brought on the stage to die, so that the audience won't miss any of the details (in this case, the cause was purely accidental; broken back, according to the coroner's verdict).

Suicide is by no means neglected: in "The Faithful," the new John Masefield play, Rollo Peters (in the rôle of Asano) commits *hari kari* as though to the manner born; and later in the same play (just when interest and appreciation seems to lag) another of the characters is butchered.

It may be said, with little exaggeration, that the theatre audience of today differs in no essential way from the crowds who patronized the Coliseum during the declining days of Rome, and accorded a cordial "thumbs down" to every gladiatorial act on the program. An aspirant for dramatic honors nowadays must step forth and die if he hopes to get any sort of a start toward stardom. It makes no difference how well he reads his lines, or how perfectly he may control his emotional faculties—if only he has a well modulated death rattle in his repertoire, his fame is assured.

(1919)

Robert Benchley

The Actor's the Thing

Five plays opened in a bunch a week or so ago, and most of them must have made perfectly frightful reading in the script. Blessed, however, with one or more excellent actors, they sneaked by the post and at any rate started with some semblance of class.

The most conspicuous example of what a good cast can do for a play is in "Anything Might Happen." Mr. Edgar Selwyn has written an extremely medium-grade farce containing nothing much that is good. True, it contains nothing much that is bad, but that is almost excessive praise for it. He has, however, had the acumen to gather together Roland Young, Estelle Winwood and Leslie Howard and get them to hoist the thing on their shoulders and prance lightly with it through three acts which, as a result, turn out to be quite amusing after all.

When we write a play (*pause for jeering to die down*), when we write a play, our first official act as author will be to get down on our chubby little knees and pray for Roland Young and Leslie Howard to act in it, for we know of no more graceful bandiers of comedy lines than they. And, to show how good Miss Winwood is, she manages to make a champagne-drinking scene not only inoffensive but funny, which just about hangs up a National Women's record.

"You and I" is the current prize play from Professor Baker's Harvard factory. It is by far the best of the group under discussion to-night, but it also owes a great deal to the gilt-edged cast which Mr. Herndon has given it. Without H. B. Warner and Lucile Watson, many of young Mr. Barry's hand-dipped phrases would be unbearable. Mr. Warner, in particular, takes long speeches, which must have been written with a T-square and compasses, and breaks them up by delightful hesitations and stumblings into normal human sounds. We have seldom admired an actor more than we did Mr. Warner in his struggle to make his salutatory address to the model approximate naturalness.

And even Geoffrey Kerr and the beautiful Miss Inescort, good as they are, can hardly bring the two representatives of the younger generation beyond a point where you are willing to concede that perhaps they have a right to escape hanging. Every line that they have to speak is a "nifty," and so gosh-darned youthful and slangy and younger-generationy that, before they are through, you long for the dulcet sounds of Elsie Dinsmore's Victorian voice talking in the interminable twilight with her Papa.

Add to these names those of Ferdinand Gottschalk and Reginald Mason and you will see what a line-up Harvard has to start the season with. We may have given the impression that we didn't like the play, but we did. Only, before he writes another, Mr. Barry ought to forget everything that Professor Baker has taught him, and also forget the fact that he is young and very clever.

In casting "Rita Coventry," Brock Pemberton was confronted by the task of getting people who were both actors and musicians. The story of the prima donna and the piano-tuner calls for an actress who can sing well and a light comedian who can play the piano well. Mr. Pemberton might have joined that group of producers who feel that, so long as the sounds of the piano come from somewhere in the same theatre with the one on which the actor is supposed to be playing, the illusion is preserved. Instead, he got Dwight Frye, who not only knows the piano, but knows acting to a remarkable degree, with a result that Patrick Delaney, the piano-tuner, takes his place as one of the most vivid characterizations of the season. Mr. Frye is a newcomer in New York, but he has already reached a stage where it is no longer necessary that he even be "watched." You won't be able to miss him.

Dorothy Francis takes care of the singing effectively and acts much better than most sopranos. Being a stickler for the genuine, Mr. Pemberton has had Deems Taylor write some charming compositions especially for "Rita Coventry;" so if you aren't enthralled by the play, you may still get your money's worth.

We are now getting down in the list to where one star, instead of a whole cast, is called upon to carry the piece. Florence Reed does this easily with "Hail and Farewell." She plays one of those women who, as the curtain goes up, are being discussed by a little group as "the most notorious woman in Europe to-day." The "to-day" in this case happens to be in the early '70's, giving a chance for the women in the audience to go "O-o-o-o" whenever a bustle appears on the stage. In fact, "Hail and Farewell," with its scented tragedy of love, is the Regular Two Dollar Dinner for a matinee audience of susceptible wives and mothers, than which there is no less stimulating sight in America today. The play is nowhere near good enough for Miss Reed, but, as a fellow said in a show I saw the other night, "'twill serve."

(1923)

Robert E. Sherwood

The Cinema Primer

The Fans
You ask me why the Films are cheap,

And why they make an Ar-tist weep,
And why they're all so Far from Pure,
And why they Man-gle Lit-'ra-ture,
And why they stress, in ev-'ry Reel,
The el-e-ment of Sex ap-peal,
And why they o-ver-flow with Bunk,
And why they're—in a Word—so Punk,
And why they run in such a Rut …
I'd solve your griev-ous Rid-dles, but
A-las—I am no Nec-ro-man-cer—
Go ask the Fans, for *they're* the An-swer.

The Critic

The Cri-tic sees a Tenth Rate Mo-vie
And, though he'd like to dis-ap-prove, he
Pro-ceeds to delve in his The-saur-us,
And spreads, in bright Ar-ray, before us
A Line of Words like "Vast, Tre-men-dous,
Un-sur-passed, Su-preme, Stu-pen-dous.
It held us Breath-less—Awed—A-ghast, —
A per-fect Work of Art at Last." …
And if, per-chance, you'd like to Know
Just why he shoots his Face off so,
And what in-spires his Gen-u-flec-tions—
Con-sult his Ad-ver-ti-sing Sections.

The Ticket Girl

This well so-phis-ti-ca-ted Al-ice
Of "Won-der-land" (a pic-ture Pal-ace)
Doth sit with-in her glaz-en Booth,
Lur-ing the waste-ful, way-ward Youth,
Who rash-ly Spends his hard-earned Nick-el
To see the Film, "Why Wives Are Fickle."
Her Pa-trons nev-er are Ex-empt
From her de-lib-er-ate Con-tempt,
For she doth Know so ve-ry Much
A-bout the Mo-vie Stars, and Such,

That when she has no Work to do
She seeks Di-ver-sion in the Zoo.

The Organist

His right Hand trills the "Mis-er-er-e"
The while his left plays "Tip-per-ar-y,"
And as he drones each mel-low Chord,
He looks un-ut-ter-ab-ly Bored.
He sees the Vil-lain thrott-le Han-nah,
And steps up-on the Vox Hu-ma-na,
Or, if the Gal falls for A-no-ther,
He sobs, "Don't Break the News to Mo-ther";
And when it all ends Hap-pi-ly,
He pounds out "Hands A-cross the Sea."
I think I'd ra-ther play the Or-gan
Than be Babe Ruth or J. P. Mor-gan.

(1921)

Robert Benchley

French, English, American

There was a time when the very fact that a play was called "La Tendresse" and was done at the Empire Theatre would have impressed us to a point where we would have felt that it must be a remarkable play. And the fact that we were privy to the information that the "l's" in Bataille's name were silent would have convinced us that he must be a great playwright.

But sixty-five years of theatre-going have cured us of this awe of French names. As we sat and twitched through the three long acts of "La Tendresse," trying first to hear Henry Miller's lines and then those of the lady behind us who had not been given a program and was thinking of suing the management, we were comforted by the firm conviction that the play which was boring us was not over our head but simply good, old-fashioned dull junk, French or no French, Empire or no Empire.

The whole thing is rabid theatre, acted with rabid theatricality, "and," as the gentleman in the story said, "for what?" To prove what every French writer has to prove at some time or other—that a middle-aged savant takes on terribly when his young mistress deceives him for a more capable man.

The one thing that kept us awake was the sound of Ruth Chatterton's voice, chiefly because it brought back memories of "Mary Rose." And somehow it seemed as if in a few minutes she must step out of that gilt scroll-work which decorates the walls in every French drama, and ask pleadingly, as she asked in "Mary Rose": "But why, why is everyone here so old?"

Another thing that we shall never assume again is that because a play is by Somerset Maugham it is going to be subtle and original. "East of Suez" might have been written by Owen Davis; at any rate, as it is presented in New York. It is said that Mr. Woods has altered it considerably from its original London form. He must have changed everything but the title if the original was written by the same Maugham who wrote "The Circle."

When Florence Reed was going through her stock apprenticeship in our hometown we were madly in love with her every Tuesday afternoon from Seat 2, Row B of the Franklin Square Theatre. She did not leave us entirely cold last week either, as we sat in the Eltinge Theatre, New York City. And there was something about "East of Suez," with its tremendous scenes of strident passion in the most approved language of strident passion scenes, that brought back memories of the plays that Miss Reed's stock company used to give in the Franklin Square Theatre along toward the end of the season, when a postal ballot of the subscribers had been taken to see which of the old favorites should be revived. "East of Suez" would have gone big in a postal ballot.

Now "The Exciters" makes no pretense of being anything but the craziest, most improbable of melodramas. Martin Brown, the author, asks you to believe nothing, which is lucky, because there is nothing in the whole thing that could possibly be believed. All he asks is that you stay in your seat, and it is quite likely that you will, for, what with being alternately amused and excited in a good-natured sort of way, you will find that the four acts have rolled along in a very pleasant manner.

A great deal of this favorable impression, after taking out credit for Allan Dinehart and others, is due to the presence in the cast of Miss Tallulah Bankhead, who seems to have concealed about her perhaps eight of a possible ten qualifications for the makings of a darned good actress. We leave a lee-way of two qualifications to make up for any possible bias we may have been led into by Miss Bankhead's good looks. The older a reviewer gets the more careful he has to be about making a fool of himself.

"Banco" is a French comedy which has been taken by Clare Kummer and shaken up with a little orange juice and vermouth. The result tastes a little queer at times, but it has an undoubted kick.

The story in the original must have been a bit wild, and with Miss Kummer's additions it has become even wilder. She has, however, abandoned for the time her delightful habit of writing lines which mean nothing. For example, when one of the men refuses to drink any more because he wants to keep his head, Alfred Lunt says: "You're welcome to it"—a good line, but with much more point than it is Miss Kummer's whimsical fashion to give us.

The leading roles in "Banco" are played by Lola Fisher and Alfred Lunt; and Francis Byrne offers something in the way of an original character creation which helps make the play one of the most entertaining so far this season.

(1922)

Heywood Broun

From "It Seems To Me"

On Actors

Nothing in the world dies quite as completely as an actor and the greater the actor the more terrifying becomes the sudden transition from radiance to darkness. One day he is there with all his moods and complexities and curious glints of this and that, and the next day there is nothing left but a few wigs and costumes; perhaps a volume of memoirs, and a scrapbook of clippings in which we learn that the dead player was "majestic in presence" that "the poise of his head was stag-like" that he had "a great voice which boomed like a bell," that he was "regal, subtle, pathetic," and that "every one who was ever associated with him loved and respected him."

Ask some veteran theatergoer "What was Booth like as Hamlet?" and he will say "Oh, he was wonderful." Perhaps the face of the old theatergoer will grow animated and Booth may live again for a moment in his mind, but we who have never seen Booth will never know anything about him. Nobody can recreate and explain the art of a dead actor to the next generation. Even men who do tricks and true magic with words are not adept enough to set down any lasting portrait of an actor on the wing.

Juvenile Fiction

A good deal of whitewash has flowed past the fence, but Tom Sawyer's trick still holds good. Even to-day it is possible to get hard work done by making people think of it as a privilege. In looking over an autumn catalogue, we came across a series of books for young persons in which we were struck by the titles, "When Mother Lets Us Help" and "When Mother Lets Us Cook." We trust that the series will be extended along these lines. If so, we intend to use as birthday gifts for H. 3rd, "When Father Lets Me Stoke the Furnace," "When Father Lets Me Shine his Shoes," and "When Father Lets Me Lend Him Money."

Polo Grounds Press Box, 1921

One of the most pathetic experiences in the world is to sit in the press box at the Polo Grounds and watch the baseball writers repress their emotions when Babe Ruth knocks a home run. They are denied the privilege of throwing their straw hats into the middle of the diamond or even of slapping anybody on the back. Good form dictates that "the longest hit ever seen on the grounds" shall be received in stony silence by the working press. Of course, this unnatural repression leads to outbursts in other directions. If you happen to hear "It's Always

Lilac Time in Lisbon" recalled for the fifteenth time some evening in the theatre, you may know that a couple of baseball writers are having a night off.

Dorothy Parker

Jacob Ben-Ami in "Samson and Delilah"

If I had thought for a moment that you would stand for it, I should start right off by saying, in full, round tones easily audible in the farthest corner of the room, that Jacob Ben-Ami, late of the Yiddish Theater and now of the Hopkins production of "Sampson and Delilah," is a great actor. I am prevented from so doing by the fear that, if I did, you would leave this department deservedly flat, and turn hurriedly over to the advertising section to lose yourself in the account of how Victor Jones improved his memory in a single evening. Were it not for that, I should go even further, if my nerve held out, and announce that Jacob Ben-Ami is one of the greatest actors on the stage today. And I should add to that statement, for the sake of dramatic effect, the purely rhetorical question, "Now what do you think about that?"

But nobody knows better than you that this is no way to start. Enthusiasm is one of the greatest dangers that menace American home life today, and is undoubtedly back of the Wall Street explosion, the Elwell case, and the feeling of discontent among the working classes. And, aside from all that, once its gets into a play review, it does show up the author so.

In particular, the use of enthusiasm in connection with Ben-Ami is not according to the best usage. It is looked upon, indeed, as little short of *nouveau*. The thing to do is to tiptoe about, finger warningly on lip, glancing furtively to right and left, and muttering through clenched teeth, "Wait—wait and see."

That is the method so successfully adopted by the various deans of newspaper dramatic critics. Do any of them lose their heads sufficiently to concede that Ben-Ami isn't bad, as actors go these days? Echo answers, "I should say not."

Some of the bolder among them may commit themselves so far as to hint that he does fairly well in "Samson and Delilah," but they hasten to cover up their recklessness by adding that it is impossible to pass any judgment upon his future competence until he has been seen in "Hedda Gabler," "Hamlet," "The School for Scandal," "Peter Pan," and "Ladies' Night." Such is the opinion of the radical element.

The conservatives dismiss the whole affair by saying that it is hardly fair to expect them to make any comment upon Ben-Ami's performance in "Samson and Delilah" until they have the opportunity to see him in "Ghosts," "Macbeth," "Ben-Hur," "Way Down East," and "The Merry Widow." They round out their critiques by implying, in considerably more than so many words, that they gravely doubt if Edwin Booth would have thought much of the methods of the newcomer.

In fact, the impression stamped upon a sensitive mind, after prolonged poring over their reviews, is that any one overheard calling Ben-Ami a good actor is liable to get five years' imprisonment or twenty-five hundred dollars' fine, or probably both, while the penalty for calling him great is the same as that for manslaughter.

Well, if it is a criminal defense, the police patrol is due to back up before our front door at any minute. It is, of course, hardly practicable for us to announce that Jacob Ben-Ami would be great in any play in which his manager might choose to exploit him in the future. But one wonders just how that ever came to be the issue, anyway, and just why it is that the hoarier critics have worked themselves into such a state about his possible future rôles. To a moderately unprejudiced observer, the question seems to be not "What would Jacob Ben-Ami be like in a revival of 'The Two Orphans,' if anyone should ever revive it?" but "How is Jacob Ben-Ami in " 'Samson and Delilah,' " And to that, we can but reply, "Great!"

In appearance, Ben-Ami is remarkably like some one you have seen somewhere; the resemblance worries you all through the play. Finally, toward the end of the evening, you discover who it is, and sink back, satisfied. His face is curiously like Charlie Chaplin's.

"Samson and Delilah" gives him his first rôle in English; one had to keep reminding oneself of that, though, for save for an unconquerable "oi" sound in such words as "first" and "work," and the substitution of "d" for "th," his seems like an experienced pronunciation. He is far easier to understand than a wide selection of native-born stars who have been playing in English, roughly speaking, all their careers. Yet his surprisingly good English cannot claim all the credit for this; it seems as if one could understand him if he were playing in Chinese. His words say much less than his movements, his gestures, his singularly mobile face.

Of his acting of the rôle of the half-mad poet, made wholly mad by the discovery of his wife's love for a blunt-witted merchant, it is difficult to speak and keep calm. Extravagant praise makes the poorest of reading; as soon as a writer begins to turn on the superlatives, his clients promptly drop off. There is nothing like an exclamation point to put a full stop to a reader's interest. So I have your own welfare at heart when I say that Ben-Ami's performance is that of an artist, and let it go at that. Doubtless, as the venerable reviewers affirm, his acting is all at variance with the old tradition; but that, in these biased eyes is no faint praise. Perhaps, as they say, he has still to prove himself and that, given a great play, he may be shown up by it to be but a mediocre actor. Possibly he will, but the entire contents of this old homestead, from the family plate to one slightly soiled, wire-haired terrier puppy, will be freely staked that will not.

It almost seems as if, in giving life to the dense and heavy "Samson and Delilah," Ben-Ami had already accommodated a far more difficult feat than those the critics have set for him to perform before they will acknowledge him. Undoubtedly, "Samson and Delilah" is a poor, stuffy, tiresome thing, when you stop to think it over. The thing is that you don't stop to think it over. All you can think about is Ben-Ami; if you think of the play at all while he is on the stage, it is only to rate it under the general head of the most interesting dramas of the decade.

"Samson and Delilah" is translated from the Scandinavian of Sven Lange. What a blessing the word "Scandinavian" is when you can't for the life of you recall whether Mr. Lange was Danish or Swedish or Norwegian! "Scandinavian" lets you out so readily. It is just another of those plays which are forever being translated from the Scandinavian.

But no one who has seen it can ever have any but the kindliest feelings for it, for it serves to bring Jacob Ben-Ami to our stage. Besides— if any "besides" is needed—it has Pauline Lord as its heroine. There is no actress who acts so painlessly Miss Lord; you keep forgetting that she is acting at all, and are apt to undervalue her performance because of its very naturalness. Her unfinished sentences, her nervous, aimless movements—real people speak and move about in just that way. Most extraordinary of all, she doesn't look like an actress. It is just as though a real woman, someone who might perfectly well live in the apartment across the hall, were up on the stage before you. Those who crave an evening of good, hard acting are inclined to feel somewhat cheated, save for her few moments of terror at the end of the play. Outside of that, they might just as well save their money and stay home and look at their wives. Miss Lord does not even appear in a complete repertory of Lucile gowns in her rôle as the wife of the impoverished poet.

The heavy-witted home-wrecker is played by Robert Haines, who, again according to the deans, is pitiably miscast. This seems however, a bit rough on Mr. Haines. It is one of those rôles in which anybody in which anybody would seem to be miscast. It is pleasant to be able to report that the piece has now been moved to the Thirty-ninth Street Theater from the Greenwich Village Theater, where it opened and every tense moment was gently smoothed over by the cheery sound of the subway train rumbling away right underneath, as if to say that no matter what was happening on the stage, God was in His heaven and business was going on as usual.

Even those who condemn "Samson and Delilah" most sweepingly can scarcely help but feel that the lady whom I overheard on the way out was a shade harsh in her comment. "Well," she summed up, "I didn't hear one bright, witty saying in the whole thing." Undoubtedly she had the right on her side, but after all—

(1921)

Ruth Hale

A Shelf of Recent Books
Two Out of a Possible Three

Experience has taught us that autobiographies are usually written by people who have been considerably picked on, and who aim to place their side of the matter before the public while there is yet time. The majestic feeling of being able to say to oneself, when the slings and arrows are flying, "Of course, I could tell you a thing or two if I would," seems to find its most satisfying outlet in an autobiography.

Well, writing a book, or copying out your love letters, is certainly a hard enough job, and we ought not to begrudge the authors even their feeblest source of energy for so doing. If we have a complaint against any of the three ladies whose lives and times are at hand: Lady Susan Townley ("Indiscretions of Lady Susan," D. Appleton and Co.), Margot Asquith ("Margot Asquith: An Autobiography, Volumes III and IV," George H. Doran Co.), and Mrs. Patrick Campbell ("My Life and Some Letters," Dodd, Mead and Co.), it is that their apologies are largely for the lives of their husbands, to whose emotions upon being so championed we can imagine nothing being added but a pained surprise.

We will say at the outset that if you should happen to want to get one or all of these chronicles, you will find in Margot a candid though somewhat chaotic tale bearing on political doings in England from 1900 on; in Mrs. Pat an obliquely revealing story of a fine if somewhat muddled woman in London's world of letters; and in Lady Susan the reason why we, for one, shrink at the very mention of her name.

Lady Susan describes her life as the wife of a diplomat who appears to have been hastened about from place to place by his Foreign Office, giving her constant new fields for the play of her sprightly temperament and subject matter for her memoirs. In her final chapter she tells how her husband failed of a deserved promotion because, so the Foreign

Office said, of "the indiscretions of Lady Susan." Therefore the book's title. The Foreign Office then, apparently, behaved very badly indeed in refusing her a hearing. But we felt sure we knew why. If they knew the half about her that her book lets out, they simply couldn't abide the woman, and yet did not have quite the heart to say so. What she actually did, on her own accounting, wasn't a patch on what we've known the wives of other diplomats to do, from a certain part of our past spent reporting in Washington; but if she was not particularly indiscreet, she was invariably arrogant and vainglorious. She hadn't the knack of doing things, and she thought she had. The combination is fatal, and we devoutly hope we have heard the last of Lady Susan.

It is a great relief to turn to Mrs. Pat. She also does what she can for her husbands: Sergeant Patrick Campbell and George Cornwallis-West. But Mrs. Pat would have to marry Moses, or Mustapha Kemal, or heaven knows whom, to get a husband who could be half as interesting as she is herself, so by virtue of this specific gravity she remains the central figure of her book. She tells of her life very honorably, not trying to make it more or less distinguished than it is. She tells of her rôles, which of them were successful and which were failures, and usually very acutely why. Then she undoes her old letters for us. Some them are splendid, and some of them, particularly those from Bernard Shaw, are positively news. Who would have thought that Shaw could sign a letter, for instance, with "Good nightest." We made great haste, when we came upon it, to fight back the impulse to gag; but after all, if Shaw could bear to write it we ought to be able to read it, and we cannot suppose that Mrs. Pat simply made it up on him. Her book is the revelation of a woman whose spirit is both large and high, whose history has been amusing, stirring, tragic, and rounded. You will be sure to like her.

You may not be so sure to like Margot Asquith, but you cannot very well help being stimulated by her. We are going a long way round to try and describe one peculiar quality of her. When Dean Kirchwey waked up one morning to find himself on one of Archie Stevenson's little lists of dangerous persons during the war, Kirchwey said promptly, "I'd like to wring his neck." The irritated informality of that phrase immediately dropped Stevenson and all his works forty fathoms beneath the serious consideration of any sane person. As far as Kirchwey was concerned,

Stevenson could contain no menace. Well, we can imagine that many English politicians must often have felt that same exasperation at Margot Asquith, accompanied by exactly that same absence of fear. She does appear to have mixed a good deal in things that did not need her. But those who thought her possessed of the slightest evil intent, to her country, to her people, or to anything else, must have been simpletons. She is an honest woman, one of personal force so great that no limitations whatever could restrain her. She is generous, tolerant, impetuous, and full of healthy inquisitiveness. And, although she might—in fact must—have injured many a statesman's sense of official dignity, she does not anywhere appear to have injured anybody's sense of personal dignity, which shows her innately and deeply kind. The rather large gesture of her dedication: *Les chiens aboyent, la caravane passé* ("Let the world say what it will"), which she credits to her son-in-law, Prince Antoine Bibesco, is of a piece with her. That was the attitude which nurtured her energy to breeze through politics. We think it grossly unfair to ascribe to her the mediocre showing of her husband in the last election. The left wing of English politics, in the last four years, has moved so violently leftward that the former outpost of the party is now a mere *embusqué*. Anyway, whether calamitous or not, the final two volumes of her autobiography are gay and interesting, and seeing that they are about politics, that is no mean testimony.

(1922)

Laurence Stallings

Celluloid Psychology

If I were a psychologist (and maybe I am) then I would straightaway begin work upon a compilation of motion picture reflexes. My concern for the psychology of the films is not founded in a deep yearning for better pictures. They surely must be perfect now. I only wish to make the celluloid principles of human conduct universal: to apply them not to a white screen in a darkened house, but to the hearts of men.

Lest the reader think I am a fanatic or a fool, let me hasten to show briefly how every jail in the United States can be razed and every police court gutted of its records of evil men. Therefore, before I get into the body of my article, I shall explain at the outset how we can obliterate the criminal instinct from the submerged section of our civilization. And by way of being controversial, I defy any motion picture addict to cite one film where the remedy I have in mind failed to effect a cure.

Lombroso and the criminologists meant no offense in damning so many of us to hereditary penitentiaries. They can be pardoned their unflattering opinions, because Lombroso and the rest did not take into consideration the enormous salutary effects of the American Northwest. The criminologists have paid close attention to faces, but oh, how they have gone by the great wide open spaces.

There is only one remedy for the criminal: he must go deep into the Heart of the Redwoods, and the state must defray the expense of the migratory reformation. I say the state must pay the cost, because I do not believe the motion picture authorities can afford to send every wrong-doer into the silent recesses of nature's forest giants. The Hollywood directors, to my certain knowledge, have sent scores of chaps into the tall timber for a twelve-month, and invariably have brought them back in the fifth reel to a perfect orgy of ethical rectitude in the sixth. How often have we seen the rude Jesse James, finally trapped by the police, shoulder his axe and march into the Northwest to become transformed into a Henry James at the end. They have convinced me from Los Angeles that out yonder under the fierce Northern lights, a new soul is hanging from every tree.

Compared to the present burden placed upon society by its erring children, the expense of the undertaking that I sponsor is a trifling one. I should like to see the state, as each man is sentenced to imprisonment, risk the experiment by freeing the culprit and furnishing him with the following requisites:

> One bright woodman's axe
> One mackinaw (cap to match)
> One pair snowshoes
> One ticket to Northwest
> One Alsatian police dog

Let us adopt this procedure; at the end of one year from the day the plan is put into effect there will be no criminals remaining in the United States, I assure you. Twenty million of my countrymen see the thing happen daily on the screen—that greatest factor in educating the masses—and we have no doubt of its success. As soon as the number of Alsatian police dogs is commensurate with the number of prisoners in our corrective institutions, I propose laying the matter before the proper authorities for immediate and wholesale action. And one year from the day will see a horde of white-faced Galahads tramping nobly back to the settlements to rejoin society, police dogs leaping madly beneath their heels.

Contingent upon the criminal's departure for the Redwoods he shall be made acquainted with one slightly shopworn maiden in one of the many reformatories now dotting our great and glorious land. While her hero is braving the vicissitudes of the frozen north, she shall undergo what the neurologists term "referred pain." For each letter that this lady dispatches from her tower to the rail head in the woods (where it will be inserted in the police dog's mouth for delivery to his master beneath the noblest of the forest giants) she will receive from the culprit in return one sprig of bayberries. None who have viewed a motion picture show will doubt that this woodsy reminder can bring the nostalgia of respectability into the maiden's nostrils. And so the state must be obligated, when the year is done, to supply the pair with the following impediments:

> One gray haired chaplain
> One black cassock for same
> Two flower girls
> One little Ringbearer
> Pair velvet pants for same
> Squad of merry young men
> Evening clothes for same

Thus at a trifling cost can we do away with the criminal instinct as fast as it appears in society. The whole expense for each pair reclaimed through the application of celluloid psychology is negligible in return for its benefits. Think of the terrible careers of the Jukes boys and girls because they avoided the woods and kept close to the cities!

These are but the beginnings of a Hollywoodland Utopia which shall, thanks to the cinema's discernment, presently descend upon mankind. Inherent in the teachings of the films are remedies equally simple for all the ills the social body is heir to. Let us get to the problem of industrial management, a simple one enough, and disposed of most readily upon the white screen. Only the other day I saw some huge shipyards put on a fair return basis without any of the absurdities of cost accounting, overhead, depreciation on plant structures, etc., through the medium of a shipowner's daughter. Do I hear shipowners from the Clyde to Kobe, Japan, pricking up their distraught ears at this piece of news? Tell them, then, that their bottoms shall beat upon the seven seas if they have blonde daughters and the perspicacity to endow them with the following resources:

> One riding crop
> One handsome superintendent
> One Arabian hunter
> One tri-cornered hat
> One evening gown
> One pipe organ

This article is just a preface to the things that are going to happen after we adopt the celluloid psychology. The question of America's position in international affairs diminishes in complexity as I follow the channel of my cinematographical experiences. I do not believe, for instance, that we liberals can ever affect the recognition of the Moscow government by Washington until we elect to the Presidency of the United States a man who has had a son in Red Cross work in Russia. If by now the reader can follow my mental processes (if he is a motion picture devotee his are probably ahead of mine) he can readily see that the Red Cross man was once imprisoned by the Soviet, and later released through the pressure brought to bear upon Trotsky by a dark-eyed ward of that great general's grandmother. It is not superfluous to paint the obligatory scene at Ellis Island where the child, praying before a rude Ikon, is interned by immigration commissioners, and the boy's impassioned harangue at the weekly meeting of his father's cabinet at the White House while the white kitten plays with a ball of yarn underneath the President's chair? Picture the following things:

The altar in the Kremlin
High dignitaries
Stars and Stripes
Blood red banner
The lace covered Metropolitan
Lohengrin
Borzoi

The thing is really so simple that I feel a bit ridiculous in advancing this solution. It looks so puerile in print.

If we want a League of Nations, there are at least a score of taffy-haired young women who will put the diplomatic mission across quicker than Lord Robert Cecil can say Geneva. The Carnegie Foundation has but to select one, and then turn the trick by issuing to the chosen damsel:

One 6-cyl roadster
One aviation helmet
One English butler (faithful)
One permanent wave
One pair riding boots (patent)
One varsity halfback (for intelligence work)

The malefactors of great wealth are still with us, despite the ironies of Mr. Marx, the bludgeonings of Mr. Roosevelt, and the shoutings of Mr. Hearst. I suspect that few of our economists have given the problem the treatment it has received in Hollywood. They must not be censured for having failed to find a solution where I have succeeded. Few of them are conversant with the films. It is not their oversight; it is my good fortune. I confess of late I have been assisting a motion picture editor in his task of reviewing the new pictures that are shown on Broadway each Sunday, and so quite by accident have witnessed test after test of the remedy. Sabbath day after Sabbath day I have seen the cinema settle labor disputes, bring about collective bargaining, relieve agricultural conditions brought by post-war deflation, and in general create an entire cordiale among rich and poor by application of simple celluloid axioms.

The rich man can go through the eye of a needle quite easily, if only he will spend one night penniless in the slums or upon a park bench. I have seen them seized by contrition so often upon the screen after they have spent one night in this fashion that I have pooled my faith with the twenty million who accept the conversion blindly each day. I realize what a target the idea makes for economists, but what are they in the face of so many of us? After all, as Abraham Lincoln or Roscoe Arbuckle said, if the mass verdict of the common people is at fault, whom else have we to trust this blessed Christmas Day?

Let us take a concrete case; and watch me apply the solution. When the next little cottages of Bethlehem and Newport are astir with mutterings about the rights of the majority and the safety of the individual, there is no need for the steel workers to go on strike. Let them, instead, prevail upon Judge Gary to cast himself adrift, penniless, for one night in New York City. This is not an exacting request, and Judge Gary should welcome any solution that obviates his writing so many ads during the lockout. Let him share a park bench at Union Square with some down-and-outer whose wife is in the charity ward of a nearby lying-in hospital. Twenty million of us know the struggles that will rend his breast as he rubs elbows with unfortunates. And equal number of us know a priori that when "the first faint streak of dawn, a-down the city's gutters, lights a new day" the Judge will have a contrite heart. Fancy the eagerness when salvaged from the once-cent coffee line of St. Vincent's, with which he will rush to the nearest Western Union station and send the telegram heard 'round the world. Let us flash that message now upon the screen of our imagination:

> SEND MEN BACK WORK AT
> DOUBLE THEIR DEMANDS
> STOP ASK FOREMAN MEET
> ME HERE SCHWAB'S LIBRARY
> FOR TEA STOP I AM CHANGED
> MAN STOP
>
> GARY

How easily we may inaugurate a five-hour day, with fair play and may the Bessemer man win.

(1919)

Alexander Woollcott

Second Thoughts on First Nights: "Love 'Em and Leave 'Em"

This next column displays all of Aleck Woollcott's tricks: logrolling for a fellow Vicious Circle friend, plugging his alma mater (Hamilton College), and taking a sidetrack from the dramatic criticism to tell a shaggy dog story.

Few of the plays that have come to town since the first curtains began to rise last August have seemed to me so nourishing as the unheralded and unpretentious comedy of life behind the counter of the department store, which has settled down behind the snowbanks at the Sam H. Harris Theater. This is the play called "Love 'Em and Leave 'Em" which was written by George Abbott and John V. A. Weaver.

Abbott is the rangy actor of cowboy type who collaborated with James Gleason in the writing of "The Fall Guy."

Weaver is the poet who has made a name for himself by writing verse in the American language. "Love 'Em and Leave 'Em" marks his first appearance in New York as a dramatist, although a quite different play of his with the same title was done to death in the suburbs about a year ago.

There have in recent years been a good many forerunners of this comedy. Such playwrights as George Kaufman, Marc Connelly, Elmer Rice, Dorothy Parker and the like, have all rather made it a point to use the American peasantry for dramatic material. They have visited the small flats, they have studied desire under the "L"; they have derived no end of amusement at the simple pastimes and pretenses of what used to be described as "life among the lowly."

But in all such ventures I have been made uncomfortable by detecting the note of the intelligentsia going slumming. I have been almost embarrassed by the consciousness that at such plays as "Close Harmony" and "To the Ladies" my humbler neighbors were being inspected through the lorgnette of sophistication.

This distraction is totally absent from "Love 'Em and Leave 'Em." In the last act of the play we are permitted to attend the rehearsal of the peasant to be given in the annual entertainment staged by the loving employees of Ginsberg's dry goods store—a fearful allegory of duty and dissipation winding up with an anthem entitled "Glory, Glory Under Ginsberg."

The authors of "To the Ladies" would have had even more fun out of this pageant than the authors of "Love 'Em and Leave 'Em" did. But I think that the difference, as impalpable and un-debatable as the difference in the tone of the voice, might be traced to this: that the authors of "Love 'Em and Leave 'Em" felt a fraternity with the clerks behind the counter at Ginsberg's and would have really worked very hard in that pageant if they had been necktie salesmen as well. I have a sneaking suspicion that "Love 'Em and Leave 'Em" is so good because you could scratch either Mr. Abbott or Mr. Weaver and find underneath only a clerk at good old Ginsberg's.

I do not know what accident of the theater threw Weaver into Abbott's arms. In the old days when Johnnie Weaver was generally regarded as the most intense undergraduate at Hamilton College, Abbott was a stalwart football player who used to visit the Hamilton Hill every fall with the Rochester team. Whether they met at that time, deponent sayeth not, not knowing. It was at that time, however, that I myself first encountered John Weaver and oddly enough that the encounter had its origins in dramatic art.

When commencement time was approaching in June, 1912, I received an impassioned telegram from the dramatic club at Hamilton College asking me to bring up with me a suit of Roman armor of such and such dimension, to be worn by one of the actors in the Latin play. Since there is nothing one cannot buy in New York, it was a matter of a few moments to telephone for a suit of Roman armor. I forget now where I got it, but I presume it was from the American Can Company. Its transportation, even so slight a distance as that lying between New

York and Utica, was not without its embarrassment. You can bootleg a suit of Roman armor into the rack over your Pullman seat, but if every swerve of the train pitches it off on the head of some irritable fellow passenger, you find yourself getting off the train at Utica as something of a social outcast.

The incident has been the more firmly branded in my memory by the circumstances that the director of the Latin play had inadvertently sent the measurements of the wrong actor, and that when the armor was actually put on Weaver's comparatively minute person, the breast plate came on down to his shin and gave him the un-warlike aspect of a Roman legionnaire clad in a tin Mother Hubbard. As we overcame by force his profound disinclination to appear before his ribald classmates in any such unbecoming a costume, I little thought that one day I would be reviewing a play of his for a New York newspaper.

Weaver is the husband of Peggy Wood in private life, if that old fashioned phrase can be used to describe the singularly candid existence led by such arch contributors to the more remunerative among the confessional magazines. In addition to the normal agitation induced by the production of a first play in New York, Weaver's attention was divided all during the first week by news from the box office and tidings from a lying-in hospital to which Miss Wood had retreated.

In "Love 'Em and Leave 'Em" the struggle is between two sisters who share a room in the boarding house not far down the street from Ginsberg's. I shall not soon forget the scene in that room at the end of the first act when the sisters put out the light and go to bed. They are at loggerheads over a bonehead of contention who works in the necktie at Ginsberg's and the fretful accusation issuing from one bed is cut short as the curtain falls by the stern voice from the other saying, "Shut your face, I'm saying my prayers." I shall not soon forget the really magnificent quarrel scene between the two sisters in the boarding house parlor in the second act, not the murderous crap game which is still in progress as the curtain of that act falls.

"Love 'Em and Leave 'Em" is the work of a young producer named Jed Harris and its cast performances which reach perfection are given by Florence Johns and Donald Meek.

(1926)

The Vicious Circle

The Indian Song Game

It is a well-known fact that the Round Table gang enjoyed word games. One of their lost gems, discovered in a desk drawer, was a challenge to insert the name of an Indian tribe into the title or lyric of a well-known song. As the game may have continued after the Round Table disbanded, exact attributions are impossible.

Cheyenne, Cheyenne, Harvest Moon

Iroquois for You, Now It's Your Turn to Cree Over Me

Arapahoe Troubles In Dreams

Narragansett Right Down and Write Myself a Letter

O, Comanche Faithful

You Took the Pottawattame That Once Was the Hottawattame

Algonquin Buy a Paper Doll That I Can Call My Own

Seminole Fashioned Song for an Old-Fashioned Girl

Osage Can You See

Piute Another Log on the Fire

I'll Be Down to Get You in Apache Honey

Aztec the High Road and You Take the Low Road

Tewa For Two

Mohawk Belongs to Daddy

Wyandotte We Do This More Often?

Shoshone the Way to Go Home

Way Down Upon the Shawnee River

Dakota Be a Moonlight Saving Time

I Navajo I Could Love Anybody Honey Like I'm Loving You

Pueblo Out the Lights and Go to Sleep

Puye Arms Around Me Honey Don't You Cry

Sioux Beats My Heart for You

Oswego, (So Goes the Nation) (Marching Through Georgia)

Erie Berie Bin

I Sent a Letter to My Love and Onondega Lost It

Ute You're Driving Me Crazy

Ol' Rockin' Cherokee's Got Me

Chippewattafall By a Cottage Small

You Ottawa See Sally on Sunday

Mohican Fight Like He Can Love

You Crow to My Head

Piuteful Dreamer

What's the Ute of Wondering

Happy Taltec

Unka Dinka Do

Huron Old Smoothie

Robert Benchley

Swing Music

One glorious element of Robert Benchley's "Melody and Madness" radio program (1938-1940, unfortunately, largely lost to history) was his off-the-cuff "explanation" of whatever struck his fancy when the director said,

"You're on." For as much as he could neither sing (except in bad Welsh) nor play a musical instrument more complex than the mandolin, various aspects of music always seemed on the tip of his tongue. In combing the ash heaps of history, we have unearthed and resurrected "Swing Music" and "Crooning," which both combine the melody and the madness.

This evening I want to give you a little talk on swing music, its origin, development and probable future, and then we might go into a short history of Italian art of the 17th Century, and possibly scramble some eggs.

I feel particularly fitted to speak on swing music, because I can't carry a tune, either.

Swing was invented by a man who went to play at a party and forgot to bring his music along: Johann Gotfried Immergluck Gesundheit was born in Japan in 1789. He was a backward child but very friendly and was taken out of school at the age of 5. This brings us up to 1794. It was long about this period of Gesundheit's life that he took up the Second Mandolin.

Now this task was made even more difficult by the fact that, instead of the usual mandolin pick made of celluloid, he used the thumb of an old mitten which he had cut off and held between the first and second fingers. This procedure really got him nowhere musically, but it kept him out of mischief.

We now come to the third period of Gesundheit's boyhood, when he came under the influence of James Watt, the inventor of the steam engine. It was a very important period in the life of the young composer, as it gave him his first feeling for dissonance and cured him of an inferiority complex which had, at one time, threatened to make him cross-eyed. He also at this period learned to tie a four-in-hand.

Students of Gesundheit have sometimes wondered at the strange, nostalgic quality in his music which comes from having the A strings tuned so that they sound like B-flat. This move can be traced directly to the fact that he fell in love shortly after learning to tie a four-in-hand and became morose and gloomy, refusing to eat or to play any other note but B-flat. This brought a certain sameness to his music and caused the police to interfere.

Between October and 1845, he managed to find time to plant and harvest several thousand radishes. Through, now, with the formative stages of his career, Gesundheit drifted into shoplifting, but he never quite forgot his first love, music, and occasionally took some tune that he had heard in life and, by way of subtle compliment, signed his own name to it. This really didn't make much difference to the original composer, however, as by the time Gesundheit had got through with his arranging it, there was nothing left of the original music.

In our next lecture we will take up the development of swing music from this point, including Gesundheit's better-known compositions, "Hurricane in F-major" for fire tongs and woodwinds; "A Day at the Dentist," arranged for D-strings only; and a complete opera score entitled "My Impressions of Parsifal." In this latter work, where Wagner used the strings, Gesundheit substituted the symphony and vice versa. (He also changed several of the melodies). We will then go on to trace swing's future (heaven forbid). I thank you.

(circa 1938-1940)

Robert Benchley

Crooning

Ladies and gentlemen, the subject of my discourse tonight is crooning.

Now, as you all know, the human throat is made up of three parts:

1) The larynx,

2) The pharynx, and

3) The Adam's apple.

The Adam's apple, of course, is the most important part of a crooner's throat, as it is the part on which the bow tie rests. Now, the ordinary singer sings with his mouth open, thusly: [*loud-ish*] Yaaah.

You notice how unpleasant that is? But the crooner, the crooner sings thusly: [*softly*] Waaah. Which is just as unpleasant but harder to hear.

Now, another important part of the crooner is the juke box. It is estimated, and I quote, "that in the twelve month period from 1939 to 1944, Americans, or people of American descent, put into juke boxes a total of 19,742,000 nickels and five cents." And I unquote.

Another phenomenon in connection with crooning is the growth of what is known as the bobby sock [*embarrassedly*] (that's no relation). In line with this, the noted psychologist at the Psychology Institute, Psychology, Pennsylvania, the head of the Outpatient Department, Dr. Erich Hoffenstummer, said, quote, "It could happen to you." Unquote.

Dr. Hoffenstummer, incidentally, has just left the institute and is now singing at the Orpheum under the name of "Perry" Hoffenstummer. Velvet rhythm, you know.

The two leading crooners of the day are Mr. Frank Sinatra and Mr. Bing Crosby. Mr. Sinatra has a huge following, which is highly enthusiastic about his singing, causing them to emit such cries as [*loudly and brashly*] "Oh, Frankie!"

Now, I have here a chart which I have just run off on my automatic pencil. Here is a red line which begins at the figure 100,000 and ends in July. From July to 200,000, we have a blue line, which is joined at Point X here by another blue line, whereupon both blue lines curve back into the red line, and here we say "Bye Bye Blues."

Now, there are various other lines here scooting up and down across the page, but these lines mean nothing. They're left over from an old chart of mine on birth rates in maternity wards.

(circa 1938-1940)

Deems Taylor

Mr. Whiteman Experiments

The New York World *gave Deems Taylor, a highly-regarded composer, a national platform when he became the newspaper's music critic. Taylor was in the audience on Feb. 12, 1924, when George Gershwin unveiled for the first time his masterpiece, "A Rhapsody in Blue," at New York's first large jazz concert.*

The audience at Aeolian Hall yesterday was as unprecedented as the concert that collected it. There was the regular music set, from Walter Damrosch and Ernest Bloch down to the critics, assembled out of curiosity to see what queer monster a serious program of jazz might be; and there was another audience that had come over from the neighborhood commonly known as the Great White Way to see its beloved jazz make a debut among the highbrows. In the intermission, learned musicologists debated heatedly up and down the aisles, while upstairs two ladies came to blows over the question of whether or not it was good form to smoke at an afternoon concert.

The occasion was a concert by Paul Whiteman and his Palais Royale Orchestra. Mr. Whiteman, whose achievements in organizing and conducting contemporary dance orchestras have made him famous even in Europe, has theories regarding the so-called jazz band. He feels that the rhythms, melodies and instrumentation of our modern popular music contain the germ of a school of genuine American composition and his concert yesterday was designed not only to exhibit jazz as it is today, but jazz as it was and may become.

One could have told that something unusual was afoot even before the playing began. For the staid rows of organ pipes that form the usual background of the Aeolian Hall platform were concealed behind a picturesque and elaborately decorated screen, and the orchestra, consisting mainly of wind and percussion instruments, with two grand pianos and a celesta thrown in, performed to an accompaniment of shifting colored lights.

First a jazz band of the now obsolete pre-war type—piano, coronet, trombone, and clarinet—played the "Livery Stable Blues" as a sort of horrible example, with the acrobatic and tonal contortions that have done so much to make "jazz" a synonym for vulgarity among the musical elect. This was immediately followed by an ancient jazz tune, "Mama Loves Papa," scored and played in the modern and subtler style.

A comedy group that followed revealed the Handelian origin of a certain famous fruit song and later permitted Mr. Ross Gorman to give an astounding exhibition of virtuosity upon the saxophone, oboe and clarinet. This was followed by a demonstration of good and bad jazz scoring, and a group of three modern pieces, including the famous "Limehouse Blues," written and scored for a modern jazz orchestra.

After Zez Confrey had displayed the possibilities of jazz playing on the piano, the first half of the program ended with a piece called "Russian Rose" that illustrated the modern arranger's skill in working with borrowed material, the material in this instance being Rachmaninoff's C-sharp minor prelude, Tchaikowsky's "Marche Slave," and the "Volga" Boat Song.

The second half of the concert, equally entertaining, contained more solid material for the serious musician. After playing a symphonic rhapsody upon three airs by Irving Berlin, Mr. Whiteman introduced a suite of four serenades by Victor Herbert that were not only charming in their thematic material but demonstrated the fact that Mr. Herbert's skill in orchestration extends to handling the unusual instrumental combinations that a jazz band presents.

This was followed by three jazz orchestrations of what Broadway calls "standard selections," the best being a delightful and irreverent transcription of MacDowell's "To a Wild Rose."

Just before the closing number—a brilliant adaptation of Elgar's "Pomp and Circumstance"—George Gershwin played "A Rhapsody in Blue" of his own composition for piano and jazz orchestra. In a way this was the most interesting offering of the afternoon, for it was an experiment in creating the jazz instrumental and thematic idiom seriously, and it was by no means an unsuccessful one. Despite its shortcomings—chief of which were an occasional sacrifice of appropriate scoring to momentary effect, and a lack of continuity in the musical structure—Mr. Gershwin's piece possessed at least two themes of genuine musical worth and displayed a latent ability on the part of this young composer to say something of considerable interest in his chosen idiom.

In a hurried and necessarily brief chronicle such as this there is no chance to attempt detailed criticism or even to formulate conclusions. These must come later. Certainly the experiment was worth the trouble; and if noise be any criterion, yesterday's audience—all of it—had a good time.

(1924)

George S. Kaufman

The Other Side of Al Jolson

The New Yorker *did not invent the "Profiles" genre of journalism. For this piece in* Everybody's Magazine, *George S. Kaufman sat down with 34-year-old Al Jolson four years before Harold W. Ross launched his magazine.*

A soft-spoken average-looking young man sat in the Hotel Biltmore in New York, and talked. His talk was of the theatre, and so, as a matter of fact, was he. But there was nothing about him to impress you unduly with that fact. Although his coat was off, no six-inch monogram could be observed on his shirt-sleeve, and he had caused not a single photograph of himself to be set tastefully here and there about the room. Certainly there was nothing to indicate that the modest occupant of the room was one of the two or three foremost entertainers of the American stage, and, exclusive of a handful of motion-picture actors, probably the highest-paid theatrical performer in the world.

Those who know Al Jolson only through his stage work will be hard put to visualize the real man. An easy and even loud assurance is so much a part of his footlight equipment that it is somewhat surprising to find this quality almost lacking between performances. To be sure, he is by no means utterly unconscious of his powers and his success, but it is mildly astonishing, in view of the eminence to which he has risen, to find that he is almost as diffident in the presence of his employers as any twenty-dollar-a-week clerk, that he is far from the robust figure that he appears to be on the stage, and that there is a good deal of the child about him in his simple enjoyment of simple matters. And, although this has been written of every comedian that ever lived, Al Jolson has an ambition to branch out a bit. No, not to play "Hamlet," or even to leave blackface forever and ever behind him, but to be an occasional performer upon the concert stage, and to produce a few plays.

He is the son of a Jewish cantor, this lusty shouter of popular ballads, and his real name is Asa Yoelson. No American player of note has had a more picturesque career, or a harder time of it getting to the top. As ballyhoo for a circus carousel, as general roustabout for the circus, as a youngster singing in the military camps during the Spanish war, as a dispenser of popular songs in the rear room of a café, required to make his nightly bed upon three or four chairs in that same back room, he has received enough hard knocks to last a lifetime. So if today, with ten thousand dollars a week or more pouring in upon him from his various activities, he finds himself a little uncertain as to just what he ought to do about it, he may be pardoned he momentary dizziness.

Al Jolson is just thirty-four, and an entertainer who stands supreme in his field. According to Lee Shubert, who has a better chance than most of us to observe the passing show and its satellites, there are only two people on the stage today who can go into any city in the United States and be sure to draw a packed house upon the mere strength of their names. The other is Fred Stone. The show doesn't matter. "Sinbad," for example, is an indifferent entertainment at best, but Jolson is now winding up his third season in it, and the production will have earned nearly a million and half dollars when it is finally packed away this summer.

And it's all Jolson. In Chicago last season, at the Auditorium, "Sinbad" was drawing seven thousand dollars a night, all that the house could hold, when Jolson felt his voice going back on him. He left for Palm Beach and a rest, while "Sinbad" continued with an understudy. But the nightly seven thousand dollars melted away to five hundred, and would have kept right on going to thirty-five cents if Jolson hadn't come back.

The people love him. They love to see him crouched over the footlights, singing with that sonorous voice of his, snapping his fingers, and in general "putting it over." "You Made Me Love You," "The Grown-Up Ladies," "Get Out and Get Under," "I Gave Her That," "Suwanee"—these are a few of the songs that Al Jolson has popularized. His may not be much of a voice, as the music critics regard voices, but it has a quality that goes over the footlights, a warmness that goes to the hearts of his audience. They love his stories, too—stories that seem to take on added point with the magnetic personality of Al Jolson as an ingredient. A good many comedians will tell you that Al Jolson "gets away with murder," that he gets uproarious laughter with material that they themselves would be afraid even to try.

He has been getting good results, lately, with the anecdote of the fastidious, middle-aged gentleman. He was sartorially perfect, this gentleman, from the exquisite set of his necktie to the discreet polish on his shoes. There was only one thing about him—he wore a toupee. But ah! even here he was the master. He had a little scheme to keep people from knowing it was a toupee. He put salt on it, to make them think it was dandruff.

It was a far cry from this sort of thing to the concert stage in Boston, but Jolson took the leap lightly and easily last fall, while "Sinbad" was playing a third or fourth engagement in The Hub. It began more or less as a joke—Jolson mentioned it to his press-agent in a kidding vein, and the latter promptly announced it. More than that, he fixed a date for it at the Boston Opera House, and put tickets on sale. Jolson laughed, and complimented the press-agent on getting the maximum out of it. Then something happened. Somebody bought a ticket. Somebody else bought another. Jolson was in for it.

He decided, accordingly, to do it properly, and engaged fifty-four members of the Boston Symphony Orchestra to appear with him. As the time approached he was probably the most nervous man in Boston. The Opera House, a great barn of a place, was packed to the rafters when Jolson came out on the stage. There was nothing of the great comedian about him—he was just an ordinary mortal scared stiff. The first thing he did was to ask the orchestra leader to keep the castanets quiet, but the conductor pointed to Jolson's knees in reply. Then the musicians went into something operatic and heavy; the Jolsonians in the audience looked at one another in surprise, and suddenly the music turned into an old coon-song, and Jolson began to sing. The audience laughed, and Jolson felt a bit easier.

He sang coon-songs, love-songs, jazz-songs, sweet old favorites—everything. He held the stage for two hours and three-quarters, and at eleven-fifteen the audience had to be sent home. News of the feat spread rapidly—it was something of an achievement for a Winter Garden black-face comic to give a concert that Boston took seriously—and next day the offers began to pour in from the music men. One of them offered five thousand dollars apiece for a series of twenty concerts. Jolson yearned to accept, for the experience and the prestige. But the producers of "Sinbad," not unnaturally, couldn't see it. And, since Jolson is under contract to them for another two years, theirs was the final word.

With the strenuous life of the concert singer denied him, Jolson drifts here and there looking for amusement. Palm Beach is his favorite playground, and hunting, fishing and golfing are the trio that loom largest in his off hours. There was a time when he played the races, but that day has passed. It passed, abruptly, when he lost $85,300 in a single afternoon at the Empire track in Yonkers, a little over a year ago. When that afternoon was over, Jolson told himself that he was through with horse-racing, and from that day he has not hazarded a dollar.

He is something better than a fair golfer—his bag of clubs goes with him on his travels, and he has played on perhaps half the golf courses in the country. For the benefit of golfers it might be added that he generally gets a ninety, which isn't bad for a black-face comedian, nor even so terrible for one in white-face.

And then, besides golf, he has one other mania. Imagine him, for example, at an orphanage just outside Philadelphia, observing the delight of the youngsters in a player-piano that he had presented to them. They lined up, on the occasion of that visit, and sang Jolson's own song, "Avalon," for him. He says it meant more to him than the thirty or forty thousand dollars that "Avalon" will bring him in royalties, and he was telling the truth. Imagine him, also, in and about the Pennsylvania coal district, going from house to house during the recent strike, and giving where it would do the most good. Al Jolson is a two-handed giver, but he likes to see where it goes. Probably his own early hardships have had something to do with that.

For there were hardships a-plenty in those early days. Young Asa Yoelson did his first singing under his father's watchful eye in a synagogue in Washington, his home, but in his heart of hearts he wasn't that kind of boy. He was inclined to be wild, with a fondness for the wharves and the railroad yards. When he was thirteen, Israel Zangwill's "Children of the Ghetto" opened in Washington, with Wilton Lackaye and Mabel Taliaferro as its stars, and an assortment of children were needed for the street scenes. So Asa made his first stage appearance as a Hester Street urchin, and did well enough for three performances. Then his father learned what was going on, and an understudy finished the week.

With his brother, Harry, he spent the next few years doing odd jobs of singing and ballyhooing in and about Washington, and then, when the Spanish war came, ran away from home to enlist. But he was only fifteen at the time, and accordingly, compromised by attaching himself to a regiment encamped at Middletown, Pennsylvania, in the capacity of general entertainer. For two months he sang for the soldiers and the miners in a variety of small towns in Pennsylvania, and then, when the Walter L. Main circus chanced to pass through Harrisburg, Jolson went in for circus life. He was engaged to render—and "render" he did—a single number in the "grand concert" that followed the performance proper.

The circus dropped him in York, Pennsylvania, and he traveled from there to Baltimore on the cow-catcher of a locomotive. Then came days as a newsboy, of singing in saloons, and of eventual discovery by the police, who were searching for him at the request of his father. In the "House of Refuge" he fed shirts to a machine until his health broke down, when he was allowed to go home. But home had scant attractions for Asa. He preferred even Al Reeves' burlesque troupe, which chanced to contain an opening for a youth to bellow the chorus of "My Jersey Lily" from the top gallery.

Never very strong, Jolson presently broke down again, and at seventeen he was once more within the ancestral walls. When he next broke loose, he made for New York, and spent a miserable six months singing for a pittance in bar-rooms and restaurants and sleeping on the riverfront. Again he went home, and again he came back, for, if there was one thing young Asa couldn't stand, it appears to have been home. When he came back a second time, he and his brother with a man named Palmer, he finally got a hold in vaudeville.

During all this Jolson never had appeared in blackface. Finally, however, a representative of the Poli circuit visited a minute theatre in Brooklyn in which Jolson was appearing, and told him his voice was so close to the negro that he should take advantage of the resemblance by blacking up. In fact, he informed him that he could have five weeks in the Poli theatres if he would appear in blackface. Jolson replied, characteristically, that he would black up permanently for two weeks and half, and the deal was on.

The ascent was easier after that. His first real success came at the Colonial Theatre in New York in 1909. Ralph Herz, dissatisfied with his billing, had refused to appear, and Jolson was rushed into the breach. His success was sensational, and there was plenty of vaudeville booking after that. He association with the Winter Garden began on the night that that playhouse opened, in the spring of 1911. It would be pleasant to record that he scored a great hit, but the plain truth is that he made his first appearance on the stage after midnight, and that no one paid any attention to him at all.

But those days have passed. Al Jolson today is on the crest of a great wave of popularity, and it is for him to say where it will sweep him.

(1921)

Edna Ferber

Old Man Minick

George S. Kaufman admired "Old Man Minick" so much that he asked Edna Ferber if they could bring it to the stage. The pair then wrote five more Broadway shows together. This 1922 story was adapted many times by Hollywood.

His wife had always spoiled him outrageously. No doubt of that. Take, for example, the matter of the pillows merely. Old man Minick slept high. That is, he thought he slept high. He liked two plump pillows on his side of the great, wide, old-fashioned cherry bed. He would sink into them with a vast grunting and sighing and puffing expressive of nerves and muscles relaxed and gratified. But in the morning there was always one pillow on the floor. He had thrown it there. Always, in the morning, there it lay, its plump white cheek turned reproachfully up at him from the side of the bed. Ma Minick knew this, naturally, after forty years of the cherry bed. But she never begrudged him that extra pillow. Each morning, when she arose, she picked it up on her way to shut the window. Each morning the bed was made up with two pillows on his side of it, as usual.

Then there was the window. Ma Minick liked it open wide. Old man Minick, who rather prided himself on his modernism (he called it being up to date) was distrustful of the night air. In the folds of its sable mantle lurked a swarm of dread things—colds, clammy miasmas, fevers.

"Night air's just like any other air," Ma Minick would say, with some asperity. Ma Minick was no worm; and as modern as he. So when they went to bed the window would be open wide. They would lie there, the two old ones, talking comfortably about commonplace things. The kind of talk that goes on between a man and a woman who have lived together in wholesome peace (spiced with occasional wholesome bickerings) for more than forty years.

"Remind me to see Gerson tomorrow about that lock on the basement door. The paper's full of burglars."

"If I think of it." She never failed to.

"George and Nettie haven't been over in a week now."

"Oh, well, young folks … Did you stop in and pay that Koritz the fifty cents for pressing your suit?"

"By golly, I forgot again! First thing in the morning."

A sniff. "Just smell the Yards." It was Chicago.

"Wind must be from the west."

Sleep came with reluctant feet, but they wooed her patiently. And presently she settled down between them and they slept lightly. Usually, some time during the night, he awoke, slid cautiously and with infinite stealth from beneath the covers and closed the wide-flung window to within a bare two inches of the sill. Almost invariably she heard him; but she was a wise old woman; a philosopher of parts. She knew better than to allow a window to shatter the peace of their marital felicity. As she lay there, smiling a little grimly in the dark and giving no sign of being awake, she thought, "Oh, well, I guess a closed window won't kill me either."

Still, sometimes, just to punish him a little, and to prove that she was nobody's fool, she would wait until he had dropped off to sleep again and then she, too, would achieve a stealthy trip to the window and would raise it slowly, carefully, inch by inch.

"How did that window come to be open?" he would say in the morning, being a poor dissembler.

"Window? Why, it's just the way it was when we went to bed." And she would stoop to pick up the pillow that lay on the floor.

There was little or no talk of death between this comfortable, active, sound-appearing man of almost seventy and this plump capable woman of sixty-six. But as always, between husband and wife, it was understood wordlessly (and without reason) that old man Minick would go first. Not that either of them had the slightest intention of going. In fact, when it happened they were planning to spend the winter in California and perhaps live there indefinitely if they liked it and didn't get too lonesome for George and Nettie, and the Chicago smoke, and Chicago noise, and Chicago smells and rush and dirt. Still, the solid sum paid yearly in insurance premiums showed clearly that he meant to leave her in comfort and security. Besides, the world is full of widows. Everyone sees that. But how many widowers? Few. Widows there are by the thousands; living alone; living in hotels; living with married daughters and sons-in-law or married sons and daughters-in-law. But of widowers in a like situation there are bewilderingly few. And why this should be no one knows.

So, then. The California trip never materialized. And the year that followed never was quite clear in old man Minick's dazed mind. In the first place, it was the year in which stocks tumbled and broke their backs. Gilt-edged securities showed themselves to be tinsel. Old man Minick had retired from active business just one year before, meaning to live comfortably on the fruit of a half-century's toil. He now saw that fruit rotting all about him. There was in it hardly enough nourishment to sustain them. Then came the day when Ma Minick went downtown to see Matthews about that pain right here and came home looking shriveled, talking shrilly about nothing, and evading Pa's eyes. Followed months that were just a jumble of agony, X-rays, hope, despair, morphia, nothingness.

After it was all over: "But I was going first," old man Minick said, dazedly.

The old house on Ellis near Thirty-ninth was sold for what it would bring. George, who knew Chicago real-estate if any one did, said they might as well get what they could. Things would only go lower. You'll see. And nobody's going to have any money for years. Besides, look at the neighborhood!

Old man Minick said George was right. He said everybody was right. You would hardly have recognized in this shrunken figure and wattled face the spruce and dressy old man whom Ma Minick used to spoil so delightfully. "You know best, George. You know best." He who used to stand up to George until Ma Minick was moved to say, "Now, Pa, you don't know everything."

After Matthews' bills, and the hospital, and the nurses and the medicines and the thousand and one things were paid there was left exactly five hundred dollars a year.

"You're going to make your home with us, Father," George and Nettie said. Alma, too, said this would be the best. Alma, the married daughter, lived in Seattle. "Though you know Ferd and I would be only too glad to have you."

Seattle! The ends of the earth. Oh, no. No! he protested, every fiber of his old frame clinging to the accustomed. Seattle, at seventy! He turned piteous eyes on his son George and his daughter-in-law Nettie. "You're going to make your home with us, Father," they reassured him. He clung to them gratefully. After it was over Alma went home to her husband and their children.

So now he lived with George and Nettie in the five-room flat on South Park Avenue, just across from Washington Park. And there was no extra pillow on the floor.

Nettie hadn't said he couldn't have the extra pillow. He had told her he used two and she had given him two the first week. But every morning she had found a pillow cast on the floor.

"I thought you used two pillows, Father."

"I do."

"But there's always one on the floor when I make the bed in the morning. You always throw one on the floor. You only sleep on one pillow, really."

"I use two pillows."

But the second week there was one pillow. He tossed and turned a good deal there in his bedroom off the kitchen. But he got used to it in time. Not used to it, exactly, but—well——

The bedroom off the kitchen wasn't as menial as it sounds. It was really rather cozy. The five-room flat held living room, front bedroom, dining room, kitchen, and maid's room. The room off the kitchen was intended as a maid's room but Nettie had no maid. George's business had suffered with the rest. George and Nettie had said, "I wish there was a front room for you, Father. You could have ours and we'd move back here, only this room's too small for twin beds and the dressing table and the chiffonier." They had meant it—or meant to mean it.

"This is fine," old man Minick had said. "This is good enough for anybody." There was a narrow white enamel bed and a tiny dresser and a table. Nettie had made gay cretonne covers and spreads and put a little reading lamp on the table and arranged his things. Ma Minick's picture on the dresser with her mouth sort of pursed to make it look small. It wasn't a recent picture. Nettie and George had had it framed for him as a surprise. They had often urged her to have a picture taken, but she had dreaded it. Old man Minick didn't think much of that photograph, though he never said so. He needed no photograph of Ma Minick. He had a dozen of them; a gallery of them; thousands of them. Lying on his one pillow he could take them out and look at them one by one as they passed in review, smiling, serious, chiding, praising, there in the dark. He needed no picture on his dresser.

A handsome girl, Nettie, and a good girl. He thought of her as a girl, though she was well past thirty. George and Nettie had married late. This was only the third year of their marriage. Alma, the daughter, had married young, but George had stayed on, unwed, in the old house on Ellis until he was thirty-six and all Ma Minick's friends' daughters had had a try at him in vain. The old people had urged him to marry, but it had been wonderful to have him around the house, just the same. Somebody young around the house. Not that George had stayed around very much. But when he was there you knew he was there. He whistled while dressing. He sang in the bath. He roared down the stairway, "Ma, where's my clean shirts?" The telephone rang for him. Ma Minick prepared special dishes for him. The servant girl said, "Oh, now, Mr. George, look what you've done! Gone and spilled the grease all over my clean kitchen floor!" and wiped it up adoringly while George laughed and gobbled his bit of food filched from pot or frying pan.

They had been a little surprised about Nettie. George was in the bond business and she worked for the same firm. A plump, handsome, eye-glassed woman with fine fresh coloring, a clear skin that old man Minick called appetizing, and a great coil of smooth dark hair. She wore plain tailored things and understood the bond business in a way that might have led you to think hers a masculine mind if she hadn't been so feminine, too, in her manner. Old man Minick had liked her better than Ma Minick had.

Nettie had called him Pop and joked with him and almost flirted with him in a daughterly sort of way. He liked to squeeze her plump arm and pinch her soft cheek between thumb and forefinger. She would laugh up at him and pat his shoulder and that shoulder would straighten spryly and he would waggle his head doggishly.

"Look out there, George!" the others in the room would say. "Your dad'll cut you out. First thing you know you'll lose your girl, that's all."

Nettie would smile. Her teeth were white and strong and even. Old man Minick would laugh and wink, immensely pleased and flattered. "We understand each other, don't we, Pop?" Nettie would say.

During the first years of their married life Nettie stayed home. She fussed happily about her little flat, gave parties, went to parties, played bridge. She seemed to love the ease, the relaxation, the small luxuries. She and George were very much in love. Before her marriage she had lived in a boarding house on Michigan Avenue. At mention of it now she puckered up her face. She did not attempt to conceal her fondness for these five rooms of hers, so neat, so quiet, so bright, so cozy. Overstuffed velvet in the living room, with silk lampshades, and small tables holding books and magazines and little boxes containing cigarettes or hard candies. Very modern. A gate-legged table in the dining room. Caramel-colored walnut in the bedroom, rich and dark and smooth. She loved it. An orderly woman. Everything in its place. Before eleven o'clock the little apartment was shining, spotless; cushions plumped, crumbs brushed, vegetables in cold water. The telephone. "Hello! ... Oh, hello, Bess! Oh, hours ago ... Not a thing ... Well, if George is willing ... I'll call him up and ask him. We haven't seen a show in two weeks. I'll call you back within the next half hour ... No, I haven't done my marketing yet ... Yes, and have dinner downtown. Meet at seven."

Into this orderly smooth-running mechanism was catapulted a bewildered old man. She no longer called him Pop. He never dreamed of squeezing the plump arm or pinching the smooth cheek. She called him Father. Sometimes George's Father. Sometimes, when she was telephoning, there came to him—"George's father's living with us now, you know. I can't."

They were very kind to him, Nettie and George. "Now just you sit right down here, Father. What do you want to go poking off into your own room for?"

He remembered that in the last year Nettie had said something about going back to work. There wasn't enough to do around the house to keep her busy. She was sick of afternoon parties. Sew and eat, that's all, and gossip, or play bridge. Besides, look at the money. Business was awful. The two old people had resented this idea as much as George had—more, in fact. They were scandalized.

"Young folks nowadays!" shaking their heads. "Young folks nowadays. What are they thinking of! In my day when you got married you had babies."

George and Nettie had had no babies. At first Nettie had said, "I'm so happy. I just want a chance to rest. I've been working since I was seventeen. I just want to rest, first." One year. Two years. Three. And now Pa Minick.

Ma Minick, in the old house on Ellis Avenue, had kept a loose sort of larder; not lavish, but plentiful. They both ate a great deal, as old people are likely to do. Old man Minick, especially, had liked to nibble. A handful of raisins from the box on the shelf. A couple of nuts from the dish on the sideboard. A bit of candy rolled beneath the tongue. At dinner (sometimes, toward the last, even at noon-time) a plate of steaming soup, hot, revivifying, stimulating. Plenty of this and plenty of that. "What's the matter, Jo? You're not eating." But he was, amply. Ma Minick had liked to see him eat too much. She was wrong, of course.

But at Nettie's things were different. Hers was a sufficient but stern ménage. So many mouths to feed; just so many lamb chops. Nettie knew about calories and vitamins and mysterious things like that, and talked about them. So many calories in this. So many calories in that. He never was quite clear in his mind about these things said to be lurking in his food. He had always thought of spinach as spinach, chops as chops. But to Nettie they were calories. They lunched together, these two. George was, of course, downtown. For herself Nettie would have one of those feminine pick-up lunches; a dab of apple sauce, a cup of tea, and a slice of cold toast left from breakfast. This she would eat while old man Minick guiltily supped up his cup of warmed-over broth, or his coddled egg. She always pressed upon him any bit of cold meat that was left from the night before, or any remnants of vegetable or spaghetti. Often there was quite a little fleet of saucers and sauce plates grouped about his main plate. Into these he dipped and swooped uncomfortably, and yet with a relish. Sometimes, when he had finished, he would look about, furtively.

"What'll you have, Father? Can I get you something?"

"Nothing, Nettie, nothing. I'm doing fine." She had finished the last of her wooden toast and was waiting for him, kindly.

Still, this balanced and scientific fare seemed to agree with him. As the winter went on he seemed actually to have regained most of his former hardiness and vigor. A handsome old boy he was, ruddy, hale, with the zest of a juicy old apple, slightly withered but still sappy. It should be mentioned that he had a dimple in his cheek which flashed unexpectedly when he smiled. It gave him a roguish—almost boyish—effect most appealing to the beholder. Especially the feminine beholder. Much of his spoiling at the hands of Ma Minick had doubtless been due to this mere depression of the skin.

Spring was to bring a new and welcome source of enrichment into his life. But these first six months of his residence with George and Nettie were hard. No spoiling there. He missed being made much of. He got kindness, but he needed love. Then, too, he was rather a gabby old man. He liked to hold forth. In the old house on Ellis there had been visiting back and forth between men and women of his own age, and Ma's. At these gatherings he had waxed oratorical or argumentative, and they had heard him, some in agreement, some in disagreement, but always respectfully, whether he prated of real estate or social depravity; prohibition or European exchange.

"Let me tell you, here and now, something's got to be done before you can get a country back on a sound financial basis. Why, take Russia alone, why ..." Or: "Young people nowadays! They don't know what respect means. I tell you there's got to be a change and there will be, and it's the older generation that's got to bring it about. What do they know of hardship! What do they know about work—real work. Most of 'em's never done a real day's work in their life. All they think of is dancing and gambling and drinking. Look at the way they dress! Look at …"

Ad lib.

"That's so," the others would agree. "I was saying only yesterday …"

Then, too, until a year or two before, he had taken active part in business. He had retired only at the urging of Ma and the children. They said he ought to rest and play and enjoy himself.

Now, as his strength and good spirits gradually returned he began to go downtown, mornings. He would dress, carefully, though a little shakily. He had always shaved himself and he kept this up. All in all, during the day, he occupied the bathroom literally for hours, and this annoyed Nettie to the point of frenzy, though she said nothing. He liked the white cheerfulness of the little tiled room. He puddled about in the water endlessly. Snorted and splashed and puffed and snuffled and blew. He was one of those audible washers who emerge dripping and whose ablutions are distributed impartially over ceiling, walls, and floor.

Nettie, at the closed door: "Father, are you all right?"

Splash! Prrrf! "Yes. Sure. I'm all right."

"Well, I didn't know. You've been in there so long."

He was a neat old man, but there was likely to be a spot or so on his vest or his coat lapel, or his tie. Ma used to remove these, on or off him, as the occasion demanded, rubbing carefully and scolding a little, making a chiding sound between tongue and teeth indicative of great impatience of his carelessness. He had rather enjoyed these sounds, and this rubbing and scratching on the cloth with the fingernail and a moistened rag. They indicated that someone cared. Cared about the way he looked. Had pride in him. Loved him. Nettie never removed spots. Though infrequently she said, "Father, just leave that suit out, will you? I'll send it to the cleaner's with George's. The man's coming tomorrow morning." He would look down at himself, hastily, and attack a spot here and there with a futile fingernail.

His morning toilette completed, he would make for the Fifty-first Street L. Seated in the train he would assume an air of importance and testy haste; glance out of the window; look at his watch. You got the impression of a handsome and well-preserved old gentleman on his way downtown to consummate a shrewd business deal. He had been familiar with Chicago's downtown for fifty years and he could remember when State Street was a tree-shaded cottage district. The noise and rush and clangour of the Loop had long been familiar to him. But now he seemed to find the downtown trip arduous, even hazardous. The roar of the elevated trains, the hoarse hoots of the motor horns, the clang of the streetcars, the bedlam that is Chicago's downtown district bewildered him, frightened him almost. He would skip across the street like a harried hare, just missing a motor truck's nose and all unconscious of the stream of invective directed at him by its charioteer. "Heh! Whatcha! … Look!"—Sometimes a policeman came to his aid, or attempted to, but he resented this proffered help.

"Say, look here, my lad," he would say to the tall, tired, and not at all burly (standing on one's feet directing traffic at Wabash and Madison for eight hours a day does not make for burliness) policeman, "I've been coming downtown since long before you were born. You don't need to help me. I'm no jay from the country."

He visited the Stock Exchange. This depressed him. Stocks were lower than ever and still going down. His five hundred a year was safe, but the rest seemed doomed for his lifetime, at least. He would drop in at George's office. George's office was pleasantly filled with dapper, neat young men and (surprisingly enough) dapper, slim young women, seated at desks in the big light-flooded room. At one corner of each desk stood a polished metal placard on a little standard, and bearing the name of the desk's occupant. Mr. Owens. Mr. Satterlee. Mr. James. Miss Rauch. Mr. Minick.

"Hello, Father," Mr. Minick would say, looking annoyed. "What's bringing you down?"

"Oh, nothing. Nothing. Just had a little business to tend to over at the Exchange. Thought I'd drop in. How's business?"

"Rotten."

"I should think it was!" Old man Minick would agree. "I—should—think—it—was! Hm."

George wished he wouldn't. He couldn't have it, that's all. Old man Minick would stroll over to the desk marked Satterlee, or Owens, or James. These brisk young men would toss an upward glance at him and concentrate again on the sheets and files before them. Old man Minick would stand, balancing from heel to toe and blowing out his breath a little. He looked a bit yellow and granulated and wavering, there in the cruel morning light of the big plate glass windows. Or perhaps it was the contrast he presented with these slim, slick young salesmen.

"Well, h'are you to-day, Mr.—uh—Satterlee? What's the good word?"

Mr. Satterlee would not glance up this time. "I'm pretty well. Can't complain."

"Good. Good."

"Anything I can do for you?"

"No-o-o. No. Not a thing. Just dropped in to see my son a minute."

"I see." Not unkindly. Then, as old man Minick still stood there, balancing, Mr. Satterlee would glance up again, frowning a little. "Your son's desk is over there, I believe. Yes."

George and Nettie had a bedtime conference about these visits and Nettie told him, gently, that the bond house head objected to friends and relatives dropping in. It was against office rules. It had been so when she was employed there. Strictly business. She herself had gone there only once since her marriage.

Well, that was all right. Business was like that nowdays. Rush and grab and no time for anything.

The winter was a hard one, with a record snowfall and intense cold. He stayed indoors for days together. A woman of his own age in like position could have occupied herself usefully and happily. She could have hemmed a sash-curtain; knitted or crocheted; tidied a room; taken a hand in the cooking or preparing of food; ripped an old gown; made over a new one; indulged in an occasional afternoon festivity with women of her own years. But for old man Minick there were no small tasks. There was nothing he could do to make his place in the household justifiable. He wasn't even particularly good at those small jobs of hammering, or painting, or general "fixing." Nettie could drive a nail more swiftly, more surely than he. "Now, Father, don't you bother. I'll do it. Just you go and sit down. Isn't it time for your afternoon nap?"

He waxed a little surly. "Nap! I just got up. I don't want to sleep my life away."

George and Nettie frequently had guests in the evening. They played bridge, or poker, or talked.

"Come in, Father," George would say. "Come in. You all know Dad, don't you, folks?" He would sit down, uncertainly. At first he had attempted to expound, as had been his wont in the old house on Ellis. "I want to say, here and now, that this country's got to …" But they went on, heedless of him. They interrupted or refused, politely, to listen. So he sat in the room, yet no part of it. The young people's talk swirled and eddied all about him. He was utterly lost in it. Now and then Nettie or George would turn to him and with raised voice (he was not at all deaf and prided himself on it) would shout, "It's about this or that, Father. He was saying …"

When the group roared with laughter at a sally from one of them he would smile uncertainly but amiably, glancing from one to the other in complete ignorance of what had passed, but not resenting it. He took to sitting more and more in his kitchen bedroom, smoking a comforting pipe and reading and re-reading the evening paper. During that winter he and Canary, the negro washwoman, became quite good friends. She washed down in the basement once a week but came up to the kitchen for her massive lunch. A walrus-waisted black woman, with a rich throaty voice, a rolling eye, and a kindly heart. He actually waited for her appearance above the laundry stairs.

"Weh, how's Mist' Minick to-day! Ah nev' did see a gemun spry's you ah fo' yo' age. No, suh! nev' did."

At this rare praise he would straighten his shoulders and waggle his head. "I'm worth any ten of these young sprats today." Canary would throw back her head in a loud and companionable guffaw.

Nettie would appear at the kitchen swinging door. "Canary's having her lunch, Father. Don't you want to come into the front room with me? We'll have our lunch in another half-hour." He followed her obediently enough. Nettie thought of him as a troublesome and rather pathetic child—a child who would never grow up. If she attributed any thoughts to that fine old head they were ambling thoughts, bordering, perhaps, on senility. Little did she know how expertly this old one surveyed her and how ruthlessly he passed judgment. She never suspected the thoughts that formed in the active brain.

He knew about women. He had married a woman. He had had children by her. He looked at this woman—his son's wife—moving about her little five-room flat. She had theories about children. He had heard her expound them. You didn't have them except under such and such circumstances. It wasn't fair otherwise. Plenty of money for their education. Well. He and his wife had had three children. Paul, the second, had died at thirteen. A blow, that had been. They had not always planned for the coming of the three but they always had found a way, afterward. You managed, somehow, once the little wrinkled red ball had fought its way into the world. You managed. You managed. Look at George! Yet when he was born, thirty-nine years ago, Pa and Ma Minick had been hard put to it.

Sitting there, while Nettie dismissed him as negligible, he saw her clearly, grimly. He looked at her. She was plump, but not too short, with a generous width between the hips; a broad full bosom, but firm; round arms and quick slim legs; a fine sturdy throat. The curve between arm and breast made a graceful gracious line … Working in a bond office … Working in a bond office … There was nothing in the Bible about working in a bond office. Here was a woman built for childbearing.

She thought him senile, negligible.

In March Nettie had in a sewing woman for a week. She had her two or three times a year. A hawk-faced woman of about forty-nine, with a blue-bottle figure and a rapacious eye. She sewed in the dining room and there was a pleasant hum of machine and snip of scissors and murmur of conversation and rustle of silky stuff; and hot savory dishes for lunch. She and old man Minick became great friends. She even let him take out bastings. This when Nettie had gone out from two to four, between fittings.

He chuckled and waggled his head. "I expect to be paid regular assistant's wages for this," he said.

"I guess you don't need any wages, Mr. Minick," the woman said. "I guess you're pretty well fixed."

"Oh, well, I can't complain." (Five hundred a year.)

"Complain! I should say not! If I was to complain it'd be different. Work all day to keep myself; and nobody to come home to at night."

"Widow, ma'am?"

"Since I was twenty. Work, work, that's all I've had. And lonesome! I suppose you don't know what lonesome is."

"Oh, don't I!" slipped from him. He had dropped the bastings.

The sewing woman flashed a look at him from the cold hard eye. "Well, maybe you do. I suppose living here like this, with sons and daughters, ain't so grand, for all your money. Now me, I've always managed to keep my own little place that I could call home, to come back to. It's only two rooms, and nothing to rave about, but it's home. Evenings I just cook and fuss around. Nobody to fuss for, but I fuss, anyway. Cooking, that's what I love to do. Plenty of good food, that's what folks need to keep their strength up." Nettie's lunch that day had been rather scant.

She was there a week. In Nettie's absence she talked against her. He protested, but weakly. Did she give him egg-nogs? Milk? Hot toddy? Soup? Plenty of good rich gravy and meat and puddings? Well! That's what folks needed when they weren't so young any more. Not that he looked old. My, no. Sprier than many young boys, and handsomer than his own son if she did say so.

He fed on it, hungrily. The third day she was flashing meaning glances at him across the luncheon table. The fourth she pressed his foot beneath the table. The fifth, during Nettie's afternoon absence, she got up, ostensibly to look for a bit of cloth which she needed for sewing, and, passing him, laid a caressing hand on his shoulder. Laid it there and pressed his shoulder ever so little. He looked up, startled. The glances across the luncheon had largely passed over his head; the foot beneath the table might have been an accident. But this—this was unmistakable. He stood up, a little shakily. She caught his hand. The hawk-like face was close to his.

"You need somebody to love you," she said. "Somebody to do for you, and love you." The hawk face came nearer. He leaned a little toward it. But between it and his face was Ma Minick's face, plump, patient, quizzical, kindly. His head came back sharply. He threw the woman's hot hand from him.

"Woman!" he cried. "Jezebel!"

The front door slammed. Nettie. The woman flew to her sewing. Old man Minick, shaking, went into his kitchen bedroom.

"Well," said Nettie, depositing her bundles on the dining room table, "did you finish that faggoting? Why, you haven't done so very much, have you!"

"I ain't feeling so good," said the woman. "That lunch didn't agree with me."

"Why, it was a good plain lunch. I don't see——"

"Oh, it was plain enough, all right."

Next day she did not come to finish her work. Sick, she telephoned. Nettie called it an outrage. She finished the sewing herself, though she hated sewing. Pa Minick said nothing, but there was a light in his eye. Now and then he chuckled, to Nettie's infinite annoyance, though she said nothing.

"Wanted to marry me!" he said to himself, chuckling. "Wanted to marry me! The old rip!"

At the end of April, Pa Minick discovered Washington Park, and the Club, and his whole life was from that day transformed.

He had taken advantage of the early spring sunshine to take a walk, at Nettie's suggestion.

"Why don't you go into the Park, Father? It's really warm out. And the sun's lovely. Do you good."

He had put on his heaviest shirt, and a muffler, and George's old red sweater with the great white "C" on its front, emblem of George's athletic prowess at the University of Chicago; and over all, his greatcoat. He had taken warm mittens and his cane with the greyhound's head handle, carved. So equipped he had ambled uninterestedly over to the Park across the way. And there he had found new life.

New life in old life. For the park was full of old men. Old men like himself, with greyhound's-head canes, and mufflers and somebody's sweater worn beneath their greatcoats. They wore arctics, though the weather was fine. The skin of their hands and cheek-bones was glazed and had a tight look though it lay in fine little folds. There were splotches of brown on the backs of their hands, and on the temples and forehead. Their heavy grey or brown socks made comfortable folds above their ankles. From that April morning until winter drew on the Park saw old man Minick daily. Not only daily but by the day. Except for his meals, and a brief hour for his after-luncheon nap, he spent all his time there.

For in the park old man Minick and all the old men gathered there found a Forum—a safety valve—a means of expression. It did not take him long to discover that the Park was divided into two distinct sets of old men. There were the old men who lived with their married sons and daughters-in-law or married daughters and sons-in-law. Then there were the old men who lived in the Grant Home for Aged Gentlemen. You saw its fine red-brick facade through the trees at the edge of the Park.

And the slogan of these first was:

"My son and my da'ter they wouldn't want me to live in any public Home. No, sirree! They want me right there with them. In their own home. That's the kind of son and daughter I've got!"

The slogan of the second was:

"I wouldn't live with any son or daughter. Independent. That's me. My own boss. Nobody to tell me what I can do and what I can't. Treat you like a child. I'm my own boss! Pay my own good money and get my keep for it."

The first group, strangely enough, was likely to be spotted of vest and a little frayed as to collar. You saw them going on errands for their daughters-in-law. A loaf of bread. Spool of white No. 100. They took their small grandchildren to the duck pond and between the two toddlers hand in hand—the old and infirm and the infantile and infirm—it was hard to tell which led which.

The second group was shiny as to shoes, spotless as to linen, dapper as to clothes. They had no small errands. Theirs was a magnificent leisure. And theirs was magnificent conversation. The questions they discussed and settled there in the Park—these old men—were not international merely. They were cosmic in scope.

The War? Peace? Disarmament? China? Free love? Mere conversational bubbles to be tossed in the air and disposed of in a burst of foam. Strong meat for old man Minick who had so long been fed on pap. But he soon got used to it. Between four and five in the afternoon, in a spot known as Under The Willows, the meeting took the form of a club—an open forum. A certain group made up of Socialists, Free Thinkers, parlor anarchists, bolshevists, had for years drifted there for talk. Old man Minick learned high-sounding phrases. "The Masters ... democracy ... toil of the many for the good of the few ... the ruling class ... free speech ... the People ..."

The strong-minded ones held forth. The weaker ones drifted about on the outskirts, sometimes clinging to the moist and sticky paw of a round-eyed grandchild. Earlier in the day—at eleven o'clock, say—the talk was not so general nor so inclusive. The old men were likely to drift into groups of two or three or four. They sat on sun-bathed benches and their conversation was likely to be rather smutty at times, for all they looked so mild and patriarchal and desiccated. They paid scant heed to the white-haired old women who, like themselves, were sunning in the park. They watched the young women switch by, with appreciative glances at their trim figures and slim ankles. The day of the short skirt was a grand time for them. They chuckled among themselves and made wicked comment. One saw only white-haired, placid, tremulous old men, but their minds still worked with belated masculinity like naughty small boys talking behind the barn.

Old man Minick early achieved a certain leadership in the common talk. He had always liked to hold forth. This last year had been one of almost unendurable bottling up. At first he had timidly sought the less assertive ones of his kind. Mild old men who sat in rockers in the pavilion waiting for lunch time. Their conversation irritated him. They remarked everything that passed before their eyes.

"There's a boat. Fella with a boat."

A silence. Then, heavily: "Yeh."

Five minutes.

"Look at those people laying on the grass. Shouldn't think it was warm enough for that … Now they're getting up."

A group of equestrians passed along the bridle path on the opposite side of the lagoon. They made a frieze against the delicate spring greenery. The coats of the women were scarlet, vivid green, arresting, stimulating.

"Riders."

"Yes."

"Good weather for riding."

A man was fishing near by. "Good weather for fishing."

"Yes."

"Wonder what time it is, anyway." From a pocket, deep-buried, came forth

a great gold blob of a watch. "I've got one minute to eleven."

Old man Minick dragged forth a heavy globe. "Mm. I've got eleven."

"Little fast, I guess."

Old man Minick shook off this conversation impatiently. This wasn't conversation. This was oral death, though he did not put it thus. He joined the other men. They were discussing Spiritualism. He listened, ventured an opinion, was heard respectfully and then combated mercilessly. He rose to the verbal fight, and won it.

"Let's see," said one of the old men. "You're not living at the Grant Home, are you?"

"No," old man Minick made reply, proudly. "I live with my son and his wife. They wouldn't have it any other way."

"Hm. Like to be independent myself."

"Lonesome, ain't it? Over there?"

"Lonesome! Say, Mr.—what'd you say your name was? Minick? Mine's Hughes—I never was lonesome in my life 'cept for six months when I lived with my daughter and her husband and their five children. Yes, sir. That's what I call lonesome, in an eight-room flat."

George and Nettie said, "It's doing you good, Father, being out in the air so much." His eyes were brighter, his figure straighter, his color better. It was that day he had held forth so eloquently on the emigration question. He had to read a lot—papers and magazines and one thing and another—to keep up. He devoured all the books and pamphlets about bond issues and national finances brought home by George. In the Park he was considered an authority on bonds and banking. He and a retired real-estate man named Mowry sometimes debated a single question for weeks. George and Nettie, relieved, thought he ambled to the Park and spent senile hours with his drooling old friends discussing nothing amiably and witlessly. This while he was eating strong meat, drinking strong drink.

Summer sped. Was past. Autumn held a new dread for old man Minick. When winter came where should he go? Where should he go? Not back to the five-room flat all day, and the little back bedroom, and nothingness. In his mind there rang a childish old song they used to sing at school. A silly song:

Where do all the birdies go?
I know. I know.

But he didn't know. He was terror-stricken. October came and went. With the first of November the Park became impossible, even at noon, and with two overcoats and the sweater. The first frost was a black frost for him. He scanned the heavens daily for rain or snow. There was a cigar store and billiard room on the corner across the boulevard and there he sometimes went, with a few of his Park cronies, to stand behind the players' chairs and watch them at pinochle or rum. But this was a dull business. Besides, the Grant men never came there. They had card rooms of their own.

He turned away from this smoky little den on a drab November day, sick at heart. The winter. He tried to face it, and at what he saw he shrank and was afraid.

He reached the apartment and went around to the rear, dutifully. His rubbers were wet and muddy and Nettie's living-room carpet was a fashionable grey. The back door was unlocked. It was Canary's day downstairs, he remembered. He took off his rubbers in the kitchen and passed into the dining room. Voices. Nettie had company. Some friends, probably, for tea. He turned to go to his room, but stopped at hearing his own name. Father Minick. Father Minick. Nettie's voice.

"Of course, if it weren't for Father Minick I would have. But how can we as long as he lives with us? There isn't room. And we can't afford a bigger place now, with rents what they are. This way it wouldn't be fair to the child. We've talked it over, George and I. Don't you suppose? But not as long as Father Minick is with us. I don't mean we'd use the maid's room for a—for the—if we had a baby. But I'd have to have someone in to help, then, and we'd have to have that extra room."

He stood there in the dining room, quiet. Quiet. His body felt queerly remote and numb, but his mind was working frenziedly. Clearly, too, in spite of the frenzy. Death. That was the first thought. Death. It would be easy. But he didn't want to die. Strange, but he didn't want to die. He liked Life. The Park, the trees, the Club, the talk, the whole show … Nettie was a good girl … The old must make way for the young. They had the right to be born … Maybe it was just another excuse. Almost four years married. Why not three years ago? … The right to live. The right to live …

He turned, stealthily, stealthily, and went back into the kitchen, put on his rubbers, stole out into the darkening November afternoon.

In an hour he was back. He entered at the front door this time, ringing the bell. He had never had a key. As if he were a child they would not trust him with one. Nettie's women friends were just leaving. In the air you smelled a mingling of perfume, and tea, and cakes, and powder. He sniffed it, sensitively.

"How do you do, Mr. Minick!" they said. "How are you! Well, you certainly look it. And how do you manage these gloomy days?"

He smiled genially, taking off his greatcoat and revealing the red sweater with the big white "C" on it. "I manage. I manage." He puffed out his cheeks. "I'm busy moving."

"Moving!" Nettie's startled eyes flew to his, held them. "Moving, Father?"

"Old folks must make way for the young," he said, gaily. "That's the law of life. Yes, sir! New ones. New ones."

Nettie's face was scarlet. "Father, what in the world——"

"I signed over at the Grant Home today. Move in next week." The women looked at her, smiling. Old man Minick came over to her and patted her plump arm. Then he pinched her smooth cheek with a quizzical thumb and forefinger. Pinched it and shook it ever so little.

"I don't know what you mean," said Nettie, out of breath.

"Yes, you do," said old man Minick, and while his tone was light and jesting there was in his old face something stern, something menacing. "Yes, you do."

When he entered the Grant Home a group of them was seated about the fireplace in the main hall. A neat, ruddy, septuagenarian circle. They greeted him casually, with delicacy of feeling, as if he were merely approaching them at their bench in the Park.

"Say, Minick, look here. Mowry here says China ought to have been included in the four-power treaty. He says——"

Old man Minick cleared his throat. "You take China, now," he said, "with her vast and practically, you might say, virgin country, why——"

An apple-cheeked maid in a black dress and a white apron stopped before him. He paused.

"Housekeeper says for me to tell you your room's all ready, if you'd like to look at it now."

"Minute. Minute, my child." He waved her aside with the air of one who pays five hundred a year for independence and freedom. The girl turned to go. "Uh—young lady! Young lady!" She looked at him. "Tell the housekeeper two pillows, please. Two pillows on my bed. Be sure."

"Yes, sir. Two pillows. Yes, sir. I'll be sure."

(1922)

153

Margaret Leech

Manicure

Saturday afternoons wrought subtle changes in the salons of Leon and Jules (Specialists in the Artistry of Coiffure). To a superficial observer all was as usual. In every orchid and green compartment a feminine form, lavishly bibbed in fresh white linen, sat before the mirror of the toilet table. Sharp little clicks came from the snapping irons of the artists in marcel. Heads were deftly molded in the plasticene dampness of finger waves. Cold cream was competently smeared on heated faces, to a murmur of "Just relax, please, Madame. Lie perfectly quiet and relax." In the booths devoted to permanent waves sat ladies with heads grotesquely bristling into huge painful coronets, like Russian headdresses. Miss Nina and Miss Hazel ran back and forth. "What's the matter with that cold air?" "Just a minute, Madame. No, I'm not going to leave you alone. It's only the steam, it won't burn you." In rows outside the compartments, the little manicure tables were crowded. Indeed, on Saturday afternoons there were so many manicures that clients often had to be "started" on stray chairs placed in the narrow aisles, with bowls of hot soapy water perilously poised on their knees.

Whatever the subtle changes of Saturday afternoons, they did not diminish the number of patrons who thronged the salons of Leon and Jules. On the contrary, these last hours of the week supported their tradition of amazing success—contributed to explain the country house toward which Mr. Leon sped at one o'clock each Saturday in a comfortable motor car with a uniformed chauffeur. For Mr. Leon—there was no Mr. Jules, and if there ever had been he was lost in the dimness of legend—did not remain in the salons on Saturday afternoons. That was a part of the subtle changes. None of "his ladies" was expected to be there.

Downstairs in the foyer of the great hotel in which the establishment of Leon and Jules was housed swirled a flux of expensive gaiety. By the entrance to the Florentine Room, a fixed point in the restless tide, stood Mr. Peter Koch, the handsome assistant manager of the hotel, smiling affably under his slight mustache. Eddies of smartly gowned women broke and rippled around him. For though his connection with the hotel was of only a year's standing, Mr. Koch had already made his impression. It was inevitable, with that face and that figure, that he should have done so. Many women paused to speak to him as he bent forward deferentially from the waist, smiled, nodded, noted things on a pad. "But, certainly, Madame, I will arrange everything. No, no, no, you must not trouble at all. I will speak to Louis myself, *parole d'honneur*. I will arrange it personally. It will be a pleasure to do it—for you, Madame."

He would glance at Madame with his full, excitable eyes, which the large lids could veil so quickly. And she, if her companion happened to be another woman, would murmur a moment later, "Isn't he marvelous? I'm afraid it's running into a flirtation. I ought to be ashamed to let him look at me the way he does."

Under the small felt hats which bobbed in the foyer or bowed across small tables in the Florentine Room were many heads shingled and waved in the salons of Leon and Jules. But none of these women ascended on Saturday afternoons. A new invasion, unfamiliar on week days, crowded the orchid compartments. These were the women who worked five afternoons of the week. On the sixth they repaired the ravages of time and exertion.

The Saturday afternoon patrons were persons well up in the world. Here were buyers, smartly dressed and deftly rouged. Here were well-informed private secretaries, in dark woolen dresses. Here were women executives with lines of worry between their brows. They looked prosperous, ever affluent. But some grace was lacking—some glaze of exquisiteness which leisure and years of infinite luxury impart. On Saturday afternoons, there was none of the casual elegance of an enameled cigarette case, of a glimpse of *binche* at the bosom, of a square emerald sliding negligently around a thin finger. And it might have been observed that on Saturday afternoons the deference of the girls at Leon and Jules fell a shade short. For these women were not silken creatures from some incredible Aladdin's palace. After all, they worked for a living. They might be wise and friendly, but they were not opening doors of vivid life, they were not clear windows through which to peep into a fairyland of riches. The young persons with the soft names—Miss Rose, Miss Nina, Miss Adele, Miss Hazel, Miss Blanche—were a little bored when Saturday afternoon came.

Miss Nina was terribly bored. She was not the prettiest of the girls at Leon and Jules, by any means. She brushed her short brown hair forward to soften her face; for, though she was only twenty-four, it was rather a pinched little face, dark-skinned. Her green-blue eyes looked surprisingly light between black lashes. Her lips were thin and avid, and she carried her head high.

But, if she was not remarkably pretty, Miss Nina undeniably had a way with her. Her figure was supple, and she had tiny feet with steep little insteps. She swished her skirts slightly when she walked. Dressed for the street in a carmine frock and hat and a plain black coat, she looked quite striking. She rouged her drooping little mouth very red, and this made her eyes look brighter and her skin less drab. The men's eyes turned as she passed through the lobby of the great hotel with her mincing, rather affected walk. It was the sort of walk which takes cognizance of the fact that men's eyes often turn.

Miss Nina was proud of working at Leon and Jules. She had striven for this job through years of initiation in lesser shops. Here she made breathless contact with something she desired, something on which her spirit fed. She looked hungrily at the women who came to the salons, appraised their jewels, their dresses, listened rapturously while they prattled of their travels, beaux, parties, appointments, shopping.

When occasion arose, Miss Nina could do more than listen. She could join in the conversation—about the cabarets, the theaters. Her evenings were not always dull. To her less conservative customers—gay debutantes, lively married women—she hinted as much: cocktails, champagne, a midnight roof. Sometimes, bending confidentially over a white hand, Nina forgot that her name was really Nellie, forgot her tiny tawdry flat, forgot long evenings spent in making clothes, or in washing, ironing, and repairing them. Almost she was able to identify herself with the other woman, to please the men that the other woman pleased, to shine in the glitter of her good fortune. They sat, half-whispering, like two friends. There was only a narrow green table between them.

When the long fantasy of her day was over Miss Nina slipped into her street clothes. Nor was disillusionment immediate. The carmine dress and hat were more becoming than the white linen uniform. She rouged her lips very carefully and buttoned her gloves and took her square shiny black purse. In the elevator she was no longer Miss Nina of Leon and Jules—she was, with some faint impertinence of lifted chin, a guest of the great hotel. The moment of traversing the foyer was pure magic every evening. Through the luxurious corridor she moved, gazing about her with her astonishingly light eyes, as though she were looking for someone. Outside the Florentine Room, where music sounded and people still lingered over tea cups among potted palms, stood Mr. Peter Koch, handsome, erect, deferential. Their eyes just met before she smiled at the doorman and was whirled into the street.

Miss Nina wandered around the airless little cloakroom, munching a very late lunch of an olive-and-cream-cheese sandwich. She was hoping that Miss Rose would forget that she had been gone quite half an hour; for her distaste for the ugly cloakroom was less than her distaste for the boredom of Saturday afternoon. Her mouth drooped as she washed her hands and dried them slowly with a towel secreted from the salons, with *Leon and Jules* straggling across it in green chain-stitching. She licked her thumb and forefinger and twisted an upturned sickle of hair on each cheek. Then from the breast of her white uniform she drew a square envelope, addressed in an angular handwriting, foreign and precise. There was more of the handwriting inside. Miss Nina ran her eyes along the lines, drawing in her chin with a mysterious smile.

"Miss Nina! Miss Nina!" The voice of Miss Rose, officiating at the appointment desk, came sharply up the stairs. Miss Nina frowned, thrust the letter into its hiding place, and minced down the stairs on her steep little feet. "Your lady's waiting," Miss Rose informed her crossly. "Manicure. Second table."

Miss Nina stifled a yawn. She took from a shelf her small crowded tray of manicure necessaries, she filled a bowl with hot soapy water. "Second table, Madame. Right this way." Miss Rose prompted the woman who had asked for Miss Nina. Her tone was a trifle brisk and businesslike, for even on a Saturday afternoon this was not an impressive customer. It was less an indication of appearance than of manner. She seemed oddly confused, ill at ease in the orchid and green salons. She stood by the appointment desk, looking about her with an exaggerated assumption of indifference. But, at Miss Rose's direction, she now moved to the second table, her head raised, as one who has outfaced many situations. Miss Nina came tripping toward her; deposited her tray and the bowl of soapy water on the glass-topped table; laid a fresh towel over the small cushion; snapped on the green-shaded light.

"Good afternoon, Madame!" she said in her eager voice. Miss Nina's eyes ran curiously over the customer. She was a new one, a stranger. Miss Nina, who had an excellent memory for faces, couldn't remember ever having seen her in the shop. She was a blonde woman, with large pale-brown eyes. The light on the table struck the flat planes of her face, cleft by fine lines about her eyes and mouth. She had neatly rubbed her thin cheeks with a brickish, dusty-looking rouge. Between the fur bands of her coat collar there was a glint of metal cloth. She laid on the table a pair of fresh kid gloves and a bag worked in blue glad beads with a German-silver mounting. Miss Nina quickly appraised the blouse, the new gloves, the beaded bag, the hat—blue velvet with a rhinestone ornament. There was that about them which spoke of Sunday, of occasion. Tissue paper seemed to rustle faintly around them. They were her "best" things. Miss Nina's upper lip curled slightly, briefly, as she took the woman's left hand, a capable hand with her large shapely nails. She ran her file experimentally around the littlest one.

"Not much shorter, Madame?" she suggested. The woman shook her head.

"You have very lovely nails. Very lovely nails, Madame," said Miss Nina absently. With mechanical skill the long file moved around the nails, shaping them. The left hand, the finger-tips dabbed with salve, was consigned to the bowl of water. Miss Nina shifted her shoulders, glanced cursorily at the customers seated at the other manicure tables. She took up the right hand, smothering another yawn.

The woman spoke so suddenly that Miss Nina was startled. Her voice had a queer husky quality, very pleasant. "Do you know a girl named Adele that used to work here?"

"Why, yes," said Miss Nina, and bit her lip. "Why, yes, of course. Yes, Adele was here for a good while. I guess, about a year or two—"

"She's not here any more, is she? Do you ever see her?" pursued the woman. Her large hazel eyes were fixed on Miss Nina's face.

The girl looked up briefly. "No," she said, twisting a fragment of cotton around an orangewood stick. "Not any more. No for—oh, two or three months. I haven't seen her since she left."

"You didn't know her very well?" asked the woman, and again Miss Nina looked at her.

"Why, yes—" she began hesitantly. Then she gave a little laugh, and leaned confidentially over the woman's hand. "Why, I'll tell you how it was, Madame. Adele was my girlfriend. Then we had a little fuss. She said something I didn't like. Will you have the white under your nails? We don't talk now." Miss Nina poked among the articles on her way for an emery board. "You knew Adele, Madame? I didn't think—"

"No," said the blonde woman. "I've never been here before. Quite some place you have, isn't it? I've never seen this Adele. But I've heard about her." She lowered her eyes, raised them again, moistening her lips. "I heard she got in some trouble here," she said and waited.

"Well!" Miss Nina threw back her head with an explosive little laugh. "What do you think of that? Well, some people say more than their prayers."

"I heard," said the blonde woman softly, "that Adele did."

"Oh, no, no," Miss Nina deprecated the entire report. "There isn't anything to that. Why, I can't believe there's anything to that. She just wanted a new place, Madame. Some place handier to where she lives."

The woman shook her head slowly. "No. That wasn't it. She got in trouble on account of some man here in the hotel. She *had* to leave."

Miss Nina drew a quick breath. Her eyes darted about the shop. A drying machine whirred behind the curtains of the nearest compartment. There was a chatter of conversation. At nearby tables Miss Blanche and Miss Myrtle bent over their customers' hands. Their backs were concentrated, oblivious. Calmly above them lay a soft haze of cigarette smoke. Miss Nina picked up her orangewood stick.

"Well, Madame," she murmured, "you know all about it, don't you? Would you put your other hand in the water, please? I did hear some gossip myself, but I don't think there was anything to it. Nothing wrong, I mean, Madame. Nothing really wrong."

"Foolish girl, wasn't she?" said the blonde woman. "Going up to his room here in the hotel and all. She might have known they'd find out."

Nina conceded the wisdom of this with a hunching of her shoulders and a sympathetic smile. "Well, of course, you know, Madame"—her voice had dropped to an eager whisper—"some girls never think how things look. You know how they are, Madame. That's what I always told Adele, she'd get in trouble if she didn't look out. I like a good time myself. But the idea, can you imagine going up to a man's room, in a hotel like this, too, where they're so careful. They have to be." Miss Nina paused, while she ran a soapy brush over the nicely groomed nails of the woman's left hand. "Will you have the medium polish, Madame? Or do you prefer the very red?" Her fingers quivered among the bottles, chose on instruction the very red. She drew out the cork, with its tiny pendant brush, and began to paint the neat finger nails.

"I got disgusted with her," Miss Nina resumed. "That's how we came to have this falling-out I spoke of. Going up to his room!" Miss Nina sniffed.

The blonde woman raised her hand, gazed intently at the shining red nails. "I suppose," she said, "you've seen this man she went with?"

"Seen him?" said Miss Nina. "Oh, yes. Yes, indeed, I've seen him." She cleared her throat. "Well, you see, Madame, Adele and I had a little apartment together last year. East Thirty-first Street. A nice little place. This man—this friend of Adele's—used to come there, see? Then sometimes, you know, my boy friend would be there, and the four of us would go out somewheres to dinner or a show or to dance somewheres. That's the way I got to know him. Of course, I wasn't paying attention to him. I had a friend of my own." Miss Nina moved her shoulders expressing hauteur. "I could see all along he was getting sick of Adele. She was just crazy about him. Silly over him. And here he was with his wife and all—"

"So he has a wife?" said the woman. And her eyes opened very wide, as she stared at the five red, shining nails of her left hand.

"Oh, sure," said Miss Nina. "I should say so. Believe me, he has a wife. Very delicate. Just relax your hand a little, Madame. She's a very delicate woman. Lives in the country, New Jersey some place. If you could just let your hand lie quiet—that's better, thank you, Madame. She's crazy about him. At least, that's what Adele used to say. He's just got to be home certain nights in the week. He has three children, too. He thinks the world of them. Quite a family man." Miss Nina laughed.

"Yes," said the woman. "It would seem that way. Well, that's hard on a man, a nagging wife."

Miss Nina was voluble, eager. "Yes, Madame, that's just what I used to tell Adele. 'Adele,' I used to say to her, 'there's no use *your* nagging at him; he's got one like that already.' And I told her, 'He's a married man, that'll never bring you luck.' But she said, 'If you like them, what can you do?' "

The woman uttered a little exclamation that was not quite a laugh. But Miss Nina did not heed. "Well, finally, she heard about Adele—the wife did. So he came to Adele and told her she'd have to leave and go some place else, because his wife, see, would make trouble if she stayed here. So that was how it happened. That's the whole story."

"Yes," said the blonde woman. "Yes, that's what I heard happened. I live in Brooklyn, and I heard about it from friends of her married sister's. I heard she got going out with this man, and then she lost her place. They all thought it was too bad, she was such a nice girl." She leaned forward across the narrow table, her lips parted. "There couldn't—you're sure that was what happened, that his wife found out about it? You couldn't be wrong about that?"

"No, I'm sure," said Miss Nina. She snipped her little scissors delicately, decisively. "Sure that was what happened. He was always scared to death his wife would find out. Why, sometimes he used to break dates the last minute. She's sick, see, and she gets suspicious. I guess she gave it to him all right."

The woman sighed. "I wonder," she said, "if Adele ever sees him now?"

"No," said Miss Nina quickly. "No, she doesn't see him any more. Hasn't seen him since she left."

"But I thought," said the blonde woman in a puzzled tone, "that you and Adele weren't friends any more? How would you know if she saw him or not? You wouldn't"—she hesitated—"I don't suppose *you* ever see him, do you? To talk to, I mean?"

"Me?" cried Miss Nina. "Why, no. No, I'd never dream—Why, what made you think—?" She laid down her small sharp scissors and ran her fingers quickly across her upper lip. The blonde woman's eyes were lowered. They stared intently at the middle finger of her right hand. And, following her gaze, Miss Nina's eyes rested on a scarlet speck beside the finger nail, which grew to a tiny bubble of blood, spreading across the whiteness of the finger. "Oh, Madame, I'm so sorry! How stupid of me! I don't know when I've done such a thing." With tremulous fingers she took the cork from a bottle of colorless fluid, and moistened a scrap of cotton which she pressed against the tiny wound. "Terribly sorry Madame. I—I must be nervous to-day."

"That's all right," said the woman. Her voice was low and quiet. "We all make mistakes. I'm afraid I've upset you, talking about your girl friend. We'll drop the subject if you'd rather."

Miss Nina pressed her palms to her cheeks. "It upsets me awfully to cut a customer. No, no, Madame, why should I mind talking about Adele? She's nothing to me any more. I don't care what she does. You needn't worry over her. She's got somebody else by now. She never cares long for anybody. That's why I was so sure, see, that she doesn't meet this man any more. Ah, you don't know what a fool she is!" Miss Nina's mouth was bitter. "Going up to his room here! If she had to see him, why couldn't she meet him someplace else? I knew she'd get in trouble. I *told* her, 'Adele,' I said, 'a manager of a hotel has his position to consider. A big hotel like this, you want to be careful about going up there to see him; he can't always be telling you, don't come up to my room—how does that look for a man to be the one to be careful?" Miss Nina was breathing fast. "I'll tell you what's the trouble with Adele, Madame. She's too easy. That's why, see, I know they don't see each other any more. A man gets sick of that, believe me."

The blonde woman bent her head. "Well, I should blame her," she said. "I should blame her. I guess every woman's been easy one time anyway—or wished she'd had the chance to be. I was easy once myself," she whispered, and her hand twitched in Miss Nina's clasp. "One time I was cashier in a hotel. There was a handsome fellow, one of the day clerks." She smiled wryly. "Well—"

She caught her lip between her teeth, with a long intake of breath, as though she were nerving herself to go on. "I fell for him," she said slowly. "A ton of bricks. I was nutty about him. His manners, you know. Always so polite and like that. He used to write me notes, lovely handwriting, like a copy book. He was educated in Europe. I'd carry those notes around with me for days—read them over and over again. He was crazy for women." She gave a nervous laugh of apology. "I thought he was crazy for me. Funny, isn't it? That's a mistake a lot of women make. Well—" After a minute she went on. "He had a wife. She was awfully delicate. That made her nagging and suspicious of him—the way they get. He couldn't bear to hurt her. And then there were the kids. He was so fond of the kids."

Miss Nina had stiffened. A confused hostility was hot in her narrowed eyes. Meeting that gaze, the woman flinched, looked away. Her lips trembled, and she bit at them to make them steady. "I stuck to him for six years," she said. "Six years out of my life, you wouldn't believe it. Every thought I had for that man, every breath I drew."

Miss Nina ran the scrub brush over the fingers of the woman's hand. Chill soapy water dripped through the fingers. Miss Nina squeezed them briefly in a towel.

"It's a bad thing to happen to a girl," said the woman. Her eyes were fastened on Miss Nina with a quivering intensity. They seemed to implore her to understand, to respond. But Miss Nina's eyes were as blank as two bits of pale-blue glass. "It's a bad thing," the woman went on, "getting mixed up with a married man. It gets a girl a bad name around. I could have married—oh, easy—before I got to going with this fellow. But after—well, after, it was different. No man's going to wait for a woman six years. Not these days. You can't blame them. And with the talk and all. There's always talk."

Miss Nina painted the last finger of the right hand with the very red polish. She thrust the cork into the bottle, busied herself with tidying her tray of small articles. The woman opened her beaded bag, awkwardly with her left hand, and took from it a mirror and a powder puff in a figured silk handkerchief. She powdered her nose and straightened her hat. "Of course, I'm not out of the running yet," she said. She snapped her bag shut, and took up her new gloves. She laughed lightly. "No, sir, I haven't given up hope yet."

But as she hesitated to rise it became clear that she had not yet finished. She was mustering the courage to go on. There was a minute of painful silence. "There's just one thing," she at last admitted. "I—I'm sorry you aren't friends with Adele any more. Because I was hoping you could take a message from me. I—I got a feeling I wanted to tell her something."

Miss Nina had raised her tray. Now she set it down with a clatter. She took the edge of the table in both hands. "Tell me," she whispered. The light from the lamp flickered sharply in her eyes. "Tell me," she repeated.

"Well, you see, I guess I know him better than you do. This man Koch—" The name fell like a stone between them. And, seeing that the woman's face was white, Nina started sharply. In her thin young throat muscles twitched.

"Oh, my God!" said Nina. "You—you're not—"

For a moment they faced each other. Then the blonde woman understood. "No," she said. "I'm not. My, do I look like a delicate wife? No, dearie, I never made it. But what I wanted to tell you was about her—Koch's wife. This sick wife of his that he can't bear to hurt." The woman swallowed, as though it hurt her. "She died four years ago," she said. "I happen to know that. You see? Well, that's all."

She did not look at Miss Nina now, stared instead at her new gloves and the blue-beaded bag. "He really did have the sick wife when I knew him. Yes, and the kids, too. Her family took them when she died. I guess he couldn't bear the idea of losing her," she said with a dreary smile. "She came in so—handy."

The woman rose, moved toward the cashier's desk, her head raised, as one who outfaced many situations. With uncertain fingers she fumbled in her bag for a crumpled bill. Outside the orchid and green salons, she paused in the gloomy carpeted silence of the hotel corridor. Almost she turned back. Her lips twisted. She clenched her hands, turning her head in panic of regret. Suddenly she pressed her stiffened palms over her eyes. She did not hear Miss Nina coming until she stood beside her.

"Oh," cried the blonde woman. There were tears in her big hazel eyes. "Oh, I shouldn't have told you. I did wrong to tell you. It's none of my business, I know, what you do. But I got so's I couldn't sleep, thinking of him giving out he was a married man—getting away with it time after time—other girls suffering the way he made me suffer." Tears spilled down her thin cheeks, across the dusty pink areas of rouge. She brushed them away angrily.

"I'm glad you told me," said Miss Nina in a queer little voice. Her aquamarine eyes were very light in her drab face. "I only wish," she said slowly, "I only wish I had known before."

The woman laid one hand on Miss Nina's arm. "Listen," she implored her. "Would you take a piece of advice? I'm older than you. Don't let this break your heart, dear. Go back to that boy friend you talked about. You get married, hear me? That's the only thing for a woman to do, get married—"

"Boy friend?" cried Miss Nina. She spat out the word in disgust. "Married? Say, what's getting married? Kids. No clothes. No fun. Washing and ironing and mending his clothes, instead of just your own. Cooking and cleaning and losing your looks. And him not as nice to you as before you were married." She thrust her face close to the blonde woman's. "I'm going to have things," she said. Her little voice was shrill and vibrant. "No thirty-dollar clerk for me when I marry. I've been studying, educating myself to speak nice, and everything. I gave the boy friend the air six months ago. Do you think I'm going to throw myself away?"

Before such indignation the woman gasped speechless. Her large hazel eyes, around which moisture still clung, looked at Nina with a hypnotized fascination which was almost fear. "What you just told me," said Nina grimly, "explains a lot of things. It's just what I needed." Her eyes narrowed as she looked at the woman. "I've got enough on

Pete Koch to put him in States Prison." And absently, thoughtfully, her fingers tapped the corner of a white envelope which protruded at the bosom of her dress.

The blonde woman drew on her new kid gloves before she stumbled from the elevator. The big foyer seemed almost quiet. The woman glanced about her. In the cashier's cage, at the end of the long hotel desk, sat a very pretty girl. And, as the blonde woman looked, she saw that a tall man stooped attentively beside the cage. His back toward the blonde woman. But she could see that he leaned forward eagerly, absorbed in his conversation with the pretty girl. The woman took an impulsive step toward him. "Oh, my God!" she whispered. The expression on her face might have been pity—as though those bland shoulders in the well-cut coat seemed suddenly pathetically vulnerable, unaware of dangers.

Then abruptly she turned and walked down the long corridor which led to the side entrance of the hotel. She kept clasping and unclasping her gloved hands as she walked. She was still laughing when she reached the street.

(1928)

Dorothy Parker

Such A Pretty Little Picture

I

Mr. Wheelock was clipping the hedge. He did not dislike doing it. If it had not been for the faintly sickish odor of the privet bloom, he would definitely have enjoyed it. The new shears were so sharp and bright, there was such a gratifying sense of something done as the young green stems snapped off and the expanse of tidy, square hedge-top lengthened. There was a lot of work to be done on it. It should have been attended to a week ago, but this was the first day that Mr. Wheelock had been able to get back from the city before dinnertime.

Clipping the hedge was one of the few domestic duties that Mr. Wheelock could be trusted with. He was notoriously poor at doing anything around the house. All the suburb knew about it. It was the source of all Mrs. Wheelock's jokes. Her most popular anecdote was of how, the past winter, he had gone out and hired a man to take care of the furnace, after a seven-years' losing struggle with it. She had an admirable memory, and often as she had related the story, she never dropped a word of it. Even now, in the late summer, she could hardly tell it for laughing.

When they were first married, Mr. Wheelock had lent himself to the fun. He had even posed as being more inefficient than he really was, to make the joke better. But he had tired of his haplessness, as a topic of conversation. All the men of Mrs. Wheelock's acquaintance, her cousins, her brother-in-law, the boys she went to high school with, the neighbors' husbands, were adept at putting up a shelf, at repairing a lock, or making a shirtwaist box. Mr. Wheelock had begun to feel that there was something rather effeminate about his lack of interest in such things.

He had wanted to answer his wife, lately, when she enlivened some neighbor's dinner table with tales of his inadequacy with hammer and wrench. He had wanted to cry, "All right, suppose I'm not any good at things like that. What of it?"

He had played with the idea, had tried to imagine how his voice would sound, uttering the words. But he could think of no further argument for his case then that "What of it?" And he was a little relieved, somehow, at being able to find nothing stronger. It made it reassuringly impossible to go through with the plan of answering his wife's public railleries.

Mrs. Wheelock sat, now, on the spotless porch of the neat stucco house. Beside her was a pile of her husband's shirts and drawers, the price-tags still on them. She was going over all the buttons before he wore the garments, sewing them on more firmly. Mrs. Wheelock never waited for a button to come off, before sewing it on. She worked with quick, decided movements, compressing her lips each time the thread made a slight resistance to her deft jerks.

She was not a tall woman, and since the birth of her child she had gone over from a delicate plumpness to a settled stockiness. Her brown hair, though abundant, grew in an uncertain line about her forehead. It was her habit to put it up in curlers at night, but the crimps never came out in the right place. It was arranged with perfect neatness, yet it suggested that it had been done up and got over with as quickly as possible. Passionately clean, she was always redolent of the germicidal soap she used so vigorously. She was wont to tell people, somewhat redundantly, that she never employed any sort of cosmetics. She had unlimited contempt for women who sought to reduce their weight by dieting, cutting from their menus such nourishing items as cream and puddings and cereals.

Adelaide Wheelock's friends—and she had many of them—said of her that there was no nonsense about her. They and she regarded it as a compliment.

Sister, the Wheelock's five-year-old daughter, played quietly in the gravel path that divided the tiny lawn. She had been known as Sister since her birth, and her mother still laid plans for a brother for her. Sister's baby carriage stood waiting in the cellar, her baby clothes were stacked expectantly away in bureau drawers. But raises were infrequent at the advertising agency where Mr. Wheelock was employed, and his present salary had barely caught up to the cost of their living. They could not conscientiously regard themselves as being able to afford a son. Both Mr. and Mrs. Wheelock keenly felt his guilt in keeping the bassinet empty.

Sister was not a pretty child, though her features were straight, and her eyes would one day be handsome. The left one turned slightly in toward the nose, now, when she looked in a certain direction; they would operate as soon as she was seven. Her hair was pale and limp, and her color bad. She was a delicate little girl. Not fragile in a picturesque way, but the kind of child that must be always undergoing treatment for its teeth and its throat and obscure things in its nose. She had lately had her adenoids removed, and she was still using squares of surgical gauze instead of handkerchiefs. Both she and her mother somehow felt that these gave her a sort of prestige.

She was additionally handicapped by her frocks, which her mother bought a size or so too large, with a view to Sister's growing into them—an expectation which seemed never to be realized, for her skirts were always too long, and the shoulders of her little dresses came halfway down to her thin elbows. Yet, even discounting the unfortunate way she was dressed, you could tell, in some way, that she was never going to wear any kind of clothes well.

Mr. Wheelock glanced at her now and then as he clipped. He had never felt any fierce thrills of father-love for the child. He had been disappointed in her when she was a pale, large-headed baby, smelling of stale milk and warm rubber. Sister made him feel ill at ease, vaguely irritated him. He had no share in her training; Mrs. Wheelock was so competent a parent that she took the places of both of them. When Sister came to him to ask his permission to do something, he always told her to wait and ask her mother about it.

He regarded himself as having the usual paternal affection for his daughter. There were times, indeed, when she had tugged sharply at his heart—when he had waited in the corridor outside the operating room; when she was still under the anesthetic, and lay little and white and helpless on her high hospital bed; once when he had accidentally closed a door upon her thumb. But from the first he had nearly acknowledged to himself that he did not like Sister as a person.

Sister was not a whining child, despite her poor health. She had always been sensible and well-mannered, amenable about talking to visitors, rigorously unselfish. She never got into trouble, like other children. She did not care much for other children. She had heard herself described as being "old-fashioned," and she knew she was delicate, and she felt that these attributes rather set her above them. Besides, they were rough and careless of their bodily well-being.

Sister was exquisitely cautious of her safety. Grass, she knew, was often apt to be damp in the late afternoon, so she was careful now to stay right in the middle of the gravel path, sitting on a folded newspaper and playing one of her mysterious games with three petunias that she has been allowed to pick. Mrs. Wheelock never had to speak to her twice about keeping off wet grass, or wearing her rubbers, or putting on her jacket if a breeze sprang up. Sister was an immediately obedient child, always.

II

Mrs. Wheelock looked up from her sewing and spoke to her husband. Her voice was high and clear, resolutely good-humored. From her habit of calling instructions from her upstairs window to Sister playing on the porch below, she spoke always a little louder than was necessary.

"Daddy," she said.

She had called him daddy since some eight months before Sister was born. She and the child had the same trick of calling his name and then waiting until he signified that he was attending before they went on with what they wanted to say.

Mr. Wheelock stopped clipping, straightened himself and turned toward her.

"Daddy," she went on, thus reassured, "I saw Mr. Ince down at the post office today when Sister and I went down to get the ten o'clock mail—there wasn't much, just a card for me from Grace Williams from that place they go to up on Cape Cod, and an advertisement from some department store or other about their summer fur sale (as if I cared!), and circular for you from the bank. I opened it; I knew you wouldn't mind.

"Anyway, I just thought I'd tackle Mr. Ince first as last about getting in our cordwood. He didn't see me at first—though I'll bet he really saw me and pretended not to—but I ran right after him. 'Oh, Mr. Ince!' I said. 'Why, hello, Mrs. Wheelock ,' he said, and then he asked for you, and I told him you were finely, and everything. Then I said, 'Now, Mr. Ince,' I said, 'how about getting in that cordwood of ours?' And he said, 'Well, Mrs. Wheelock,' he said, 'I'll get it in soon's I can, but I'm short of help right now,' he said.

"Short of help! Of course I couldn't say anything, but I guess he could tell from the way I looked at him how much I believed it. I just said, 'All right, Mr. Ince, but don't you forget us. There may be a cold snap coming on,' I said, 'and we'll be wanting a fire in the living-room. Don't you forget us,' I said, and he said, no, he wouldn't.

"If that wood isn't here by Monday, I think you ought to do something about it, Daddy. There's no sense in all this putting it off, and putting it off. First thing you know there'll be a cold snap coming on, and we'll be wanting a fire in the living-room, and there'll we'll be! You'll be sure to tend to it, won't you, Daddy? I'll remind you again Monday, if I can think of it, but there are so many things!"

Mr. Wheelock nodded and turned back to his clipping—and his thoughts. They were thoughts that had occupied much of his leisure lately. After dinner, when Adelaide was sewing or arguing with the maid, he found himself letting his magazine fall face downward on his knee, while he rolled the same idea round and round in his mind. He had got so that he looked forward, through the day, to losing himself in it. He had rather welcomed the hedge-clipping: you can clip and think at the same time.

It had started with a story that he had picked up somewhere. He couldn't recall whether he had heard it or had read it—that was probably it, he thought, he had run across it in the back pages of some comic paper that someone had left on the train.

It was about a man who lived in a suburb. Every morning he had gone to the city on the 8.12, sitting in the same seat in the same car, and every evening he had gone home to his wife on the 5:17, sitting in the same seat in the same car. He had done this for twenty years of his life. And then one night he didn't come home. He never went back to his office any more. He just never turned up again.

The last man to see him was the conductor on the 5:17.

"He come down the platform at the Grand Central," the man reported, "just like he done every night since I been working on this road. He put one foot on the step, and then he stopped sudden, and he said, 'Oh, hell,' and he took his foot off the step and walked away. And that's the last anybody see of him."

Curious how that story took hold of Mr. Wheelock's fancy. He had started thinking of it as a mildly humorous anecdote; he had come to accept it as fact. He did not think the man's sitting in the same seat in the same car need have been stressed so much. That seemed unimportant. He thought long about the man's wife, wondered what suburb he had lived in. He loved to play with the thing, to try to feel what the man felt before he took his foot off the car's step. He never concerned himself with speculations as to where the man had disappeared, how he had spent the rest of his life. Mr. Wheelock was absorbed in that moment when he had said "Oh, hell" and walked off. "Oh, hell" seemed to Mr. Wheelock a fine thing for him to have said, a perfect summary of the situation.

He tried thinking to himself in the man's place. But no, he would have done it from the other end. That was the real way to do it.

Some summer evening like this, say, when Adelaide was sewing on buttons, up on the porch, and Sister was playing somewhere about. A pleasant, quiet evening it must be, with the shadows lying long on the street that led from their house to the station. He would put down the garden shears, or the hose, or whatever he happened to be puttering with—not throw the thing down, you know, just put it quietly aside—and walk out of the gate and down the street, and that would be the last they'd see of him. He would time it so that he'd just make the 6:03 for the city comfortably.

He did not go ahead with it from there, much. He was not especially anxious to leave the advertising agency forever. He did not particularly dislike his work. He had been an advertising solicitor since he had gone to work at all, and he worked hard at his job and, aside from that, didn't think about it much one way or the other.

It seemed to Mr. Wheelock that before he had got hold of the "Oh, hell" story he had never thought about anything much, one way or another. But he would have to disappear from the office, too, that was certain. It would spoil everything to turn up there again. He thought dimly of taking a train going West, after the 6:03 got him to the Grand Central, he might go to Buffalo, say, or perhaps Chicago. Better just let that part take care of itself and go back to dwell on the moment when it would sweep over him that he was going to do it, when he would put down the shears and walk out the gate—

The "Oh, hell" rather troubled him. Mr. Wheelock felt that he would like to retain that; it completed the gesture so beautifully. But he didn't quite know to whom he should say it.

He might stop in at the post office on the way to the station and say it to the postmaster; but the postmaster would probably think that he was only annoyed at there being no mail for him. Nor would the conductor of the 6:03, a train Mr. Wheelock never used, take the right interest in it. Of course the real thing to do would be to say it to Adelaide just before he laid down the shears. But somehow Mr. Wheelock could not make that scene come very clear in his imagination.

III

"Daddy," Mrs. Wheelock said briskly.

He stopped clipping, and faced her.

"Daddy," she related, "I saw Doctor Mann's automobile going by the house this morning—he was going to have a look at Mr. Warren, his rheumatism's getting along nicely—and I called him in a minute, to look us over."

She screwed up her face, winked, and nodded vehemently in the direction of the abandoned Sister, to indicate that she was the subject of the discourse.

"He said we were going ahead finely," she resumed, when she was sure that he had caught the idea. "Said there was no need for those t-o-n-s-i-l-s to c-o-m-e o-u-t. But I thought, soon's it gets a little cooler, some time next month, we'd just run into the city and let Doctor Sturges have a look at us. I'd rather be on the safe side."

"But Doctor Lytton said it wasn't necessary, and those doctors at the hospital, and now Doctor Mann, that's known her since she was a baby," suggested Mr. Wheelock.

"I know, I know," replied his wife, "But I'd rather be on the safe side."

Mr. Wheelock went back to his hedge.

Oh, of course he couldn't do it; he never seriously thought he could, for a minute. Of course he couldn't. He wouldn't have the shadow of an excuse for doing it. Adelaide was a sterling woman, an utterly faithful wife, an almost slavish mother. She ran his house economically and efficiently. She harried the suburban trades people into giving them dependable service, drilled the succession of poorly paid, poorly trained maids, cheerfully did the thousand fussy little things that go with the running of a house. She looked after his clothes, gave him medicine when she thought he needed it, oversaw the preparation of every meal that was set before him; they were not especially inspirational meals, but the food was always nourishing and, as a general thing, fairly well cooked. She never lost her temper, she was never depressed, never ill.

Not the shadow of an excuse. People would know that, and so they would invent an excuse for him. They would say there must be another woman.

Mr. Wheelock frowned, and snipped at an obstinate young twig. Good Lord, the last thing he wanted was another woman. What he wanted was that moment when he realized he could do it, when he would lay down the shears—

Oh, of course he couldn't; he knew that as well as anybody. What would they do, Adelaide and Sister? The house wasn't even paid for yet, and there would be that operation on Sister's eye in a couple of years. But the house would be all paid up by next March. And there was always that well-to-do brother-in-law of Adelaide's, the one who, for all his means, put up every shelf in that great big house with his own hands.

Decent people didn't just go away and leave their wives and families that way. All right, suppose you weren't decent; what of it? Here was Adelaide planning what she was going to do when it got a little cooler, next month. She was always planning ahead, always confident that things would go on just the same. Naturally, Mr. Wheelock realized that he couldn't do it, as well as the next one. But there was no harm in fooling around with the idea. Would you say the "Oh, hell" now, before you laid down shears, or right after? How would it be to turn at the gate and say it?

Mr. and Mrs. Fred Coles came down the street arm-in-arm, from their neat stucco house on the corner.

"See they've got you working hard, eh?" cried Mr. Coles genially, as they paused abreast of the hedge.

Mr. Wheelock laughed politely, making time for an answer.

"That's right," he evolved.

Mrs. Wheelock looked up from her work, shading her eyes with her thimbled hand against the long rays of the low sun.

"Yes, we finally got Daddy to do a little work," she called brightly. "But Sister and I are staying right here to watch over him, for fear he might cut his little self with the shears."

There was general laughter, in which Sister joined. She had risen punctiliously at the approach of the older people, and she was looking politely at their eyes, as she had been taught.

"And how is my great big girl?" asked Mrs. Coles, gazing fondly at the child.

"Oh, much better," Mrs. Wheelock answered for her. "Doctor Mann says we are going ahead finely. I saw his automobile passing the house this morning—he was going to see Mr. Warren, his rheumatism's coming along nicely—and I called him in a minute to look us over."

She did the winks and the nods, at Sister's back. Mr. and Mrs. Coles nodded shrewdly back at her.

"He said there's no need for those t-o-n-s-i-l-s to c-o-m-e o-u-t," Mrs. Wheelock called. "But I thought, soon's it gets a little cooler, some time next month, we'd just run into the city and let Doctor Sturges have a look at us. I was telling Daddy, 'I'd rather be on the safe side,' I said."

"Yes, it's better to be on the safe side," agreed Mrs. Coles, and her husband nodded again, sagely this time. She took his arm, and moved slowly off.

"Been a lovely day, hasn't it?" she said over her shoulder, fearful of having left too abruptly. "Fred and I are taking a little constitutional before supper," she called back.

Sister, weary of her game, mounted the porch, whimpering a little. Mrs. Wheelock put aside her sewing, and took the tired child in her lap. The sun's last rays touched her brown hair, making is a shimmering gold. Her small, sharp face, the thick lines of her figure were in shadow as she bent over the little girl. Sister's head was hidden on her mother's shoulder, the folds of her rumpled white frock followed her limp, relaxed little body.

The lovely light was kind to the cheap, hurriedly built stucco house, to the clean gravel path, and the bits of closely cut lawn. It was gracious, too, to Mr. Wheelock's tall, lean figure as he bent to work on the last few inches of unclipped hedge.

Twenty years, he thought. The man in the story went through with it for twenty years. He must have been a man along around forty-five, most likely. Mr. Wheelock was thirty-seven. Eight years. It's a long time, eight years is. You could easily get so you could say that final "Oh, hell," even to Adelaide, in eight years. It probably wouldn't take more than four years for you to know that you could do it. No, not more than two …

Mrs. Coles paused at the corner of the street and looked back at the Wheelock's house. The last of the light lingered on the mother and child group on the porch, gently touched the tall white-clad figure of the husband and father as he went up to them, his work done.

Mrs. Coles was a large, soft woman, barren, and addicted to sentiment.

"Look, Fred: just turn around and look at that," she said to her husband. She looked again, sighing luxuriously. "Such a pretty little picture."

(1922)

Frank Sullivan

The Cub Reporter
Or The Scoop, or A Slice of Life,
or Zaza

It was midnight in the city room of the *Morning Morning*, a big metropolitan daily with a great many agate lines of advertising; more, in fact, than any other three big metropolitan dailies combined.

Below, in the basement, the presses hummed. They were humming "Tenting on the Old Camp Ground," for it was 1865 and the Civil War was just over. All the reporters wore Dundreary whiskers and plaid pants.

"So you want to be a cub reporter?" said Phineas Dalrymple, the editor, to a rosy-cheeked, bright-eyed lad who had just graduated from either Harvard, Yale, Princeton, or Cornell. The grizzled scribe regarded the youth with a not unfriendly (that is to say, a friendly) eye. The editor had been a newspaperman himself, once.

"Oh sir," said young Ned Medfellow, "I have wanted to be a member of the Fourth Estate since I was knee-high to a grasshopper. And the girl of my choice says she will marry me the moment I score my first beat."

Dalrymple did not answer for a moment.

"Ah," he said, finally. "There were grasshoppers in those days."

He sighed.

"Well," he added, "there isn't much advice I can give you, Perkins. Perkins *is* your name, isn't it?"

Medfellow thought it best to humor the noted wiseacre, so he replied that it was.

"Well, it's not much of a name," said Dalrymple pettishly, for he had been married at various times to women named Perkins, "Why don't you get a good name, like Medfellow, for instance?"

Ned smiled. Here was his own name back again. Funny, he thought, how things always work out all right, somehow.

"All I can tell you," said Dalrymple, "is that if a man bites a dog it's news. Now go out and scoop the town, like a good cub reporter. By the way, before you go—you couldn't spare a couple of dollars until pay day, could you?"

Ned could, nay, did; he sallied forth, his hopes high.

"Hurray," he told Clara, the girl of his choice, "I've got my first assignment!"

"Superb!" she shot back, "And what a break, too, for I just met that charming John Wilkes Booth and he tells me he is going to Washington tomorrow to shoot Mr. Lincoln. Wouldn't that be a fine scoop if you got it first?"

(Richard Harding Davis had not been invented yet.)

Ned laughed indulgently.

"Ah, you women," he said, chucking her under the chin, "How should you pretty creatures know about such things as scoops?"

"Well, all I know is, he had a pistol," said Clara.

The next day, Mr. Booth shot Mr. Lincoln, and Ned's fiancée decided it might be just as well if they didn't wait until he got his first scoop before they got married. So they got married right away.

Thirty years passed. Again the city room, but this time the presses were humming, "Goodby, Dolly, I Must Leave You, Though It Breaks My Heart To Go." It was '98 and Ned was still a cub reporter.

"I'm glad we didn't wait about the marriage," Clara often said.

Another thirty years pass. It is 1928 and the presses are now humming "I Can't Give You Anything But Love, Baby."

Ned is still a cub reporter and has three sons and seven grandsons, all cub reporters. Ned now has a large mustache and three chins and is the only cub reporter in New York so equipped. He is quite proud of this and is looked up to by cub reporters of only one chin or less.

It is the den of the Medfellow's cozy apartment. Clara is adjusting Ned's tie, lovingly.

"Where are you off to tonight, my love?" she inquires.

"Don't you know?" he asks.

"If I did, I wouldn't ask, would I?" says she, untying the necktie in a great huff.

"Well, I'm off to the banquet. The League of Authors Who Write Stories About Cub Reporters Who Invariably Scoop the Town is giving me this banquet in my honor, I being the exception proving the rule."

The little woman's eyes glowed with pride.

"I knew you'd make good," she said, tying the tie again, "I knew you had it in you from the day I told you about Booth and Lincoln. Promise me you will always be my Cub Reporter."

"I do," he said tenderly, "I promise, if you'll promise always to be my Red, Red Rose."

She promised, and arm in arm they went down Life's Autumn.

(1929)

Laurence Stallings

Turn Out the Guard

In World War I, writers Frank Adams, Harold Ross, Johnny Weaver and Aleck Woollcott all served in the army, but never saw action. Laurence Stallings was the only member of the Vicious Circle to experience actual combat. Stallings was a lieutenant in the U.S. Marines at the Battle of Belleau Wood near the Marne River; he was wounded in June 1918 and his right leg was amputated. Stallings often wrote about the military in books, stories, plays and movies. His Army-Navy fable "Turn Out the Guard" was written 10 years after the Armistice for The Saturday Evening Post.

Col. Stonewall Jackson Butt was cooling his heels in the Canal Zone in April, 1917. He was an undersized officer with all the truculence of a terrier, having entered West Point some thirty years before by a scant half inch. After achieving his colonelcy he had taken up sideburns of a whitish texture, and they conferred upon him the distinction of a finely bred Sealyham terrier.

In 1903, on the Island of Luzon, a Moro had thrown a bolo at him and cocked one eye for him. This lent the colonel one utterly doggy side—which he chiefly turned at naval officers. His apathy toward seafaring men was the result of a youth spent in the household of an ancient family of military tradition, where it was dinned into his ears that failure to grow would inevitably result in his attending the United States Naval Academy at Annapolis. He had made the necessary West Point height through terror lest he be confined at Annapolis, a place seemingly designed to school dwarfs for duties in the cramped spaces aboard a man-o'-war.

There were two things rankling in Colonel Butt's heart as he cooled his heels in Colon some two weeks after America's active interest in European army matters: Chiefly, there was a deep mortification of pride because his colleagues at Washington had declined to recall him for service in France. Secondly, it galled him to realize that Stonewall Jackson Butt, Jr., was an officer in the United States Navy.

The colonel might have been even more deeply mortified to have overheard Butt, Jr., in the wardroom of the U. S. S. *Collier O'Leary*, explain his father's failure to be among the first officers to go.

"My father," he said, "is a Bayardist—a fellow who believes in leading his troops. If he were sent to France, his bloody pugnacity would result in his being made a major general. But regardless of rank, he would lead the first wave of any operation he might be supposed to direct. This would result in his death. But the War Department believes that the only bad major general is a dead major general. Obviously, it will keep him at Panama for the duration."

Lieutenant Butt, junior grade, United States Navy, came ashore at Panama in May 1917, his ship being en route to Guam for a two-year cruise on the Asiatic Station.

"How are you, lieutenant?" asked the colonel, accepting the naval officer's salute from his doggy side.

"Shipshape," said Lieutenant Butt, smiling pleasantly and taking the other side.

The colonel was astonished to find the lad the handsomest Butt in all the annals of the house. His four years at Annapolis had filled him out and his face was that of the young Saint John. In the service a handsome son is a distinct asset. The colonel relaxed the Sealyham look and began to be charming.

"Shall we go drink to each other's health?" said the colonel, who rarely began drinking before sundown.

"The old swab," thought Lieutenant Butt affectionately, "must be getting a little rummy." He had been told years before at Annapolis that army officers drank themselves into retirement when inevitably they perceived the folly of their careers.

The colonel was busy thinking up ways to be kind to his son. Colonel Butt thought the surest road to his trust lay through the neck of a bottle, since he believed navy men to be sots once the full disaster of a life at sea broke upon them.

"Let's go," said the colonel, "to the Panama side and have a glass of Pernod *fils*. I know a café where they make a beautiful absinth frappé."

"Absinth in the morning?" thought the naval officer. Yes, it must be true that colonels were rummies. But he did not wish to offend the old gentleman. He spoke politely:

"Don't you think it would be better to lay a keel of pilsner first? Then we can fit her with the Pernod armor plate and toss a few brandies down the hatch for ballast. You used to stow away the brandy, I recall."

With difficulty, the colonel overcame his disgust for nautical metaphors. He was an abstemious man, drinking only a little brandy and water before and after meals. His son's ready willingness to acquire a stinko bun at noon smacked of a navy man's two hours' liberty ashore from a cruiser.

"Oh," said the colonel with terrific bonhomie, "we'll just feel out the enemy before we issue rations. After that we'll deploy and engage the whole Barleycorn army in detail." The colonel was proud of his repartee. Trust the old army lingo to match any seafaring gab!

"Righto," said Butt, Jr. "My ship's bound for the Asiatic Station for a two-year hitch in hell. I want to be poured on her tonight, full and by."

"You dislike going to the Asiatic Station?" the colonel asked the lieutenant, keenly watching that Saint John face.

"I'd rather be scuttled in forty fathoms," the sailor said bitterly; cruelly adding: "After all, one of us ought to be in this war, father."

"It is the very question I wish to discuss with you," the colonel said, and lapsed into unbroken silence until they presently came to a striped awning jutting from a plaster wall. Beneath the awning were iron tables and the uncomfortable little chairs that drinkers must occupy in foreign countries.

The colonel raised his watered cognac and the lieutenant blew the froth from his brew.

"Army," said the naval officer, raising his glass.

"And Navy forever!" the army officer countered, clinking rims. They drank down deep. Lieutenant Butt caught the waiter.

"Stand by for boarders," he said.

"Reload 'em," said Colonel Butt. They smiled at each other.

"Stonewall," said the colonel to his son, half an hour later, as they were throwing in a third Grand Marnier for ballast, the Pernod armor plate being fitted tightly to their ribs, "there is a very lovely girl stopping here with her father."

The lieutenant was silent. He remembered that his father used his given name only on portentous occasions.

"She is," said the colonel, "of a most distinguished Middle-Western family."

The lieutenant preserved his silence. He had been taught at Bancroft Hall to make no important strategic dispositions until the enemy gave a hint of his mission. That his father regarded any Middle-Western family as distinguished was odd for one who considered all things west of the Shenandoah Valley as unworthy of any distinction whatsoever.

"Above all," said the colonel, boldly unmasking his true disposition, "her father is a member of the House Committee on Naval Affairs."

This was tantamount to revealing the left flank, and the naval officer immediately changed his course. "The Naval Affairs Committee?" He looked his father over shrewdly. "Where is she, you say?"

"Her father," the colonel said, "usually brings her here at noon. He is very fond of a sweet red Spanish wine they sell here. Marquis de Riscal I think it is called. That is why I brought you here."

"Ask the waiter," he requested his father, "if he has any chewing gum or cloves—and let's not have that onion soup."

The colonel knew the Spanish word for cloves, and he changed the soup to consommé Madrilene.

"After all," said the army officer, showing his doggy side in the warmth of the ballast he had taken aboard, "a naval officer's wife does not matter. He grows to love her and is afforded the pleasure of her company half his days. If he dislikes her, he is away at sea and free of her half his time. It is fifty-fifty either way a navy man may take it." The colonel laughed.

The naval horizon was clouding up. Visibility was low. Colonel Butt changed his attack. "When I married your mother," he said, "I had only your interests at heart. I had my whole military career before me, but her father was one of the original stock-holders of the Pullman Company and I had to think of the future of my child."

"I know," said Lieutenant Butt with some bitterness. "That's why my class at Annapolis always refers to me as Gawdge. I'd wake up as a plebe to find fifty pairs of boots standing outside my door."

The colonel was hardly sympathetic. "The girl I have chosen for you," he said, "is charming, and her father is not bad for a congressman. He has immense political power. If you marry his daughter, you have only to keep sober and refrain from striking your admiral when you are drunken, to become an admiral yourself some day; whereas I married solely for your welfare and am still a colonel."

Lieutenant Butt reflected: "The girl might not have me."

"The young lady is exactly your height," responded his father immediately.

"If I thought," said the younger man, his handsome dark eyes narrowing and his clean jaw squaring nautically, "that it would really be possible for her to get me duty on one of the destroyer patrols with Sims, I'd marry a pituitary monster, congressman father and all."

"I'm sure she will," the colonel said.

"No, father," Lieutenant Butt said patronizingly. "When women marry naval officers for love, they keep 'em at home the first cruise. After that, they keep 'em at sea."

"Sometimes I think you are too stupid even for the naval service," Colonel Butt exploded instantly.

"You forget yourself," the Annapolis man said angrily. "It is a pity West Point deprives a man of his manners."

The father bowed an apology in some heat. "The young woman would dearly love to spend the war years in Paris. Can you not see her cheering up the wounded French officers, happy that her husband is commanding one of the patrol boats operating out of Brest?"

The colonel sprang to his feet and clicked his heels, for a large man and a lovely girl had entered the café. The large man wore a sleazy linen suit that bagged over a statesmanlike belly festooned in watch charms of secret orders. Behind the man walked a girl in pink organdie—a fairly young and large-calved girl who seemed to propel and control the man ahead of her by waves of a Hertzian vitality. She smiled for the colonel's bow, exposing strong teeth and large snapping blue eyes. The eyes rested finally upon the lineaments of the young Saint John.

"The lady is here," said Colonel Butt. "I should be happy to beg the pleasure of an introduction."

Lieutenant Butt was inspecting the girl, who now sat three tables away and facing him.

"The old hulk's a water-logged windjammer," he said. "But she's as pretty as a racing ketch."

"You'll be bound for Admiral Sims' division," the colonel coaxed, "the day after your marriage."

"She's the kind," said Lieutenant Butt, "that you make love to without any thought of marriage." He spoke admiringly, as if directly to the object of criticism.

His father rose. "I shall ask the honor of presenting you," said Colonel Butt.

"Please ask her to forgive the impetuousness," his son said, his eyes speaking whole logarithm tables to her across the tables. The colonel walked over to the other table and briefly was back again.

"I said you were timid," he explained.

"The truth is," exclaimed the son, fluffing his white cap cover jauntily, "I don't know how to thank you, father." He was simulating a fresh natural timidity. "And I am keel-hauled if I see where you expect to haul up on this maneuver."

Colonel Butt revealed the ultimate mission of a perfect campaign. "She will never rest," he said, taking his son's arm and starting him for the enemy, "until her distinguished father-in-law, the major general, is commanding his own division in France."

"Particularly," said Lieutenant Butt, hanging back and blushing like a bugler at retreat, "if presently there is an heir to the Butt tradition."

"There has been a Butt to lead a charge in every war in our history," said the colonel, advancing.

The two officers arrived. "My son," exclaimed Colonel Butt proudly, "I am presenting you to the man we call the Savior of the American Navy." The lieutenant bowed low to the man in linen. "And this, Miss Wanda," the colonel said, twinkling, "is the most timid sailor that was ever shipped away to long exile at Guam."

"Guam?" said the Savior of the American Navy. "Good Lord! Where's that?" He was displeased. "I say, let the English police their own possessions."

"I wondered who you were when father inspected your ship this morning," said Miss Wanda, devil may care in the large blue eyes.

"I was trying to get your eye," the lieutenant retaliated impishly. "But we of the Navy have so much respect for your father that we were all on our best behavior this morning."

"Did you think it was funny for me to make the inspection with him?" she asked, grinning devilishly. "You seemed sort of snippy when I knocked over that range finder and broke the prism."

"You already had the range on me and had smashed more than a prism," the naval lieutenant, suddenly abandoning his timidity, declared with forthright bluntness.

"You sailors!" said Miss Wanda, enjoying Lieutenant Butt's cavalier dismissal of an incident that would occasion the filing of fourteen separate requisition sheets.

"After all," said Butt, Jr., "Venus rose from the sea, you know."

The congressman took a paternal hand. "Never trust a navy man," he said, laughing with sardonic implication and slapping the young man on the back.

"Why not?" said Lieutenant Butt, j. g., U. S. N., with Virginia's own darling manners. "We navy men trust our statesmen." He reeked with simple patriotism, and Colonel Butt looked at his son with a gathering admiration.

The Lieutenant had turned back to Miss Wanda. "You and I," he was saying, "must go over to the old fort in the moonlight. We'll drag the two heroes along." He indicated army duck with breasted ribbons and sleazy linen with watch charms in an embracing gesture. "But we'll make 'em keep their interval."

"Keno!" shrieked Miss Wanda. "There'll be a lovely moon."

Butt, Jr.'s face was clouded for the first time. "Then I'd better not go," he said.

"Why?" said the girl anxiously.

"It'll break my heart to remember it," he said soberly, "when I'm way down below—in Guam."

The colonel was tart. "Never criticize your duty, lieutenant," he said. "Your family keeps its silence when favoritism momentarily triumphs over fitness."

The elder man was every inch a Butt at that moment. But he dropped the matter instantly. He soon was listening attentively to the congressman's exposition of the strategy board's confidential plans for transporting troops to France.

II

Brigadier General Stonewall J. Butt, United States Army, stood upon the deck of the *Leviathan*, having emerged from his cabin deluxe to watch the great transport thread the narrows of Brest and drop anchor under the green hills of Brittany. The harbor was alive with bunting, for on the *Leviathan's* decks were twenty thousand yelling Americans, and destroyers played beneath her sides as billowing narwhals play in the vast deep. The millionth American had arrived to settle that old score with Lafayette. They would presently pay it and open new accounts with half his descendants.

Brigadier General Butt for the first time in his life thrilled with pride at naval display as he watched the U. S. S. *Romboid* reverse her screws and heel sharply, smart angles of her destroyer's bow breasting green water as her tired crew cheered. The *Romboid* was in from patrol, the great *Leviathan* safely disposed in snug harbor behind the subnets. Lieutenant—senior grade—Butt could handle the new type destroyer. Brigadier General Butt, for all his landsman's eyes, could not mistake the master of the *Romboid's* seamanship as the narrow craft knifed her way to her berth behind the breakwater, her forestack flaunting the chevron that boasted at least one enemy submarine sent down to Davy Jones.

Father and son examined each other as they drank warm cognac at a *brasserie* in the Rue de Siam. The brigadier general had not seen his son since Lieutenant Butt had literally swept Wanda off her feet in a whirlwind courtship beneath the very walls of old Panama. The general was wistful and the Sealyham looked more like a tired Airedale's. The three ribbons on his breast, withal they were for valor, were not so choice as the single blue-and-white one on his son's tunic. Lieutenant Butt was ruddy and bronzed, and there were weather lines around the mouth of the young Saint John, and seamy strains in the corners of eyes that had followed the channel foam in February's patrolling.

"I'd enjoy spending the week-end with you here," the general said, eying the son's ribbon wistfully, "but I must take the night train for Chaumont. I am eager to be with my brigade." He drank cognac pensively. "After all," he said, "war is war."

The naval veteran smiled. "I'm going to Chaumont with you," he said.

The general hastily sought to prevent him. "It is kind of you to wish to escort me," he said.

The lieutenant broke in as an old mustache might interrupt a village boy: "It's not that. It's that I'm to be in naval guns from now on." He explained bitterly, "You see, Daniels chucked me the Navy Cross for that U-78 thing off Cherbourg. But Wanda won't rest until I've copped a D. S. C. Lord knows, I don't want their army dud. I hear they award it to every general that supervises potato transport."

The general coughed savagely. "You forget your present company," he said.

The navy man smiled. "Anyway, Wanda says her French friends never heard of a Navy Cross. So it's up to me." He grinned. "If it's a boy, Wanda thinks it would mean something for me to have an army D. S. C. after Butt." He laughed. "I'd be a unique parent." He caught the strained look in his father's eye and dropped the matter. "By the bye," he asked the general, "what luck did you draw?"

His father was apologetic. "Just at present I suppose I'll be acclimatized in the Service of Supply." Then he spoke the whole truth, for a Butt could not lie in line of duty. "Potatoes," he said, with some bitterness.

"When Wanda hears of this she'll have Pershing recalled from France!" exclaimed the submarine sinker in horror.

"Then don't let her hear of it," said the general, hastily setting down his glass.

Young Butt looked at Old Butt curiously. "Father," he said, after a silence, "why not let Wanda get you a combat command? Those trenches can't be so bad."

The potato brigadier's hand trembled and the Sealyham returned flashing and seemed about to spring. The general stood erect.

"You are thick-skulled," he said, the old service animosity reviving, "even for an Annapolis man."

The lieutenant's ruddy face grew white. "I was never confined in those stone prisons at West Point," he said evenly. "Possibly I may seem curious to an army man."

He saluted and waited dismissal. The general returned the salute and started down the Rue de Siam, and was instantly followed by two old girls from the café.

One of the girls tugged at his sleeve and said, "I like dear-boyes, yas?"

Young Butt ran after his father. "Look here, sir," he said, putting his hand across the girl's face and pushing her away from the general's arm, "let's bury this service hatchet. Tell me why Wanda mustn't know you are in potatoes?"

The elder man took the other's arm gently. "I was about to say that Wanda mustn't hear of my post. She must see me in it—find her father-in-law in some warehouse swinging sacks of potatoes." He spoke with the wisdom of thirty years in harness. "There is nothing so disconcerting to high command, my son, as an irate woman who suddenly breaks into the office of the chief of staff, smarting with injustice."

The lieutenant seemed to relish some inner vision, for he laughed loudly. "What would you like in this man's Army?" he said. "You can have it."

Brigadier General Butt spoke his dream. "I'd like a cavalry brigade," he said. "For sooner or later this war will be fought in the open, with lightning movements on a grand scale in Napoleonic fashion. But Pershing is prejudiced against infantry officers. He always puts cavalrymen at the head of cavalry brigades."

The naval officer was loath to discuss the probability of another Waterloo. "You haven't seen Wanda recently," he said instead.

"How is the dear girl?" the general asked.

"About a month now," the lieutenant replied.

"Then we shall have to be quick about her finding me in potatoes."

"Wanda goes anywhere any time," Butt, Jr., assured his parent. "An amazing person. Two weeks ago she made an address in French to the disabled officers of the First Foreign Legion—presented 'em with soap kits." He smiled. "Rode thirty miles in a flivver, she wrote me."

"Your mother was that way," the general said, looking old and sad. He was thinking of her. He wished her success in reorganizing the drainage system of whatever Elysian army post she was at present re-landscaping.

III

Major General S. J. Butt, U. S. A., was making an inspection of heavy ordnance, railway and field, by request of G. H. Q. at

Chaumont before the great guns took the road for the Meuse-Sedan front. The major general was severe in his scrutiny of personnel and *matériel*, for his was a bitter task about which he held no illusions. He knew that the post had been created to send him into limbo.

News of his severity had reached the officers of a naval-artillery battalion which, fresh from St. Mihiel, lay doggo in a small town above Chalons. The general, it was said, had performed the unheard-of rite of inspecting the automatic strapped to the leg of a rear admiral and had publicly reprimanded that naval functionary when the weapon was discovered to be in a deplorable state of rust and disuse.

Lieutenant Commander Stonewall J. Butt, Jr., U. S. N., who had the battalion, spoke with some heat of the approaching ordeal. His battalion family was resting in a large oak-paneled room in the only château the town afforded.

"Now, gentlemen," he said decisively to their assembly, "we are to be inspected by a foot-slogging meddler from G. H. Q. tomorrow. Doubtless some of you know that the general inspecting us has the honor to be related to me."

The lieutenant commander cut short an incipient growth of applause and continued: "But for God's sake don't think that because of my unfortunate blood relationship he'll be easy on us! He is opposed, by accident of birth and breeding, to webbed feet and seagoing guns, to scuttle butts and salty water. So ease off knocking Joey Daniels long enough to have your sections privvy up the guns. And have every man shave his head to the regulation quarter-inch tuft. When Major General Butt accompanied one of the divisions last month as an observer, I understand he had the second wave of an attacking battalion cut one another's hair at the very parallel of departure. Later, when he was back in hospital recovering from his wound, I understand he even ordered the army nurses to conform."

Ensign Snoddy, the lieutenant commander's adjutant, Annapolis, 1918, was unwise enough to ask a question: "Did they conform, sir?"

Lieutenant Commander Butt turned upon him with pity. "So much so," he said, "that the German prisoners in the hospital mistook them for nuns." The meeting dispersed amidst cheers.

"My wife," the lieutenant commander said later to Snoddy, "is bringing that congressional party down to luncheon tomorrow to meet the inspecting general. She'll be rather tired, and of course she'll want some things that are not carried by a naval battalion as regular equipment." He gave a list to Snoddy. "Will you please get a motor bike and go to Chalons this afternoon and get these?"

Snoddy studied the list. "I never saw the pumps at Brest," said the ensign, with the innocence of one whose maternal lore was limited to contact with boatswains and masters at arms since early adolescence. "But there's an auxiliary pump on that condenser, sir. I'm afraid we can't detach it until after inspection."

"I'll have to go with you," his superior said. "Get the bike and you can drive me. While you are scouting around in Chalons, I'll drink to your health in that café near the library."

A few hours later Snoddy was discovering that his commander, despite his youthful distinction, was a human being, after all. "These hoggish legislators," Butt, Jr., was saying, "always like sweet red fizz water. I've bought 'em a case of sparkling Chambertin. My father-in-law put sugar in Beaune 1903 last week." The lieutenant commander shuddered "And my own father puts water in Napoleon brandy." He grimaced. "This is a young man's war, Snoddy."

Snoddy thrilled at such confidences.

"We'd better start back," he was told. "We'll take our time. I want you to teach me the new verses to "I Knew My Cousin Nellie from Childhood's Brightest Hour." I know only the first seventy-five."

It was a pleasure to serve under Lieutenant Commander Butt—a man who could win a D. S. C. from the Army and still keep his interest in the old Annapolis songs.

"Are you going to send your boy to Crabtown when he grows up, Commander?" said Snoddy.

"Mrs. Butt," said her husband with feeling, "has already entered him on the junior admiral's list for the Naval Staff College at Newport."

IV

The overt incident that actually precipitated the Great War came in Galley Number Four, which was attached to the château itself. The ice that laved the Chambertin was melting rapidly in the heat of September. Heat was particularly oppressive for a congressional party. The American style of tin hat which they proudly wore as denizens of the zone of advance had been soundly made by British steelmasters in 1915 and was irksome to the bald dome of Congressman Porcinus.

Wanda sensed the gathering war cloud and offered to change with him, tendering her French *poilu* model copied in papier-mâché by Reboux from regulation steel. It would not go on his head. He and his four colleagues of the House had followed the inspecting general the first four hours. But frock coats and tin hats were too much for September weather in the Côte d'Or and consequently the congressional party was a little dampened by two o'clock in the afternoon. Major General Butt had found immense fault with both equipment and personnel. Lieutenant Commander Butt had followed, tight-lipped but broiling.

Major General Butt strode into Galley Number Four, where luncheon itself was waiting. Running a glove around the lip of a copper kettle, the inspecting officer detected grease along the seam of the index finger and asked for some vinegar and soda to show the naval personnel how corrosion comes off metal. In a place redolent of food and wine, the situation acquired the tension of a piano wire.

"You fellows never clean anything in the Navy," he told the cook, third class, who presided over the tureens and buzzicots of Galley Number Four. The cook, who could remember ten days' bread and water because an admiral once tasted kerosene in a chicken he had ordered broiled on an oil stove, answered with an "Aye, aye, sir," in an infuriating manner. As he did so, the major general detected the odor of lemon extract on the cook's breath. This led to a further thirty-minute delay, the cook being carried away to await specifications.

Wanda broke the tension. "Father," she said, to Major General Butt, as two services shuddered, "you've been pottering around, sticking your nose into everything. Luncheon is spoiling. So put down that rag and get out of this kitchen and let Stony Wally serve his luncheon. You can stick your head in those silly guns afterward."

Major General Butt straightened up without regard for his daughter-in-law and turned to his aide-de-camp, Colonel Hoskins.

"Have them stand by the howitzers," he said. He whirled to Major Cordovan, his assistant aide-de-camp. "We will first inspect the ammunition stores," he said. The general thrust the Savior of the American Navy from his path and walked past him. A score of hirelings outside in olive drab followed him down the village street. They seemed to bear the pall of Wanda's pride as they passed out of sight.

The Savior of the American Navy became choleric. "I'll stand no more falderal from the military," he said, seizing a bottle of Chambertin and drawing from his pants pocket a large buckhorn-handled corkscrew. "I'll lunch now." He caught the arm of Lieutenant Commander Butt, who was turning with Snoddy to follow dutifully after his father. "Order lunch now," he said.

"I can't," said Butt, Jr., stonily.

Wanda had not chosen her husband for an ambitious career for nothing. "He really can't, daddy," she said.

Porcinus thrust his daughter aside. "Why can't you?"

The naval officer swelled. Saint John turned into Saint Michael. "You, here," he said, "behave yourself!"

The congressman seemed bitten by something sharper than a serpent's tooth. His colleagues, despite the chin straps of their helmets and the warmth of the kitchen, contrived to blanch.

"I'll stand no nonsense from the Navy, either," said Porcinus, taking a half *poulet meunière* smoking from a warmer over the stove.

The naval officer struck it from his hand. "Look here, you civvy," he said, "there's a war on! Damn your manners! You'll stick to routine in this outfit or I'll have you thrown out of the area!"

"Stony," cried Wanda proudly, "aren't you ashamed?"

"I am tired," continued Lieutenant Commander Butt warmly, "of having my relatives fight this way for me! It's my own father sticking his nose in my soup kettles one minute and my father-in-law telling me when to eat the next. Take those silly scuttles off your head and stand by until you are called!"

"I'll have you recalled from France!" the congressman cried angrily. "I'll order an investigation of your career by a special committee of the House!"

"Investigate and be damned!" said Butt, Jr. He strode from the kitchen, Snoddy following him as Greek lads once followed Prince Achilles. They reached the street, to observe the inspecting party returning. The naval officer's tired face relaxed.

"Maybe they're coming to luncheon, after all," he said to Snoddy. "Get ahead and see. Run back."

Snoddy had no chance to report back, for the general came on apace. As Lieutenant Commander Butt saluted and stood by to fall in line, the general shouted:

"Typical navy style, sir! That's right! Ball up your inspection like a bunch of tramps!" He strode to his son. "Where are the keys to the ammunition stocks, sir?"

The naval officer's face was a mask. "With me, sir, where they belong, sir."

"I give you to understand," the general said, "that this is my inspection, sir."

"I give you to understand," cried Lieutenant Commander Butt in fury, "that it is my ammunition, sir."

Major General Butt turned his doggy side to the naval personnel. He seemed gentle. "I want a telegraph," he said. "Where is Communications, sir?"

Butt, Jr., knew the game was lost. His influence lay with the *poulet* on the kitchen floor, struck by himself from the hand of Porcinus. Communications meant nothing but a last-hour relief from his command. He took his medicine.

"Around the corner, sir," he said. "By the guardroom, sir."

Major General Butt relentlessly marched around the corner toward the telegraph office. As he did so, a marine sergeant who had been watching for his passage since sunrise bawled, "Turn out the guard!"

And a section of marines, rehearsed to the last notch of impromptu simulation, came tumbling from the guardroom and fell into a faultless line. "Present—arms!" cried the sergeant.

"Will the general inspect the guard, sir?" Lieutenant Commander Butt said to Colonel Buskins with automatic deference. The general stopped at the guard.

"Inspection," cried the sergeant, "arms!"

The general snatched the rifle of the right guide as if he meant to defend himself from attack.

"Rust on the floor plate," he began, before he had looked at the floor plate. "Dust around the upper band. Bayonet swivel and studs filled with petrolatum. Grit in the cartridge guide. Firing pin's corroded." He held the rifle gingerly, as if it were contaminating and he feared to look at any part he had so clairvoyantly pronounced in bad condition. "Do you men never clean the bore of the piece?" he said to the sergeant of marines.

The sergeant was mum. He knew these raty old army bloaters from way back in China. "He'd better pray," he said—some hours later, of course—"that the underside av his undershirt was as clean as the bit av their pieces this marnin'."

"A rifle," said the general, "is a soldier's best friend." He thrust the rifle back scornfully, with a straight right jab to the face that the guide parried with practiced apathy.

Lieutenant Commander Butt had hopes that Communications had been forgotten in the new duties of inspecting rifles. At that moment, however, the general perceived that a button was missing from the breast of the sergeant. There was no mistaking it. The tunic gaped, exposing the top of a white singlet and a half moon of furry tattooing.

"My God!" cried the general in awe, extending the gap in the tunic until the head of Buffalo Bill shone clear on the sergeant's breast.

"This man," began Lieutenant Commander Butt smoothly, "reported the loss of a button this morning. The only alternative he had was to use an army button, for there are no stocks of marine buttons in this area. He had lost the button in line of duty, while forcing some

German prisoners to uncover to the colors of an infantry regiment passing through town yesterday."

The naval officer was weightily reporting a serious thing. "He quite rightly reported to me that he had no authority to replace the marine button with an army button. For though he is at present acting under orders of the Secretary of War, he is actually an enlisted member of naval forces under the direct authority of the Secretary of the Navy." It was a nice point he made. "And I recognized the Army's right to restrict jealously its own insignia to members of its own service. We of the Navy agreed that it was better to risk reprimand at an inspection by a ranking general of the Army, sir, than to violate an army regulation."

"Take his name," said Major General Butt to his aide, "and send this man to the noncommissioned officers' school at Gondrecourt as first choice from this area for a commission." The general turned to the sergeant. "I congratulate you, sergeant," he said. "Dismiss your guard."

The heat was oppressive and the general felt the need of brandy and water. "I think we might lunch, sir," he said. "It's been a perfect inspection."

Wanda had the list made out perfectly. Major General Butt was seated at the head, between a bottle of Evian and a bottle of Corvoissier. She sat on his left and her father on his right. Lieutenant Commander Butt sat at the far end, between Snoddy and a forlorn second lieutenant who spoke French. Outside, the regimental band broke into "Army and Navy Forever," as Major General Butt rose and proposed a toast that Wanda had whispered to him.

"To the Democratic Party," the general said, raising his glass, "that is making the world safe for democracy."

Lieutenant Commander Butt winked at Snoddy as Snoddy drank the Medoc 1917. Of course he'd have to make it up with Wanda and the baby. He was beginning to love Wanda, just as Wanda was probably preparing to send him to sea. Easiest way to make it up would be to get a wound. Wounds, though, were as scarce as hen teeth in howitzers. He knew Wanda, though. She'd never rest until she had christened her own battleship. His father and Porcinus seemed to be hitting it off. Of course Porcinus would be difficult to handle in the future. The future?

Well, the Germans were cracking and the war wouldn't last forever. Probably the Democratic Administration wouldn't either.

Wanda was winking solemnly at Snoddy as Porcinus was explaining to an eager major general the exact position of General Pershing in the Argonne Forest.

(1928)

Dorothy Parker

Women: A Hate Song

I hate women.
They get on my nerves.

There are the Domestic ones.
They are the worst.
Every moment is packed with Happiness.
They breathe deeply
And walk with long strides, eternally hurrying home
To see about dinner.
They are the kind
Who say, with a tender smile, "Money's not everything."
They are always confronting me with dresses,
Saying, "I made this myself."
They read Woman's pages and try out the recipes.
Oh, how I hate that kind of woman.

Then there are the human Sensitive Plants;
The Bundles of Nerves.
They are different from everybody else; they even tell you so.
Someone is always stepping on their feelings.
Everything hurts them—deeply.
Their eyes are forever filling with tears.
They always want to talk to me about the Real Things,
The things that Matter.
Yes, they know they could write.
Conventions stifle them.

They are always longing to get away—Away from it all!
—I wish to heaven they would.

And then there are those who are always in Trouble.
Always.
Usually they have Husband-trouble.
They are Wronged.
They are the women whom nobody—understands.
They wear faint, wistful smiles.
And, when spoken to, they start.
They begin by saying they must suffer in silence.
No one will ever know—
And then they go into details.

Then there are the Well-Informed ones.
They are pests.
They know everything on earth.
And will tell you about it gladly.
They feel it is their mission to correct wrong impressions
They know Dates and Middle names.
They absolutely ooze Current Events.
Oh, how they bore me.

There are the ones who simply cannot Fathom
Why all the men are mad about them.
They say they've tried and tried.
They tell you about someone's husband;
What he said
And how he looked when he said it.
And then they sigh and ask,
"My dear, what is there about me?"
—Don't you hate them?

There are the unfailingly Cheerful ones.
They are usually unmarried.
They are always busy making little Gifts
And planning little surprises.
They tell me to be, like them, always looking on the Bright Side.

They ask me what they would do without their sense of humor?
I sometimes yearn to kill them.
Any jury would acquit me.

I hate women.
They get on my nerves.

(1916)

Dorothy Parker

The Gunman and the Debutante

A wild and wicked gunman—one who had a gang in thrall—
A menace to the lives of me and you,
Was counting up, exultingly, the day's successful haul—
As gunmen are extremely apt to do.
A string of pearls, a watch or two, a roll of bills, a ring,
Some pocketbooks—about a dozen, say—
An emerald tiara—oh, a very pretty thing!
Yes, really, quite a gratifying day.

A dainty little debutante came tripping along,
With wistful, trusting eyes of baby blue;
She softly hummed a fragment of a most Parisian song—
As debutantes are very apt to do.
That wild and wicked gunman felt he couldn't miss the chance
To end his busy day triumphantly:
"Though scarcely in the habit of attacking debutantes,
Your money or your life, my dear," said he.

The dainty little debutante was trembling with alarm,
Appealingly she looked him through and through,
And laid her helpless little hand upon his brawny arm—
As debutantes are very apt to do.
Then earnestly she prayed the wicked gunman to be good,
She begged that he'd reform that very day,

Until he dropped his wicked gun, and promised that he would,
And bade her go her sweet and harmless way.

The wild and wicked gunman sat considering it all,
"At last," he cried, "I've met my Waterloo."
He vowed he'd give to charity the day's successful haul—
As gunmen are extremely apt to do.
But when he tried to find his gains and give to those in want—
The pocketbooks, the watches, bills and ring—
He found, to his amazement, that the little debutante
Had taken every solitary thing!

(1916)

Dorothy Parker

Song of the Open Country

When lights are low, and the day has died,
I sit and dream of the countryside.

Where sky meets earth at the meadow's end,
I dream of a clean and wind-swept space
Where each tall tree is stanch old friend,
And each frail bud turns a trusting face.

A purling brook, with each purl a pray'r,
To the bending grass its secret tells;
While, softly born on the scented air,
Comes the far-off chimes of chapel bells.

A tiny cottage I seem to see,
In its quaint old garden set apart;
And a Sabbath calm steals over me,
While peace dwells deep in my brooding heart.

And I thank whatever gods look down

That I am living right here in town.

(1921)

Dorothy Parker

Love Song

Suppose we two were cast away
On some deserted strand.
Where in the breeze the palm trees sway—
A sunlit wonderland:
Where never human footstep fell,
Where tropic love-birds woo.
Like Eve and Adam we could dwell,
In paradise, for two.
Would you, I wonder, tire of me
As sunny days went by,
And would you welcome joyously
A steamer? ... So would I.

Suppose we sought bucolic ways
And led the simple life,
Away—as runs the happy phrase—
From cities' toil and strife.
There you and I could live alone,
And share our hopes and fears,
A small-town Darby and his Joan,
We'd face the quiet years.
I wonder, would you ever learn
My charms could pall on you,
And would you let your fancy turn
To others? ... I would, too.

Between us two (suppose once more)
Had rolled the boundary deep;
You journeyed to a foreign shore,

And left me here to weep.
I wonder if you'd be the same,
Though we were far apart,
And if you'd always bear my name
Engraved upon your heart.
Or would you bask in other smiles,
And, charmed by novelty,
Forget the one so many miles
Away? … That goes for me.

(1921)

Dorothy Parker

The Flapper

The playful flapper here we see,
The fairest of the fair.
She's not what Grandma used to be,—
You might say, *au contraire.*
Her girlish ways may make a stir,
Her manners cause a scene,
But there is no more harm in her
Than in a submarine.

She nightly knocks for many a goal
The usual dancing men.
Her speed is great, but her control
Is something else again.
All spotlights focus on her pranks,
All tongues her prowess herald,
For which she well may render thanks
To God and Scott Fitzgerald.

Her rule is plain enough—
Just get them young and treat them rough.

(1922)

John V. A. Weaver

Élégie Américaine

In 1921 H. L. Mencken wrote of John V. A. Weaver's talents, "His realism is very careful ... Its language is naïve, clumsy, grammarless—the vulgate of poor and hopeless folk, and yet folk who can feel ... He opens the way for a ballad literature in America, representative of true Americans and in the American language ..."

I wished I'd took the ring, not the Victrola.
You get so tired of records, hearin' an' hearin' 'em,
And when a person don't have much to spend
They feel they shouldn't ought to be so wasteful.
And then these warm nights makes it slow inside,
And sittin's lovely down there by the lake
Where him and me would always use ta go.

He thought the Vic'd make it easier
Without him; and it did at first. I'd play
Some jazz-band music and I'd almost feel
His arms around me, dancin'; after that
I'd turn out all the lights, and set there quiet
Whiles Alma Gluck was singin' "Home, Sweet Home,"
And almost know his hand was strokin' my hand.

"If I was you, I'd take the Vic," he says,
"It's somethin' you can use; you can't a ring.
Wisht I had ways ta make a record for you,
So's I could be right with you, even though
Uncle Sam had me." ... Now I'm glad he didn't;
It would be lots too much like seein' ghosts
Now that I'm sure he never won't come back ...

Oh, God! I don't see how I ever stand it!

He was so big and strong! He was a darb!
The swellest dresser, with them nifty shirts
That fold down, and them lovely nobby shoes,
And always all his clothes would be one color,
Like green socks with green ties, and a green hat,
And everything ... We never had no words
Or hardly none ...

                    And now to think that mouth
I useta kiss is bitin' into dirt,
And through them curls I useta smooth a bullet
Has went ...

                    I wisht it would of killed me, too ...

Oh, well ... about the Vic ... I guess I'll sell it
And get a small ring anyways. (I won't
Get but half as good a one as if
He spent it all on that when he first ast me.)
It don't seem right to play jazz tunes no more
With him gone. And it ain't a likely chanst
I'd find nobody ever else again
Would suit me, or I'd suit. And so a little
Quarter of a carat, maybe, but a real one
That could sparkle, sometimes, and remember
The home I should have had ...

                    And still, you know,
The Vic was his idea, and so ...

                    I wonder ...

                                        (1919)

John V. A. Weaver

Carpe Diem

Why're you always pullin' sob-stuff?
Honey, what's the big idear?
"Will I never love no others?—
How many girls do I get a year?"
What's the good o' borryin' trouble?
Damn tomorrow! What's it worth?
Just this lovin' night can give us
Everythin' there is on earth.

Say, you know old Apple Annie,
Blurry-eyes, and nose all blue?
Oncet she was a knock-out looker,
Oncet she was as sweet as you.
While she's creepin' 'round the alleys
Why d'ye think she smiles all day?
'Cause her old bean's all chuck full with
Things no years can't take away.

Kiss me like you want to kiss me,
Lock your arms around me tight!
Don't be fightin' what you're feelin'—
Nothin' matters but tonight!
When you're dry, and white, and pinched-up
You'll remember times like this—
You'll be glad and glad, I tell you,
For the joys you didn't miss.

(1920)

John V. A. Weaver

When I'm All Through

When I'm all through, and you got to get rid of me,
Don't go shootin' the bunk, or makin' prayers,
And all that stuff. And don't go stickin' me
Into no stuffy cemetery lot.
I want some room … I got to have room … I got to!

So if you really want to take the trouble,
You take what's left, and put it in a fire,
The hottest you can find—and let 'er burn!
Till I ain't only a handful of grey somethin'.
"Ashes to ashes"—aint' that a whole lot cleaner
Than "dust to dust" ? You let old fire have me.

Then you just cut them ashes in four parts.
Take the first ashes to the side of a mountain,
Heave 'em up to the wind … I used to love
The way it's quiet and strong and big up there.

The second ashes, take 'em down to the ocean;
And when the waves come pilin' up the beach,
Scatter 'em where the green starts to get foamy.
They used to sing me songs about havin' nerve,
And never getting' tired, or givin' in—
Let 'em run, and take me with 'em.

And the third part, you go out to the country,
Into some wide, long field, and spread 'em round.
Maybe they'll help the grass to climb a little.
I can remember how I used to roll,
And dig my face down in, and sniff and bite it,
And lay back on it, just a crazy kid,

And watch the clouds go skippin' over the sky,
And the bees, and the crazy birds, and everything
Would get so perfect I would want to cry.

Then they'll be one part left. You take that down
Where's they's the thickest crowds, right in the city.
And when nobody's lookin', give it a sling
Onto the sidewalk, underneath their feet.
The pore things, always hoofin' it along,
Somewheres, they don't know where, and I don't either.
Always lookin' for somethin'—wonder what?
I never got very near 'em. A person can't,
Even when you want to. Everybody's scared,
So scared, you know … so scared! But a bunch of ashes
Maybe might get real close to somebody once.

Just once …

(1922)

Franklin P. Adams

A Tennis Player's Garden of Verses

How do you like to get out on a court,
Out in the August sun?
Oh, I think that is the pleasantest sport
Ever a boy has done.

Every night I say a prayer
That I shall be a better player;
And every day it's not too wet
I knock the balls across the net.

The child who has a little nerve
Will have a fairly decent serve;
He'll win a match, I'm pretty sure,

Unless his forehand drive is poor.

A birdie who observed me play
Stopped a minute just to say,
As I sent a service out,
"Ain't you 'shamed, you clumsy lout?"

The world is so full of a number of parks.
I'm sure we should all be as happy as larks.

The friendly court all green and white
I love with all my heart;
I hit the ball with all my might,
But precious little art.

Franklin P. Adams

Revised

Then here's to the City of Boston,
The town of the cries and the groans,
Where the Cabots can't speak to the Kabotschniks,
And the Cabots won't speak to the Cohns.

Franklin P. Adams

A Wish

I do not yearn for prairies wide;
I crave to tramp no tangled wood;
I hunger for no hills. I tried …
It did no good.

And yet I wish I wished to roam;

I wish I craved the open sea;
Or loved the meadow for my home,
The life that's free.

I wish I craved to see the corn,
Or ached to glimpse some native spot;
And yet to be where I was born
I hanker not.

I wished I yearned to see the hut
Of boyhood, if for but a minute.
Not that I like this wishing, but
There's money in it.

Franklin P. Adams

Mr. Irving Berlin Rewrites "Paradise Lost"

"With thee conversing I forget all time,
All seasons, and their change,—all please alike."
—Milton

Honey, when I talk to you, O gee whiz!
I don't ever know what time it is;
I don't know if it's night or day;
I don't know if it's March or May;
I can't remember
If it's December;
I don't know if it's twelve or nine;
I don't care if it's rain or shine.
But when you go away from me,
I'm just as low as I can be.
And I weep because my sweetie I did lose
'Cause I got those Paradise Blues.

CHORUS
The stars would glisten to me
When you would listen to me,
Dear.
The sky was bluer
The when you were
Here.
And every minute
That had you in it
Was gay.
Now I'm magenta
Because you went a-
Way.
(Sweet mamma!)
I never married;
Life is dry and arid.
For I got the Paradise Blues!

Franklin P. Adams

Journalism

From *The World*, Feb. 27, 1931. Its last issue.

Journalism's a shrew and a scold;
I like her.
She makes you sick, she makes you old;
I like her.
She's daily trouble, storm, and strife;
She's love and hate and death and life;
She ain't no lady—she's my wife;
I like her.

Franklin P. Adams

Palm Beach

Mr. and Mrs. Martin Foss,
Catherine Fox and Eleanor Goss,
Mr. and Mrs. James W. Cox,
Mr. and Mrs. Lyttleton Fox,
Mr. and Mrs. E.F. Hutton,
Mr. and Mrs. Arthur Cutten,
Mrs. Finley Peter Dunne,
Grover A. Whalen and Gurnee Munn,
Mr. and Mrs. Alfred Hearn,
Mr. and Mrs. Jerome D. Kern,
Gerald Brooks and Gerhard M. Dahl,
Mr. and Mrs. Lessing Rosenthal,
Leopold Stokowski and James T. Pope,
Mr. and Mrs. H.B. Swope,
Edward T. Stonesbury and Mrs. Frank Case,
Barclay Warburton, Eleanor Chase,
Mr. Dudley Field Malone,
Mr. Percy Mendelsohn,
Milton Florsheim and Percy Pyne,
Mr. and Mrs. Arthur Hammerstein,
Addison Mizner and Elsie Cripps,
Mr. and Mrs. Henry Phipps,
Mrs. Thomas Chadbourne and Frank X. Shields,
Robert Schaffner and the Rosenfields,
The Harvey Shaffers and the Westport Helds,
The Ziegfelds, the Felds, and the Rosenfelds,
Francis T. Hunter and Bruno Huhn,
Mrs. Vincent Astor and Heywood Broun,
Mr. and Mrs. McAneeny,
Mrs. Bruce Powell and Miss Marion Sweeney,
James P. Donahue and T.L. Jones,

The Pittsburgh Kaufmans and the Syracuse Kohns,
Mr. and Mrs. William Norris,
Mr. Ina Nelson Morris,
Mr. and Mrs. Edgerton Freeman,
R.L. Goldberg and William Seeman,
Mr. and Mrs. Harrison Stoach,
Mr. and Mrs. Arthur Somers Roche,
The Mitchells, the Hardings, the Snowdens, and the Peaveys,
The Baches, the Beaches, the Kahns, and the Levys,
Evangeline Johnson and Alice De Lamar,
Mr. Josef Urban and S.T. Carr,
The Riddle, the Biddles, and the Henry Reas,
The Parks, the Clarkes, and the Alfred Kays,
The Mayers, the Thayers, the Marstons, and the Dillmans,
The Seligmans, the Slaters, the Stehlis, and the Stillmans
Lie on the beach to get an umber tint
With nothing to do but get their names in print.

Franklin P. Adams

Precocity
A Collaboration by A. A. Milne, E. A. Poe, Dorothy Parker, and Ye Editor

James James
Morrison Morrison
Weatherby
George Dupree
Took
Great
Care of his mother,
Though he
Was only three.
James James
Morrison Morrison

Said to his mother,
"Mother," he said,
Said he:
"So all
The night tide
I lie down
By the side
Of my
Beautiful
Annabel Lee."

Franklin P. Adams

To Dorothy Parker Campbell, And Alan

Dottie, dear, when life was sour,
Sad, and aching all the time,
You would send The Conning Tower
Many a rhyme.

When beset with brier and bramble
Was the path, you wrote and how!
But, O Mrs. Alan Campbell,
Never now.

I'm no foe to nuptial beauty,
Yet I'm certain, Mr. C.,
That you owe a definite duty
Unto me.

Hit her, slap her, sock her, shake her,
Till she take the rusted pen;
Beat her, and her woe may make her
Write again.

Donald Ogden Stewart

The Courtship of Miles Standish
In the Manner of F. Scott Fitzgerald

This story occurs under the blue skies and bluer laws of Puritan
New England, in the days when religion was still taken seriously
by a great many people, and in the town of Plymouth where the
"Mayflower," having ploughed its platitudinous way from Holland, had
landed its precious cargo of pious Right Thinkers, moral Gentlemen of
God, and—Priscilla.

Priscilla was—well, Priscilla had yellow hair. In a later generation,
in a 1921 June, if she had toddled by at a country club dance you would
have noticed first of all that glorious mass of bobbed corn-colored locks.
You would, then, perhaps, have glanced idly at her face, and suddenly
said "Oh my gosh!" The next moment you would have clutched the
nearest stag and hissed, "Quick—yellow hair—silver dress—oh Judas!"
You would then have been introduced, and after dancing nine feet
you would have been cut in on by another panting stag. In those nine
delirious feet you would have become completely dazed by one of the
smoothest lines since the building of the Southern Pacific. You would
then have borrowed somebody's flask, gone into the locker room and
gotten an edge—not a bachelor-dinner edge but just enough to give
you the proper amount of confidence. You would have returned to the
ballroom, cut in on this twentieth century Priscilla, and taken her and
your edge out to a convenient limousine, or the first tee.

It was of some such yellow-haired Priscilla that Homer dreamed
when he smote his lyre and chanted, "I sing of arms and the man"; it

was at the sight of such as she that rare Ben Johnson's Dr. Faustus cried, "Was this the face that launched a thousand ships?" In all ages has such beauty enchanted the minds of men, calling forth in one century the Fiesolian terza rima of "Paradise Lost," in another the passionate arias of a dozen Beethoven symphonies. In 1620 the pagan daughter of Helen of Troy and Cleopatra of the Nile happened, by a characteristic jest of the great Ironist, to embark with her aunt on the "Mayflower."

Like all girls of eighteen Priscilla had learned to kiss and be kissed on every possible occasion; in the exotic and not at all uncommon pleasure of "petting" she had acquired infinite wisdom and complete disillusionment. But in all her "petting parties" on the "Mayflower" and in Plymouth she had found no Puritan who held her interest beyond the first kiss, and she had lately reverted in sheer boredom to her boarding school habit of drinking gin in large quantities—a habit which was not entirely approved of by her old-fashioned aunt. Although Mrs. Brewster was glad to have her niece stay at home in the evenings, "Instead," as she told Mrs. Bradford, "of running around with those boys, and really, my dear, Priscilla says some of the *funniest* things when she gets a little—er—'boiled,' as she calls it—you must come over some evening, and bring the governor."

Mrs. Brewster, Priscilla's aunt, is the ancestor of all New England aunts. She may be seen today walking down Tremont Street, Boston, in her Educator shoes on her way to S.S. Pierce's which she pronounces to rhyme with *hearse*. The twentieth century Mrs. Brewster wears a highnecked black silk waist with a chatelaine watch pinned over her left breast and a spot of Gordon's codfish (no bones) over her right. When a little girl she was taken to see Longfellow, Lowell, and Ralph Waldo Emerson; she speaks familiarly of the James boys, but this has no reference to the well-known Missouri outlaws. She was brought up on blueberry cake, Postum, and *The Atlantic Monthly*. She loves the Boston *Transcript*, God, and her relatives in Newton Centre. Her idea of a daring joke is the remark Susan Hale made to Edward Everett Hale about sending underwear to the heathen. She once asked Donald Ogden Stewart to dinner with her niece; she didn't think his story about the lady mind reader who reads the man's mind and then slapped his face, was very funny; she never asked him again.

The action of this story all takes place in MRS. BREWSTER'S *Plymouth home on two successive June evenings. As the figurative curtain rises* MRS. BREWSTER *is sitting at a desk reading the latest installment of Foxe's "Book of Martyrs."*

The sound of a clanking sword is heard outside. MRS. BREWSTER *looks up, smiles to herself, and goes on reading. A knock—a timid knock.*

MRS. BREWSTER: Come in.

(*Enter* CAPTAIN MILES STANDISH, *whiskered and forty. In a later generation, with that imposing mustache and his hatred of Indians, Miles would undoubtedly have been a bank president. At present he seems somewhat ill at ease, and obviously relieved to find only* PRISCILLA'S *aunt at home.*)

MRS. BREWSTER: Good evening, Captain Standish.

MILES: Good evening, Mrs. Brewster. It's—it's cool for June, isn't it?

MRS. BREWSTER: Yes. I suppose we'll pay for it with a hot July, though.

MILES (*nervously*): Yes, but it—it is cool for June, isn't it?

MRS. BREWSTER: So you said, Captain.

MILES: So I said, didn't I?

(*Silence.*)

MILES: Mistress Priscilla isn't home, then?

MRS. BREWSTER: Why, I don't think so, Captain. But I never can be sure where Priscilla is.

MILES (*eagerly*): She's a—a fine girl, isn't she? A fine girl.

MRS. BREWSTER: Why, yes. Of course, Priscilla has her faults—but she'd make some man a fine wife—some man who knew how to handle her—an older man, with experience.

MILES: Do you really think so, Mrs. Brewster? (*After a minute.*) Do you think Priscilla is thinking about marrying anybody in particular?

MRS. BREWSTER: Well, I can't say, Captain. You know—she's a little wild. Her mother was wild, too, you know—that is, before the Lord spoke to her. They say she used to be seen at the Mermaid Tavern in London with all those play-acting people. She always used to say Priscilla would marry a military man.

MILES: A military man? Well, now tell me Mrs. Brewster, do you think that a sweet delicate creature like Priscilla—

A VOICE (*in the next room*): Oh DAMN!

MRS. BREWSTER: That must be Priscilla now.

THE VOICE: Auntie!

MRS. BREWSTER: Yes, Priscilla dear.

THE VOICE: Where in hell did you put the vermouth?

MRS. BREWSTER: In the cupboard, dear. I do hope you aren't going to get—er— "boiled" again tonight, Priscilla.

(*Enter* PRISCILLA, *infinitely radiant, infinitely beautiful, with a bottle of vermouth in one hand and a jug of gin in the other.*)

PRISCILLA: Auntie, that was a dirty trick to hide the vermouth. Hello Miles—shoot many Indians today?

MILES: Why—er—er—no, Mistress Priscilla.

PRISCILLA: Wish you'd take me with you next time, Miles. I'd love to shoot an Indian, wouldn't you, auntie?

MRS. BREWSTER: Priscilla! What an idea! And please dear, give Auntie Brewster the gin. I—er—promised to take some to the church social tonight and it's almost all gone now.

MILES: I didn't see you at church last night, Mistress Priscilla.

PRISCILLA: Well I'll tell you, Miles. I started to go to church—really felt awfully religious. But just as I was leaving I thought, "Priscilla, how about a drink—just one little drink?" You know, Miles, church goes so much better when you're just a little boiled—the lights and everything just kind of—oh, its glorious. Well last night, after I'd had a little liquor, the funniest thing happened. I felt awfully good, not like church at all—so I just thought I'd take a walk in the woods. And I came to a pool—a wonderful honest-to-God pool—with the moon shining right into the middle of it. So I just undressed and dove in and it was the most marvelous thing in the world. And then I danced on the bank in the grass and the moonlight—oh, Lordy, Miles, you ought to have seen me.

MRS. BREWSTER: Priscilla!

PRISCILLA: 'Scuse me, Auntie Brewster. And then I just lay in the grass and sang and laughed.

MRS. BREWSTER: Dear, you'll catch your death of cold one of these nights. I hope you'll excuse me, Captain Standish; it's time I was going to our social. I'll leave Priscilla to entertain you. Now be a good girl, Priscilla, and please don't drink straight vermouth—remember what happened last time. Good night, Captain—good night, dear.

(*Exit* MRS. BREWSTER *with gin.*)

PRISCILLA: Oh damn! What'll we do, Miles—I'm getting awfully sleepy.

MILES: Why—we might—er—pet a bit.

PRISCILLA (*yawning*): No. I'm too tired—besides, I hate whiskers.

MILES: Yes, that's so, I remember.

(*Ten minutes' silence, with* MILES *looking sentimentally into the fireplace,* PRISCILLA *curled up in a chair on the other side.*)

MILES: I was—your aunt and I—we were talking about you before you came in. It was a talk that meant a lot to me.

PRISCILLA: Miles, you mind closing that window?

(MILES *closes the window and returns to his chair by the fireplace.*)

MILES: And your aunt told me that your mother said you would some day marry a military man.

PRISCILLA: Miles, would you mind passing me that pillow over there?

(MILES *gets up, takes the pillow to* PRISCILLA *and again sits down.*)

MILES: And I thought that if you wanted a military man why—well, I've always thought a great deal of you, Mistress Priscilla—and since my Rose died I've been pretty lonely, and while I'm nothing but a rough old soldier yet—well what I'm driving at is—you see, maybe you and I could sort of—well, I'm not much of a hand at fancy love speeches and all that—but—

(*He is interrupted by a snore. He glances up and sees that* PRISCILLA *has fallen fast asleep. He sits looking hopelessly into the fireplace for a long time, then gets up, puts on his hat and tiptoes out of the door.*)

THE NEXT EVENING

PRISCILLA *is sitting alone, lost in reverie, before the fireplace. It is almost as if she had not moved since the evening before.*

A knock, and the door opens to admit JOHN ALDEN, *nonchalant, disillusioned, and twenty-one.*

JOHN: Good evening. Hope I don't bother you.

PRISCILLA: The only people who bother me are women who tell me I'm beautiful and men who don't.

JOHN: Not a very brilliant epigram—but still—yes, you *are* beautiful.

PRISCILLA: Of course, if it's an effort for you to say—

JOHN: Nothing is worthwhile without effort.

PRISCILLA: Sounds like Miles Standish; many things I do without effort are worthwhile; I am beautiful without the slightest effort.

JOHN: Yes, you're right. I could kiss you without any effort—and that would be worthwhile—perhaps.

PRISCILLA: Kissing me would prove nothing. I kiss as casually as I breathe.

JOHN: And if you didn't breathe—or kiss—you would die.

PRISCILLA: Any woman would.

JOHN: Then you are like other women. How unfortunate.

PRISCILLA: I am like no woman you ever knew.

JOHN: You arouse my curiosity.

PRISCILLA: Curiosity killed a cat.

JOHN: A cat may look at a—Queen.

PRISCILLA: And a Queen keeps cats for her amusement. They purr so delightfully when she pets them.

JOHN: I never learned to purr; it must be amusing—for the Queen.

PRISCILLA: Let me teach you. I'm starting a new class tonight.

JOHN: I'm afraid I couldn't afford to pay the tuition.

PRISCILLA: For a few exceptionally meritorious pupils, various scholarships and fellowships have been provided.

JOHN: By whom? Old graduates?

PRISCILLA: No—the institution has been endowed by God—

JOHN: With exceptional beauty—I'm afraid I'm going to kiss you. Now.

(They kiss.)
(Ten minutes pass.)

PRISCILLA: Stop smiling in that inane way.

JOHN: I just happened to think of something awfully funny. You know the reason why I came over here tonight?

PRISCILLA: To see me. I wondered why you hadn't come months ago.

JOHN: No. It's really awfully funny—but I came over here tonight because Miles Standish made me promise this morning to ask you to marry him. Miles is an awfully good egg, really Priscilla.

PRISCILLA: Speak for yourself, John.

(They kiss.)

PRISCILLA: Again.

JOHN: Again—and again. Oh Lord, I'm gone.

(An hour later JOHN leaves. As the door closes behind him PRISCILLA sinks back into her chair before the fireplace; an hour passes, and she does not move; her aunt returns from the Bradfords' and after a few ineffectual attempts at conversation goes to bed alone; the candles gutter, flicker, and die out; the room is filled with moonlight, softly stealing through the silken skein of sacred silence. Once more the clock chimes forth the hour—the hour of fluted peace, of dead desire and epic love. Oh not for aye, Endymion, mayst thou unfold the purple panoply of priceless years. She sleeps—PRISCILLA sleeps—and

*down the palimpsest of age-old passion the lyres of night
breathe forth their poignant praise. She sleeps—eternal
Helen—in the moonlight of a thousand years; immortal
symbol of immortal aeons, flower of the gods transplanted
on a foreign shore, infinitely rare, infinitely erotic. *)*

*For the further adventures of Priscilla, see F. Scott Fitzgerald's stories in
the "Girl With the Yellow Hair" series, notably "This Side of Paradise,"
"The Offshore Pirate," "The Ice Palace," "Head and Shoulders," "Bernice
Bobs Her Hair," "Benediction" and "The Beautiful and Damned."

(1922)

Robert Benchley

The Rapeseed Oil Letters

*In the late Thirties, Robert Benchley was a well-known columnist. But
apparently not well-known enough that a pair of lobbyists wouldn't venture
naively into his web by asking for his support of some legislation. He just
couldn't help himself.*

Dear Mr. Benchley:

With full cognizance of your deep interest in the social and political
welfare of our great country, we know you will be delighted to learn of
the successful efforts to bring relief from the heavy tax burden to a large
cross-section of our citizenry. In the Revenue Bill of 1938 (HR 9682)
as reported by the Senate Committee on Taxation, April 5, 1938, it is
provided that:

"Effective July 1, 1938, rapeseed oil is exempted from the import
tax on oils where used in the making of rubber substitutes ... Sec.
702(a)."

Once again, an alert public stands as a bulwark to democracy and has brought about the repeal of this iniquitous tax.

With renewed assurances of our esteem, permit us, dear sir, to remain

Your obt. Servants,

Irving I. Schachtel, William G. Shoemaker, Jr.

Messieurs Schachtel and Shoemaker:

Either you were being very rude or ignorant of the fact that my father happens to make a product called "incest oil" and has spent a great deal of money to fight the repeal of the rapeseed oil import tax, which you seem to hail with so much glee. The so-called "making of rubber substitutes" is, as you must know, merely a sop to the Catholic Church. I feel that your taunting of me in this connection was either deliberate or just sheer bitchery.

Thank you for nothing,

Robert Benchley

Frank Sullivan

Style Hints for Meticulous Paupers

I have just completed a round of the rummage sales and ash cans in the fashionable New York faubourgs and I must admit that never in my experience as an advisor to the well-dressed man have I seen a greater variety or more tempting array of—shall we say—duds for the choice of man who wishes to dress well at a cost of nothing, or practically less.

Of course, if there ever was a time when it was important to dress well, that time is now. The man who is well dressed has a feeling of self-confidence, and that is what we cannot have too much of today—self-confidence, and a good five cents.

Because I have lost my shirt, is that any reason why I should immediately say to myself, "Oh, the Hades, or heck, with it! I won't wear a shirt"? Ah no. Because if I am craven enough to give up my shirt that easily, then the next step in my moral disintegration is obvious. What will I do when I lose my pants?

Look at Germany. Yes, look at Germany, and blush! No shirts over there, and no pants, either. A lot of people running around without a stitch of clothes on. Germany offers the well-dressed man an ominous example of the very point I am trying to make. Overwhelmed by disaster and having lost their shirts, our good German cousins also lost their morale. Discouraged, they let the shirt go without a struggle. So, when the German pant started to go, they were, Hamlet-like, unable to do anything about that. And today they are a nation of nudists!

Unless my information about Germany is far more inaccurate that usual, great crowds of Teutons now go about in what, when it was considered uptown, used to be called The Alltogether. The Germans today seem to be trying to make Mahatma Gandhi look as if he were bundled up to go out into a blizzard, and indeed sometimes I think that is just exactly what he does look like.

Yet Germany is the nation that gave us Goethe, Beethoven and Wagner, three of the greatest men who ever lived; geniuses who, however much they may have disregarded the conventions in other respects, yet never appeared in public without trousers except on rare occasions such as fires, raids, etc. As I said to my grandmother the other night, "Well, the mark may have practically disappeared in Germany, but the birthmark is certainly plain to be seen there." And as my grandmother said to me, on that very same night, as she reached at me with her cane, "If I could get at you with this, my buck, I'd give you a birthmark."

No. This is no time for men to grow careless in dress. This is the time when you, and you, and I should be devoting our every energy to getting a *new* shirt, on the principle that a man who is freezing to death in a snowdrift should at all costs pinch himself to keep awake; or, better, get up out of the snowdrift and hurry home to a warm bed.

Not only is it important to myself that I dress well at this time, but it is important to my friends who are in the same boat with me, because demoralization is contagious. If my friend, who may be of weaker calibre than I (which would be bogey for that course) should see me carelessly dressed, down at the heels, might he not with reason say to himself, "Well, Beau Sullivan, the best dressed man in Greenwich Village has given up. Why shouldn't I?"

That is why I have made a special point, ever since the depression started, of continuing to be the dandy. I have not allowed myself to relax one iota toward shabbiness. As religiously as ever, I apply bear grease to my hair every morning, despite the difficulty of getting good bears these days, or, after you've got them, of getting any grease from them. I trim my cuffs, rub yesterday's grime from my collar, and put shoeblack on my heels so the holes in my socks won't show—all just as painstakingly as in the good old days.

I referred to Mr. Gandhi. It reminded me that I once had a most interesting talk with him on the subject of clothes. I was staying in India at the time, with my cousin, "Mr. A." A slight figure of a man, Mr. Gandhi just came up to my shoulder, and you may well believe that I was flattered at that, for it is a rare occasion indeed when Mahatma Gandhi comes up to *anybody's* shoulder. Let alone a believer in Osmosis like myself. You either come up to *his* shoulder or you don't meet him, for he is not only an extremely busy man but a shy one, and he rarely goes out.

We talked of "cabbages and kings" for a while. I found him very broad-minded about both, because of course his religion forbids him to eat either. Were he to take even the tiniest bite of a king or a cabbage, Gandhi would lose caste. This may seem like a silly taboo to us king and cabbage eaters of the Occident, yet I daresay some of our western customs, such as dipping your sister in brandy on New Year's Eve, would seem to the Oriental to have slight basis in reason or logic. But I wander from my subject. I asked Mr. Gandhi what he thought of clothes, and I am glad to report that he declared himself for them.

"Without my loin cloth," he told me, "I should certainly feel lost."

And we American men might well learn from the famous Indian pundit and his learn cloth, the important reason of being well dressed.

Who was it said clothes make the man? Probably nobody. Probably at some time someone passed a remark in fun about clothes and some busybody overheard it, and repeated it. Then it got bandied about by gossips until it had no resemblance at all the original remark. That's the trouble with this country, today, too much gossip. And too many dancing grandmothers. And too much petting, and peanut politics. And lack of respect for our gangsters. The family is disintegrating. For ages the family has been the bulwark of civilization, and now it's disintegrating. A fine time to pick to disintegrate, too, with the buffalo only twenty years extinct. Scarcely cold in his grave. And a fine time for gossip, too, and for repeating things about clothes making the man. Oh, sometimes when I think about how the world is going to pot, I could burst into a flood of billingsgate.

(1932)

Robert Benchley

Ivy Oration

In Robert Benchley's day, the president of the Harvard Lampoon *was tasked with delivering the Ivy Oration at the Class Day ceremonies preceding Commencement. (In subsequent years, a safer system of tryouts became the norm.) In typical fashion, he spent many hours fretting over and drafting the speech, only to discard his prepared text and ad-lib most of it. The legend of the speech grew over the decades, with those who were present embellishing the tales of the reactions of the audience as they attempted to follow him. Eventually, most of them just surrendered themselves to his whimsy. Printed versions are rare. What follows is cobbled together from a few different sources.*

Surprise! . . . is not the name for the emotion with which I am overcome at being just now called upon to address you at this meeting. It is nothing short of confusion. Nothing could have been farther from my thoughts as I sat listening to the other speakers here this afternoon, than that my modest voice should be desired to lend a touch of dignity to this occasion. Why, a quarter of an hour ago I was sitting in my room, looking for a position for next year, when the Bursar, that Prince of Good fellows, that Shylock of Melancholy Dane, came bounding up the stairs, and, laying a sympathetic hand on my shoulder, said, "Bob, old man, aren't you coming down to say a few words to the Big Red team? The boys are all calling for you down there." Then it all came over me like a flash—this was Class Day! I did remember having seen a program of the week, in which somewhere between ball-games with Yale and Phi Beta Kappa Exhibits there was made casual mention of a Class Day Exercise, but I understood that it was to be held only in case the ball-game at New Haven was called off on account of rain. And besides, I really did not dare to leave the Yard, for fear lest I had not the right colored ticket and that, once out, I could never get back in again to get my clean clothes for the summer vacation. So here it was Class Day, and there I was in my room, hemming napkins. Quickly I drew on a pair of shoes and my cap and gown, and breaking into a run—and a perspiration—soon found myself, unless I am mistaken, here.

On this day, when all minds are turned to the National Prize Ring in Chicago, where Harvard and Yale are again demonstrating that the rules of the game need changing before next season, and at a time when the air is so charged with personal politics that it threatens to destroy the crops, what could be more out of place or thoroughly disagreeable, than for me to give my speech a political flavor? With true Harvard indifference then, I shall proceed to deliver a political speech which our paternal and conservative Administrative Board refused me permission to deliver in the Thayer Common-room, stigmatizing it as unnecessarily impolite and improper propaganda.

I shall divide my speech into three quarters, or halfs: first, the Peroration, containing what I consider to be one of the most virulent attacks against the Malefactors of Great Health yet voiced in the present campaign; second the Oration Proper, or Improper, dealing in the large with the great issues of the day, such as the Class Day Issue of the Lampoon and the Recall of Faculty Decisions. In this I shall embody a sweeping denunciation of the goodies. Thirdly, and inevitably, will come the Anti-Climax, or Oporation, in which, with a burst of mature rhetoric seldom found in one so young, I shall revile in bitterest terms the Social Usurpation of our Colleges, dealing with the underground method in which the Social Set at Harvard derives its stimulus from Boston, the annual, exclusive five-day cruise of the Yale crew along the Themes [*sic*], to be celebrated again Friday, and the recent election and inauguration of Sam White as President and Fellows of Princeton on the magnanimous endorsement of our intrepid cheer-leader, our heritage from the class of 1911. These are visual questions, Classmates, and must be met at Harvard Squarely.

You have my ultimatum. If you are resigned and ready, I shall proceed, without further parsley, to dissect my Peroration. If there are any timid or super-sensitively nervous ladies or members of the Harvard Equal Suffrage League present in the arena, they may retire now inconspicuously by the trap-door opposite, where the elephants enter. I will answer any questions that may be put to me after the lecture.

1ˢᵗ Peroration: Roman numeral I—small letter (a).

Voters and Votaries—and Conservative Republicans.

We are gathered here today in this June sunshine (if it had been raining I should have been quick-witted enough to substitute for that, "We are gathered here in this June rain." By a lucky coincidence the "June" part would be equally fitting in both cases, you see). We are gathered here in this June sunshine, under the leafy boughs of the grand old elms, to celebrate the fourth anniversary of the passing of our entrance English examinations. As our witty Latin orator so aptly puts it, "Non sequebantur, sed in felicitate demonstrandum nunc nobis ad libitandum esse." What more can be said? Father Garcelon, in his prime, from his taxi-chariot, could say no more. Were it not for the fact that all you nice people had melted all the way down here just to hear my words and to say that they weren't nearly so funny as you had expected them to be, I should let it go at that, and call the whole thing right off now. But I will not. Rather will I turn from this, our Peroration, to the second section of the speech—the Oration Proper.

If the Malefactors of Great Health do not like what I have just said about them, they may petition the Administrative Board at its next secret practice.

Oration Proper: Section A, under the general heading of Cotton Goods and Steel Rails. Roman numeral V. (Personally, I think the speech drags a little at this point.)

As I look into your bright young faces here in the shade of these grand old rock-maples, I am oppressed with the conviction that never before in her history has our country been face to face with such a grave financial crisis. It is with the customary Class Day mingled emotions of pleasure and regret that we bask here today, and with eyes dimmed by Boylston St. dust look back over the seventeen pre-digested courses that have constituted our educational banquet. Let us ponder ponderously on these things. What have we accomplished? What new visions have we seen? When and why does all this mean? O, Brothers, we are all unthinking in this extremity. We have waited and the innumerable caravan has gone without us. We have sung, and the echo has not come back. And now I ask you, what has the Republican party ever done for you, the working man? Temporary platforms, unfilled pledges and dinner-pails, and these mute, defenseless colonnades confront us, and with tier upon tier cry out "Give us the man."

You are brave men. You have given your lives without a murmur to the Class Album Committee, lives padded, it is true, by Vice-Presidencies of the Soap and Brush Club, but lives, nevertheless, young, virile lives. Even now, with that intrepid fearlessness born of youth you recline here in the new-mown grass before this altar raised to machine-made wit, defying at once hay-fever, and Owen Johnson's accusation that Harvard's social set is based on the dry grass of fields, which, like Memorial toast, is cast into the oven and withereth away.

You have heard with calmness the dictatorial warnings of the Class Day Committee that pajamas are not to be worn under the caps and gowns until the caps and gowns have been removed, and that anyone attempting to leave the Yard by more than one gate at a time without a yard mileage ticket properly endorsed by the Secretary of the Navy, will have to stay in the Yard all night and cry himself to sleep under the red-oak saplings, or else leave the Yard immediately. And yet we are

Romans, and this is Rome, that from her throne of beauty ruled the world! O, ingrates! Sluggards! Undesirable citizens!

And now I think that you will agree that I have come logically to the crux of my argument on which I base my claim for the nomination. You have gone through much, besides your June allowances. You have survived the embroidered salmon of last night's spread, where your classmates and their classmates tread on your light fantastic toe. You have gone through that most democratic of institutions, the Senior Picnic, where one sees more of the other men in one's class than at any other gathering. And right in connection with the Senior Picnic I wish to make the announcement that I have learned the name of the man who slapped me on my sun-burned back the morning after the picnic, and I give him warning that I shall hound him today, from spread to spread, forcing him to eat one dollar's worth of food at each place, till at last I see him sink bubbling beneath the banana-strewn Red Sea at Beck.

And now, as Tupper's lightning artist says, as the one-thirty bell rings on a lunchless noon, "Now for the last and best!" My speech so far has dealt mainly with the economic aspects of the matter at hand. I shall now close by a few concrete references to the proposed Freshmen Sanitarium, and the Conservation of our National Resources in general.

As a result of a clubbing offer with the Harvard Advocate I shall omit this section of my speech in delivering it here this afternoon, but a complete copy of it, with footnotes and errata, may be found in the current issue of the Advocate on page 409. It is for sale almost anywhere, and offers two prizes—a second and a third prize, the amounts to be announced at its awarding for the best essay on "How the Ivy Oration (printed in this number) might be improved."

I do not claim that the principles enunciated in this speech will take effect immediately. You are young men yet. But think them over, Brothers. Take them home and confront yourselves with them when you are alone tonight shaking the confetti from your clothes, standing on a packing box full of old neck-ties which Max won't buy and which you hate to throw away. Then, in the silence, ask yourself if your life has been such that you could face with calmness a disclosure to the world of all that Terry knows about you.

When the time comes to fee the goody with an I. O. U. and when, with someone else's diploma in one hand, and a Bursar's card, to show that you are a real Harvard man, in the other, you sit on the old college fence, and gaze over your Lyendecker Arrow collar across the old college campus to where the sun is setting in a crimson glow behind the old college pharmacy, then allow a tear to tickle unnoticed down your cheek, and thinking of what I have said today about the Ideal College man and the community, give a regular Harvard cheer for yourself, gird up your loins and be brave.

Go forth now, and, like the gypsy-moth, spread to your heart's content. The only distressing feature of Class Day is now over. Go and live today out to its fullest measure, rejoice and be glad, for you are exiting today in that Golden Age, to which, when again we assemble here as a class, we shall longingly refer as the good old Halcyon Days when we were in college.

Marc Connelly and George S. Kaufman

Life's Calendar For December 1921

1—Th.—Baltimore, Md., lighted by gas, 1816. Mayor Hylan tries the same thing in New York, 1921. Christopher Sholes invents typewriter, 1867.

2—Fri.—Battle of Austerlitz, 1805. Christopher Sholes gets his hands covered with ink changing typewriter ribbon, 1867. John Brown hanged; popular songwriters get busy, 1859. Monroe Doctrine born, 1823. First Pullman car bed patented, 1856. First Pullman car joke, 1856.

3—Sat.—Illinois admitted to Union. Chicago celebrates with 87 murders, 1818. First cases of ante-Christmas politeness among elevator men and apartment telephone operators noticed in New York, Utah, and parts of southern Connecticut, 1921.

4—Sun.—Washington bids farewell to his officers, 1783. Citizen of Duluth, Minn., loses mind trying to fish short spoon out of mustard bottle, 1919. Three hundred and fourteen British novelists, playwrights, war correspondents and poets arrive in America for lecture tours, 1920.

5—Mon.—Martin Van Buren, eighth president, born 1782. Female lawyer breaks into newspaper without being referred to as Portia, 1906. Christopher Sholes calls in man to change typewriter ribbon, 1867.

6—Tu.—Delaware, with consent of Du Ponts, ratifies Constitution, 1787. Chinese labor exclusion act passed; China takes it coolie, 1894. Three hundred and fourteen British novelists, playwrights, war correspondents and poets complete books on conditions in America, 1920.

7—Wed.—Congress declares war on Austria-Hungary, 1917. Austria-Hungary doesn't much care by this time, 1917. One-thousandth book on South Seas completed by Harold L. Pleevey, of South Bend, Ind., 1921. Ten-year-old boy reads entire inscription on streetcar transfer, New York, 1919. Christopher Sholes sells the typewriter, 1921.

8—Th.—President Jefferson sends first message to Congress, 1801. Green and red glass jars for drugstores invented, 1743. Six million, eight hundred and fifty thousand people still wonder what that stuff is that's in them, 1921.

9—Fri.—Three men light cigarette from same match and are immediately struck dead by lightning, 1889. Judge Gary predicts era of prosperity, 1908, '10, '11, '12, '13, '14, '15, '16, '17, '18, '19, '20, '21. New York telephone directory issued in four volumes, 1924.

10—Sat.—Mississippi admitted to Union, 1817. Frances White learns to spell, 1917. Spanish War ends, 1898.

11—Sun.—Plato begins lecture course, 399 B.C. Husbands bring home something new in explanations, 399 B.C. Indiana admitted to Union, 1816.

12—Mon.—First National Republican Convention. Elihu Root refuses to see reporters, 1831. Record for output of Christmas cigars smashed by Alex Portland Cement Co., 1920.

13—Tu.—Battle of Fredericksburg, 1862. Mean temperature grows meaner, 1921.

14—Wed.—First number of Boston, Mass., *Gazette* published, 1719. Constant Reader makes a complaint, 1719. George Washington dies, 1799. Alabama admitted to the Union, 1819. First banquet photograph taken, forty diners coming out on the dais, 1871. South Pole discovered, 1911.

15—Th.—Battle of Nashville, 1864. Hotels stop starching towels, 1956.

16—Fri.—Boston Tea Party; British guests arrive late, 1773. Managers pronounce it the worst theatrical season in years, 1912, '13, '14, '15, '16, '17, '18, '19, '20, '21. Great fire in New York, 1835. Janitors celebrate it by turning off heat, 1921.

17—Sat.—Eighteenth Amendment passed, 1917. Eighteenth Amendment passed up, 1918, '19, '20, '21. First successful flight of aeroplane, 1903. Six million, four hundred and thirteen thousand persons say it will never work, 1903.

18—Sun.—Thirteenth Amendment, abolishing slavery, passed, 1865. *Monah*, new Arrow collar, invented, 1922. Motion picture magnate sends representative to see D. Alighieri about film rights to "Inferno," 1919.

19—Mon.—Library at Alexandria opened to public; first sixteen patrons asking for Harold Bell Wright, 283 B.C. Elephant in circus winter quarters at Bridgeport, Conn., kills great-grandson of man who gave him bad peanut in Salt Lake City, Utah, 67 years before, 1899.

20—Tu.—South Carolina secedes from Union, 1860. Seventy-five extra beds put in New York hospitals to take care of Christmas card buyers, 1920, '21.

21—Wed.—Cambridge, Mass., founded, 1630. Yale men take steps, 1630. Man checks hat and coat with management of Child's restaurant, 1916. First optimist-pessimist joke, 1453.

22—Th.—Pilgrims land at Plymouth Rock, 1620. Shuberts build Plymouth Theatre, 1917.

23—Fri.—Dials for telephones invented, 1916. Shopping rush breaks all records; manufacturers hurriedly make 100,000 more art calendars, 1921.

24—Sat.—Treaty of Ghent ends war with England, 1812. Hearst resumes same, 1912. Seventeen thousand parodies on " 'Twas the night before Christmas and all through the house, etc.," appear in newspapers, 1890-1921, incl.

25—Sun.—CHRISTMAS DAY; extra matinees.

26—Mon.—George Dewey born, 1837. Ground broken for first transcontinental railway; Pathé news scooped, 1863. Apartment house attendants resume normal manners, 1921.

27—Tu.—John C. Calhoun, vice-president of U.S., resigns, probably to seek fame and fortune, 1832. Six hundred thousand Christmas neckties worn for last time, 1921.

28—Wed.—Iowa admitted to Union, 1846. Woodrow Wilson born, 1856. Government takes control of railroads, 1917. Complaints of food begin, 1917. Thousands of homes gladdened by return of relatives to their own homes, 1921.

29—Th.—Texas admitted to Union, 1845. East Liverpool, Ohio, woman claims to have seen entire 22 installments of 22-installment movie serial, 1918.

30—Fri.—King George III succeeds to English throne; Brisbane editorial demands recount, 1760. Gadsden Purchase, 1853. Twenty-two million-dollar movie theaters erected on same day, 1920.

31—Sat.—Assault on Quebec, 1775. Thirsty Americans resume attack, 1919. Ring out, Wild Bells! In one Year and out the other!

Robert Benchley

The Iron Pipe Ad

Robert Benchley's parody of an advertisement in The Saturday Evening Post.

I Am the Strength of the Ages

I have sprung from the depth of the hills.

Before the rivers were brought forth, or even before the green leaves in their softness made the landscape, I was your servant.

From the bowels of the earth, where men toil in darkness, I come, bringing a message of insuperable strength.

From sun to sun I meet and overcome the forces of nature, brothers of mine, yet opponents; kindred, yet foes.

I am silent, but my voice re-echoes beyond the ends of the earth.

I am master, yet I am slave.

I am Woonsocket Wrought Iron Pipe,
"the Strongest in the Long Run"
(trademark).

Send for illustrated booklet entitled "The Romance of Iron Pipe"

Robert Benchley

Have You Tried These New Memory Courses?
Here Is the Story of How I Doubled My Salary in One Evening

Five weeks ago I had such a bad memory that my friends all called me "Bad Memory Joe." There was practically nothing too important for me to forget. I would even forget how forgetful I was, and make dates which I should have remembered that I could never remember to keep. It was terrible.

I began to go downhill. Black spots would appear before my eyes, and then they would disappear and other black spots would take their place. My friends shunned me. Time and again I was on the point of calling up the doctor, but I could never remember his telephone number.

Then, one night, as I lay in bed trying to remember something (it didn't matter what, so long as I could remember it), I saw a great light. It flashed upon me like a dream. I leaped out of bed with a bound, and, landing on the toy train which my baby boy had left there the night before, I leaped back into bed again. But in that short fraction of a second, I had decided to take the step which was to mean so much in my life. I had decided to send for Prof. Womble's Memory Course (ten lessons in the privacy of your own room).

Well, I sent for the course—and studied it.

The effect was electrifying. Before I had read the first four paragraphs of the first lesson I was summoned to the telephone to answer a call from my office. At the conclusion of the conversation, I called my wife to me.

"Olga," I said, my voice quavering with emotion, "Olga, here is an extra fifty cents on this week's allowance. Mr. Golightly, my employer (as you know), has just called me up and told me that my salary has been raised fifty per cent. We can now afford that extra tire on our runabout."

And, at the moment when I closed the book containing the third lesson, I received a telegram saying that I been elected Vice-President and General Manager of the company. This was too much. I kissed my wife and gave her another fifty cents.

To-day I am getting a salary of $150,000 a year—and extras. Five weeks ago I was getting $14 a week. And yet I do not consider myself any brighter than any other man. What I have done, you can do. Perhaps you would like to hear just how Professor Womble's Memory Course gave me the self-confidence that I now have. Whether you would like to hear it or not, you are going to.

The Secret for Remembering Names

Let us take, for instance, the matter of remembering names. Before taking this course I was utterly unable to connect names with faces, or vice versa. And, as the two almost always go together, it will be seen that I was not very well equipped for social congress. I have been known, while acting as an usher at a reception of honor, to be obliged to ask both the guest and the hostess what their names were, before I could perform the ceremony of introducing them to each other. This, of course, was *gauche* of me, and I felt it keenly.

But now, after studying the lesson on How to Remember Names and Faces, I am practically a new man. All I have to do is this:

Every day, before I leave my house, I memorize the names of sixty familiar household or barn-yard objects, making a mental picture of each one as I impress its name on the delicate surface of my brain. You have no idea how delicate and impressionable the surface of your brain is until you have taken the course. It makes one go hot and cold all over to think of the collection of scandalous impressions that must have accumulated there after thirty years of knocking about New York,—or Bangor, for that matter.

Thus, as I leave my front-door, I am muttering to myself: "Hen, bran-mash, sofa, silo, what-not, doggie, gas-stove-lighter, antimacassar, souvenir-ash-tray, camel, cat, percolator, egg-shell, etc., etc." And, as I say each name, I shut my eyes and picture it in my mind's eye. I sometimes fall down the front steps while walking thus with my eyes shut, but I certainly do visualize those hens and souvenir-ash-trays.

The Way the System Works

By the time I reach my office, I have the sixty names of household and barn-yard objects pretty fairly well visualized. Then I tuck them away in a corner of my brain that has nothing in particular to do just at that moment, and wait for something to turn up.

Soon a customer of the firm comes in, bringing with him a friend from Tacoma who is interested in our little proposition with the North Star Smelting & Smelting Company. The friend is introduced as Mr. Conchman. He has a blonde, disorganized beard, of which I make immediate mental note. Then, just to make sure of myself and ostensibly to start the conversation pleasantly, I say:

"What was the name again, please? I didn't quite get it."

The repetition of the name gives me time to go through the following mental process, establishing a train of associations between this man and my list of barn-yard objects:

The man's beard is blonde and sparse. It might be said (if one were anxious to say it) that it resembles ensilage. Ensilage is found in a *silo*, and *silo*, you will remember, is one of the list of sixty mystic words I memorized this morning. It was, in fact, fourth in the list. Next to it came *what-not*. Now, let us review the objects that are usually found on a what-not. There may be a hand-painted china shepardess, a mother-of-pearl paper-cutter bearing a picture of a ferris-wheel and the legend "Greetings from the Centenary," a sweet-grass miniature demijohn, a conch-shell,—that's it,—a *conch-shell*, and the man's name is Conchman!

While you are evolving this train of associations, you can be shaking his hand up and down, unless the mental process should be too complicated, in which case you could motion him to be seated and give him a post-card album to look at until you got his name indelibly fixed on the delicate surface of your brain.

Then, when Mr. Conchman's business is transacted, he goes out and I go on with my work.

Let us say that it is seven years later, and that I meet him in a hotel in Mobile, Ala. Approaching me with a smile, he says:

"I don't suppose you remember me, do you?"

Quick as a wink I am on my feet.

"Why, of course, I remember you!" I say, delightedly, holding him off at arm's length in order to get a better perspective of all his characteristics. "Your beard reminds me of ensilage. Ensilage, ensilage, *silo, silo,* the fourth word in my list, the fifth of which is *what-not!* You're something that goes on a what-not. Yes, you are, you old rascal, don't deny it. *What-not.* Hand-painted china shepardess? No ... mother-of-pearl paper-cutter? No ... sweet-grass demijohn? It isn't Mr. Demi-john, is it? No, no, of course not. ... Wait, I've got it! It's Mr. Conch-shell! That's it, Conch-shell, or rather Conchman. How are you, Mr. Conchman? I remember you perfectly."

Sometimes, the man has gone before I can complete my train of associations, but usually I can hold his interest until I reach the end. And then I disclose to him that the secret of my remarkable memory is nothing more or less than Dr. Womble's Memory Course (ten lessons in the privacy of your own room).

This, of course, is just one branch of the course. Before I had finished reading lesson number eight I could remember numbers and dates with the same facility. This is done by somewhat the same method, only the numbers are personified and made to talk and act like human beings. There being only one hundred numbers that are used in ordinary combinations, one has to visualize only one hundred little men and women, doing one hundred different things. If, for instance, I want to remember that my watch number is 18,648,590 (just why anyone should ever want to remember his watch number is not clear, but it seems to be the thing to do, according to all diaries) I make the following little picture in my mind:

A fat little man wearing a suit of armor, piling three little Czecho-Slovaks into a basket of laundry which is being carried by a member of the Senate Foreign Relations Committee and one of the Isadora Duncan dancers. You see the principle of the thing? It is so simple as to be almost ludicrous, or perhaps, so ludicrous as to be almost simple.

Inspiration for Table Talk

Thus, in an ordinary conversation, I am able to supply interesting side-lights on the topics under discussion, which completely baffle the other parties to the affair. Let us say that I am attending a dinner-party. Turning to the lady on my right I say:

"Would you mind passing the salt, please? Salt is perhaps the chief product of Salzburg, Austria (latitude 45° 30"—longitude 10° 45") the mines in that district having produced, in the month of August, 1915, 12,000 tons of this precious saline formation. It has been estimated that no less than 120,000 people are given employment by this industry, and one pound of salt, in the bean, contains 4,500,000,000 grains, or as many grains as there were dollars in the Victory Loan."

I have acquired quite a reputation as a dinner-guest in this manner, and I can truthfully say that whatever I am, in a business or social way, I owe to Dr. Womble's Memory Course. What I have done, others can do.

(1919)

Franklin P. Adams

My Invisible Cloak

I used to think that the airplane was the closest I'd ever come to a fairy tale come true. It was like the Wishing Ring: Whir-r-r-r! and there I was. In less time than it took to write "Dixie" the author of that song would have jumped into his plane and gone to the yearned-for Land of Cotton, Cinnamon Seed, etc. There would never have been that frequently expressed wish—what we who shout the Battle Cry of Freuddom call the Southland Libido.

But now, for a long time, I have been wearing the Invisible Cloak. But, unlike the lads in the fairy tales, I don't wear it when I want to. I'd like to don it, for example, when I am a linesman in an important lawn tennis match and I call one of Bill Tilden's drives "out" that everybody in the stands thinks was good, or when I fail to fill a four-flush and one of the contestants calls me; or when a barber, looking at my face with bored and contemptuous pity, says, "Shave yourself, I see."

No, I wear the Invisible Cloak when I don't want to. I am invested with it the instant I try to catch the waiter's eye to ask him why that party at the next table, who came in after I came and who gave their order twenty minutes after I gave mine, should get their Broiled Whitefish, To Order (15 min.), before I get my Lamb Hash au Gratin, which, as everybody knows, is one of the Dishes Marked with a Star Are Ready. I wear it when I go to one of those places with a Free Air sign to ask the man whether he'd mind inflating the left front to 45 pounds. I wear it when I walk up to a soda water fountain at which one clerk is washing glasses and the other two clerks are standing, with their backs to me, discussing whether Dempsey will kill the Smoke. I wear it—everybody, though, wears it here—whenever I go into a hardware store for anything whatsoever.

And sometimes my manuscripts—yes, even mine—walking into an editorial office seem to be invested with it.

(1922)

Robert Benchley

The Woolen Mitten Situation
A Confidential Report
Of An Investigation Conducted, Strictly
According To The Best Established
Traditions

Asking me here to speak tonight was nothing short of inspiration on your part, for I have some very important data for all advertising men. I might as well admit right at the start that my first job on leaving college was with the advertising department of the Curtis Publishing Co. I am probably the only ex-Curtis advertising man who has not gone into the agency business for himself. As a matter of fact, when I left Curtis (I was given plenty of time to get my hat and coat) I was advised not to stick to advertising. They said I was too tall, or something. I forget just what the reason was they gave.

But one of my last jobs before leaving Curtis was to go out on a commercial research trip for Mr. Charles Coolidge Parlin, the well-known Curtis commercial research sharp. Most of you have been shown some of Mr. Parlin's reports—in strict confidence—giving you the inside dope on the distribution of your own product and proving that, by using exclusively the Curtis publications—their names escape me at the moment—you will not only reach all the public that you want to reach but will have enough people left over to give an amateur performance of "Pinafore."

I used to have a hand in making up these Parlin reports. My report on the gingham situation was perhaps considered my most successful, owing to the neat manner in which it was bound. It has been estimated that my gingham report retarded by ten years the entrance of the gingham manufacturers into national advertising.

Looking through an old trunk last week I came upon a report which I made for Mr. Parlin, but which was never used. I would like to read it to you tonight. It is a report on the woolen mitten situation in the United States and was intended to lead the way for a national campaign in the Curtis publications to reach mitten consumers all over the country.

In making this report I visited retail stores and jobbers selling mittens in 49 states, asking the following questions:

Of the retailers, I asked:

1) Does the average woman, in buying mittens, ask for them by brand or just ask for mittens?

2. Does she try on the mittens for size?

3. Is there any appreciable consumer demand for mittens during the summer? If so, what the hell for?

4. Is there any appreciable consumer demand for mittens during the winter?

5. Isn't it true that a mitten with a nationally advertised trade-name—like "Mitto" or "Paddies"—provided the Curtis publications were used exclusively—would sweep the field!

6. How many mitten buyers demand that the mittens be attached together with a string?

Of the jobbers, we asked the following questions:

1. How do you like jobbing?

2. Are you a college man?

3. Wouldn't you be happier doing something else?

4. Do you ever, by any chance, sell any mittens?

Out of the 4,846 jobbing establishments visited, only eight jobbers were found in. Jobbing establishments are always on such dark streets and there never seems to be anybody in the store. I finally got so that I would sit in my hotel and make up the jobbers' answers myself.

Now, as a result of this investigation, the Curtis Company was able to place the following facts at the disposal of the various mitten manufacturers. Each mitten manufacturer was blindfolded and taken into a darkened room where he was made to promise that he would never tell anyone the facts about his own business that he was about to be told. Then he was turned around and around until he was dizzy, and then hit over the head by the Curtis advertising director.

Following is the result of the mitten investigation:

1. In 49 states, it was found that 615,000 women do not buy mittens at all. At first, these statistics would seem to be confusing. But, on being analyzed, it is found that 82 percent of these 615,000 women live in towns of a population of 50,000 or over, which means that they can keep their hands in their pockets and do not need mittens. Here, then a consumer demand must be created.

2. From 5.6 percent to 95 percent of the department store sales of men's mittens are made to women. This just shows what we are coming to.

3. In the New England states, one woman in ten buys ready-to-wear mittens instead of piece goods from which to make her own mittens.

4. In the Middle West, one woman in eleven buys mitten piece-goods. This extra woman is accounted for by the fact that an aunt of mine went to live in Wisconsin last year.

In the South, they had never heard of mittens. At one place in Alabama we were told that they had drowned the last batch they had, thinking the inquiry had been for "kittens." This gave us an idea, and we made a supplementary report on kitten distribution. In this investigation it was found:

A. That there is no general consumer knowledge of breeds of kittens. In other words, a kitten is a kitten and that's all.

B. Four out of five kittens never do anything worthwhile in the world;

C. The market for kittens is practically negligible. In some states there are no dealers at all, and hardly any jobbers.

D. A solution of the kitten dealer-problem might lie in the introduction of dealer helps. In other words, improve the package so that the dealer can play it up. Give him a kitten he will be proud to display.

But to return to our mittens:

We have shown that a nationally advertised brand of mittens *if* given the proper distribution and *if* adapted to the particular consumer demand in the different localities ought to dominate the field.

We now come to the problem of the proper medium for such a campaign. In the chart on the opposite page we have a pyramid representing the Curtis circulation. Eleven million people, of whom 25,000 are able to lift the paper high enough to read it.

In this shaded section here is where the country club is going to be. This is all made land … We come down here to a circle showing consumer demand 49 percent … Curtis quota 48 percent and here is the state of Kansas, which was admitted as a free state in 1856.

To continue: in 1902, the year of the war, there were 160,000 of these sold in Michigan alone. Bring this down to present day values, with time and a half for overtime, and you will see what I mean. Of these, 50,000 were white, 4,600 were practically white and 4,000 were the same as those in Class A—white.

We have now pretty well lined up the channels of distribution for mittens and have seen that there is only one practical method for reaching the mitten consumer, namely 52 pages a year in the *Post*, and 12 pages in color in the *Journal* and *Country Gentleman*. There will be no duplication here as the readers of the *Country Gentleman* go to bed so early.

In addition to the benefit derived from all this, the mitten manufacturers will be shown all over the Curtis building in Philadelphia and allowed to peek into Mr. Lorimer's office. And, if they don't like this plan for marketing their product, they can lump it, because it's all they are going to get.

This report was the start of the big campaign which put the Frivolity Mitten Co. where it is today. And, for submitting it, I was fired. That is why I was especially glad to be able to read it to you tonight and why I wish that Mr. William Boyd could have been here, too.

(1926)

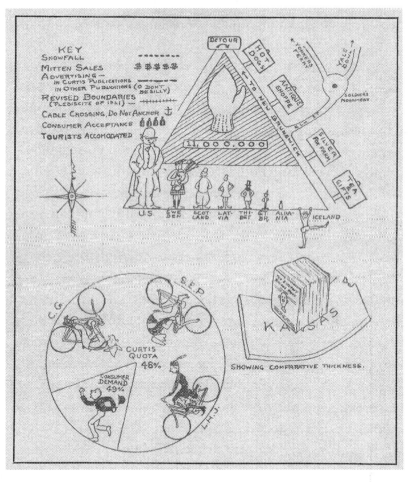

(1926)

Appendix I
Biographical Sketches of Round Table Members

FRANKLIN P. ADAMS (1881-1960) was the dean of the Round Table and the oldest member when it launched in 1919. His nickname—F.P.A.—was known in every household in New York for more than thirty years because of his popular newspaper column "The Conning Tower." Adams discovered and published scores of fledgling writers when they were virtual unknowns, among them George S. Kaufman, James Thurber, Edna St. Vincent Millay and E. B. White. "He raised me from a couplet," proclaimed another frequent contributor, Dorothy Parker. When his newspaper career wound down, F.P.A. was among the first radio stars, appearing as a panelist on "Information Please," an early quiz show. In his lifetime, Adams published more than 20 books. Today every one of them is out of print.

ROBERT BENCHLEY (1889-1945) was a quivering mass of contradictions. Perhaps the most interesting of the discrepancies was the vast chasm between the public's perception of him as an idler who could barely be bribed to turn out any work and the reality of his productivity. To be fair, he cultivated the misperception. He crafted an image of himself as a *flâneur*, an idler allergic to actual work. In numerous stories, he built an image of a professional postponer (the irony, of course, being that he actually finished those stories). In fact, his "Theory of Work" stated that "anybody can do any amount of work, provided it isn't the work he is supposed to be doing at that moment."

Still, he wrote and/or acted in 48 short films and 38 features between 1928 and 1945, winning an Academy Award for "How To Sleep;" starred on his own radio show for three years (1938-1940) with Artie Shaw as his bandleader; was a frequent guest artist on other radio shows, such as "Amos 'n' Andy" and "The Fred Allen Show" and recorded a classic version (Thurber's avowed favorite) of James Thurber's "The Secret Life of Walter Mitty;" in the late Nineteen Thirties was writing three syndicated magazine columns simultaneously, while making films; published 73 "Wayward Press" (criticism) columns for *The New Yorker* under the pseudonym "Guy Fawkes," 1927-1939; from 1920-1929 was the weekly drama critic for *Life* magazine; was the regular drama critic for *The New Yorker* from 1929-1940; published 12 books of short stories in 21 years (three more were published posthumously); published more than 600 stories in various magazines (and had several hundred others which were not published until long after his death).

HEYWOOD BROUN (1888–1939) was an icon among newspapermen and the general public alike. A true iconoclast, Broun was fiercely liberal and fought for the underdog, the disenfranchised and the common man for more than 25 years in New York's busiest newspaper cityrooms. Born in Brooklyn Heights, Broun was an easygoing raconteur who could spend an afternoon at the Polo Grounds playing checkers with Christy Mathewson and then review an Ethel Barrymore drama a few hours later. He founded the American Newspaper Guild and was its first president, and was a tireless labor organizer. Broun's column "It Seems To Me" was a standout in the *Tribune* and later the *World*, and he was famously fired by publisher Ralph Pulitzer for fighting with management. Perhaps his greatest accomplishment was his long marriage to another rebel, Ruth Hale. When Broun died in 1939, more than 3,000 jammed St. Patrick's Cathedral to say good-bye.

MARC CONNELLY (1890-1980) was the quiet at the center of the noisy Round Table. Taciturn by nature, of sparkling personality, he burned brightly early on and survived all the other members to prolong the legend well into the latter half of the 20th Century. In the Twenties, with George S. Kaufman, he wrote "Dulcy," "To the Ladies," "Merton of the Movies" and "Beggar on Horseback." He won a Pulitzer Prize in 1930 for "The Green Pastures," an imagining of the Negro version of heaven. In the Fifties he spent time as an actor in films and stage productions. His autobiography, "Voices Offstage," was published in 1968. His lack of driving ambition provoked Kaufman to proclaim once (upon hearing that a new story by Charles Dickens had just been discovered and published) "Dickens, dead, writes more than Connelly, alive."

EDNA FERBER (1887–1968) had to be the hardest-working member of the Round Table, and arguably the most successful. She liked to say that she only dropped into the Algonquin on Saturdays for lunch, because the rest of the week she was tied to her typewriter on the Upper West Side. She wrote 12 novels, eight plays, and more than 100 short stories. Ferber's 1924 novel "Showboat" was the basis for the first great American musical comedy. With George S. Kaufman she collaborated on numerous hit plays, such as "Minick," "The Royal Family" and "Dinner At Eight." She was among the highest-paid short story writers in the nation. Ferber's greatest accomplishment was "So Big" (1924), a novel that celebrated life in rural Illinois. Among the classic movies based on her books is "Giant" (1955), James Dean's last film.

RUTH HALE (1887–1934) has fallen into the deep cracks of history, but in 1922 most New Yorkers recognized her name in headlines as the preeminent combatant in the fight for equal rights for women. Hale was a Tennessee native who came to New York and worked as a Broadway press agent, book critic on the Brooklyn *Eagle* and freelance writer for major magazines. Hale tirelessly campaigned to pass the Nineteenth Amendment giving women the right to vote and fought to use her maiden name professionally. With Jane Grant, she co-founded the Lucy Stone League, a forerunner of the women's rights movement. Hale married Heywood Broun in 1917; their son, Heywood Hale Broun, was a popular sportscaster, actor and writer.

GEORGE S. KAUFMAN (1889-1961) was all throughout American entertainment for much of the 20th Century. He was a playwright, director, drama critic and producer. He wrote plays with Marc Connelly, Ring Lardner, Edna Ferber, John P. Marquand, Howard Teichmann and (most successfully) Moss Hart. With various collaborators, he wrote stage musicals for The Marx Brothers and others, and his writing (what has been called "intelligent nonsense"), combined with Groucho's improvisation provided many of American comedy's most memorable moments. He won two Pulitzer Prizes for Drama ("Of Thee I Sing" [the first ever awarded to a musical] and "You Can't Take It With You") and a Tony Award for directing ("Guys And Dolls"). Despite his prediction that he would not be well treated by posterity, his plays continue to enjoy successful revivals. A more complete listing of his accomplishments and plaudits can be found at www.georgeskaufman. com.

MARGARET LEECH (1894–1974) hit Manhattan straight out of Vassar and quickly found her niche as a writer of piercing and insightful urban stories. It was among the Vicious Circle that her writing career took off. Leech (nicknamed by Marc Connelly "Peaches and Cream") turned out three successful novels, including "Tin Wedding" and "The Back of the Book," before she switched to non-fiction for the remainder of her career. Leech collaborated with Heywood Broun on a searing biography of the notorious anti-vice crusader, Anthony Comstock, that is still read today. In her late thirties Leech took up deep historical research about presidents Lincoln and McKinley. After years of hard work she won two Pulitzer Prizes in history: "Reveille in Washington" (1942) and "In the Days of McKinley" (1960). Leech was the first historian to accomplish this feat.

DOROTHY PARKER (1893–1967) may be the poster child for the Algonquin Round Table, but it was notoriety that in later life she came to detest. Parker's public persona as a witty jokester and pun-loving party girl belied her more serious side. For someone who never made it through high school, Parker ran with fast company: Hemingway, Fitzgerald, Ring Lardner and Elinor Wylie. She could write in any genre: light verse, short fiction, literary criticism, screenplays and playwriting. The one thing to elude Parker was completing a novel. Parker helped give *The New Yorker* its identity from its debut issue in 1925 and was associated with the magazine for more than 30 years. In her thirties Parker became deeply political and gave more time to left-wing causes than to deadlines; she ended up on J. Edgar Hoover's watchlist, with an FBI file that's three inches thick. In 1999 the Dorothy Parker Society was founded. In 2005 it got her birthplace in Long Branch, New Jersey, named a national literary landmark by the Friends of Libraries USA, with a nice bronze plaque to mark the spot where Parker entered the world. Her official web site is www.dorothyparker.com.

ROBERT E. SHERWOOD (1896–1955) collected more accolades and awards than any other member of the Vicious Circle. Immediately after World War I, where he saw combat as a soldier fighting with the Commonwealth forces, Sherwood landed a job at *Vanity Fair*, working in a legendary triumvirate with Robert Benchley and Dorothy Parker. Sherwood followed this with a stint at the humorous weekly *Life*, where he was one of America's first motion picture critics. But it was the stage that was Sherwood's true passion. A supremely gifted storyteller, Sherwood had a knack for realistic dialogue and creative scenarios. He had boundless energy for creating plays and won three Pulitzer Prizes for his Broadway hits: "Idiot's Delight" (1936), "Abe Lincoln in Illinois" (1939) and "There Shall Be No Night" (1941). During World War II he wrote speeches for President Roosevelt, which led to his fourth Pulitzer for his biography "Roosevelt and Hopkins" (1949). Sherwood went to Hollywood and was a success there, too. He was nominated for an Academy Award for writing "Rebecca" in 1940 and won for "The Best Years of Our Lives" in 1946.

LAURENCE STALLINGS (1895–1968) was a Wake Forest graduate who participated in heavy combat in World War I. The experience provided him with a lifetime of material to inspire him to write about war, peace and human conflicts. He never strayed too far from the themes of freedom and liberty, even when writing satirical pieces about the military. Stallings did not join the Round Table until 1922, the same year he came to New York for a job on the *World*. In 1924 Stallings was tapped to be on the "Op. Ed" page with F.P.A., Woollcott and Broun. He shared an office with Maxwell Anderson, at the time a fellow editorial writer. The pair collaborated on an anti-war play, "What Price Glory?" for the powerful Broadway producer Arthur Hopkins. It was a smash hit. Edna Ferber's "So Big" beat Stallings' battlefield novel "Plumes" for the Pulitzer Prize in 1924. His novel was adapted for the silent movie epic "The Big Parade" that same year and was among the first blockbusters in the pre-talking pictures era. Stallings went to Hollywood and worked as a screenwriter for almost thirty years. Stallings lived to be 73 and see his beloved Marines go to Vietnam. He was buried with full military honors at Fort Rosecrans National Cemetery in San Diego.

DONALD OGDEN STEWART (1894–1980) is virtually forgotten today, but in the 1930s and 1940s he was a popular screenwriter and master of light humor. A Princeton graduate from Ohio, Stewart arrived in New York at the peak of the era of Wonderful Nonsense. He was closest to Robert Benchley, so close that Benchley broke his leg at Stewart's wedding. Early in his career Stewart wrote numerous parodies and satirical sketches for *Life, Vanity Fair* and *The New Yorker*. He joined the flock that went to Hollywood in the Thirties for the easy money the studios provided. He adapted his friend Philip Barry's play "The Philadelphia Story" as a movie for Katharine Hepburn, Cary Grant and Jimmy Stewart in 1940 and won his only Academy Award. This was the pinnacle of his career, and the beginning of a 40-year downward slide. He was active in Communist Party and left-wing activities, and the State Department and FBI were monitoring his activities. In 1951 he went to London at the height of the Red Scare. Stewart never returned to the United States.

FRANK SULLIVAN (1893-1976) had the lightest touch of any newspaper writer working in New York. The Saratoga native famously got into humor writing when he erroneously reported that a prominent socialite had passed away; when she proved to be very much alive, his editor took him off the news beat. Sullivan substituted for F.P.A. on the *World*, and wrote humor pieces for *Life* during the 20s. It was on the *World* that he began a tradition of writing a humorous roundup of newsmakers each December; when the *World* was sold, Harold Ross hired him. Sullivan wrote *The New Yorker's* Christmas greeting from 1932 to 1974.

DEEMS TAYLOR (1886–1966) is only remembered for one thing in American popular culture: his star turn with Mickey Mouse as the Narrator in "Fantasia." It was a different story in the Twenties, when he was a popular musical composer of light opera. Taylor was a New

York University graduate infatuated with classical music in an era when jazz was the rage. Taylor eked out a living as a composer, and turned to music criticism as a way to pay the bills. On the *World* he excelled as a reviewer, and this led to him getting work as a radio commentator on CBS. His national radio popularity helped him become the most famous composer of the 30s and 40s. Taylor wrote the libretto for "The King's Henchmen" with Edna St. Vincent Millay in 1925; it was called the first American opera written by an American. Taylor was an early president of the American Society of Composers, Authors and Publishers [ASCAP]; for the past 40-plus years the Deems Taylor Award has been the organization's highest honor.

JOHN V. A. WEAVER (1893–1938) burned brightly for 15 years as the "slang poet" who wrote "in American" as a free-verse pioneer. He also proved an axiom: If a writer goes out of print and is not taught in schools, he will be quickly forgotten. Weaver was a sullen, moody, cantankerous 26-year-old when he moved to New York and joined the Round Table as a friend of Alexander Woollcott. He became the literary editor of the Brooklyn *Daily Eagle*; he wooed and married Peggy Wood, also a member of the Vicious Circle. Weaver contributed poems to *The Smart Set, Life, Harper's* and many other literary magazines. His first book, "In American" (1921), was a bestseller, going through seven printings in its first year, a huge accomplishment for a collection of poetry. Weaver's other books of verse were "Finders" (1923), "More In American" (1926), "To Youth" (1927), "Turning Point" (1930) and "Trial Balance" (1931). He wrote about soda fountain workers, department store clerks, unhappy girlfriends and truck drivers. Weaver had an uncanny ear for dialogue, and it is this vivid writing style that makes him unlike others. Weaver went to Hollywood in the Thirties, but just like for so many others of the time, it was deeply unfulfilling to him. His career was cut short by tuberculosis at age 44.

ALEXANDER WOOLLCOTT (1887–1943) was among the most powerful dramatic critics in New York from World War I up through the Great Depression. Writing for the *Times* and later the *World*, Woollcott curried favor with the big stars of the day and was as much a celebrity on Broadway as the actors. His column "Second Thoughts on First Nights" was a must-read. Woollcott was among the handful of New York soldier-journalists in Paris during the war, and it was his welcome-home party that was the impetus to get the Round Table started at the Algonquin Hotel. The Marx Brothers owed him a huge debt for discovering them early in their career. Woollcott was an early and popular contributor to *The New Yorker*; he created the "Shouts and Murmurs" column. Woollcott's style translated perfectly to the airwaves; he pioneered talk radio in the Thirties on CBS. Somewhere on an American stage in the 21st Century the spirit of Woollcott lives on: He was the model for the character of Sheridan Whiteside in Kaufman and Hart's "The Man Who Came to Dinner."

Other Members of the Algonquin Round Table
Not Featured in This Collection

MARGALO GILLMORE (1897–1986): This beautiful A-List Broadway actress was nicknamed "the baby of the Round Table." She starred in early Eugene O'Neill plays.

JANE GRANT (1892–1972): The first female reporter in the *New York Times* city room. Grant co-founded *The New Yorker* with her first husband, Harold W. Ross. She was a staunch feminist.

BEATRICE BAKROW KAUFMAN (1894–1945): Editor, writer and socialite. In 1917 she married George S. Kaufman and was instrumental in his success.

NEYSA McMEIN (1888–1949): At one time McMein was the highest-paid and most popular magazine cover artist in the industry. Her West 57th Street studio functioned as a salon for the Vicious Circle.

HERMAN J. MANKIEWICZ (1897–1953): He went from press agent to the *New York Times*, and was among the first writers on *The New Yorker*. He co-wrote plays with George S. Kaufman and produced

Marx Brothers movies. Mankiewicz earned eternal glory by co-writing "Citizen Kane," for which he won his only Academy Award.

HARPO MARX (1888–1964): Actor, comedian, musician and card player. His shtick was that he was the silent one, but that was only an act.

WILLIAM B. MURRAY (1890-1949): *Brooklyn Eagle* writer who left to become a publicist and talent agent. He was a big name on the business side of entertainment, ran the William Morris Agency and was a pioneer in radio sponsorships.

BROCK PEMBERTON (1885–1950): Broadway producer and director. Founded the Tony Awards.

MURDOCK PEMBERTON (1888–1982): Broadway press agent, first art critic for *The New Yorker*.

HAROLD W. ROSS (1892–1951): Founded *The New Yorker* with his first wife, Jane Grant, and members of the Round Table. He ran the magazine from 1925 until his death.

ARTHUR SAMUELS (1889–1938): Editor of *Harper's Bazaar* and popular songwriter.

JOHN PETER TOOHEY (1880–1946): Theater press agent for "Dinner at Eight," "You Can't Take It with You," "Of Mice and Men," "The Man Who Came to Dinner." Credited with coming up with the name for *The New Yorker* for Harold Ross.

DAVID H. WALLACE (1889–1955): Theatrical press agent who got into theater publicity during Broadway's Golden Age. On his personal client list were John Barrymore, Ethel Barrymore and Laurette Taylor.

PEGGY WOOD (1892–1978): Glamorous Brooklyn-born actress in musical comedies, plays, early TV star. In 1965 she was nominated for an Academy Award for co-starring in "The Sound of Music." Her first husband was John V. A. Weaver.

Appendix 2
A Note on the Text and the Writers
By Kevin C. Fitzpatrick

Since the pieces in this collection are derived from a wide variety of sources spread out over many years, there will necessarily be different styles of punctuation, spelling and grammar. The editors have left the original pieces as they were printed.

In a writing career that spanned 40 years, **Franklin P. Adams** generated more than one million words for newspapers and magazines. With his daily columns and frequent magazine pieces, Adams went about the business of writing with workmanlike zeal. Except for an annual summer break, he wrote year-round from 1900 until after World War II. The pieces chosen for this collection are almost all from his "Conning Tower" column. Adams, a master of light verse, frequently drew on the classics for inspiration. He was never a hearty practitioner of free verse. These poems all have three things in common: he wrote about his friends, interests (tennis and poker) and daily routine. The longest piece of Adams' in this book, "Women I'm Not Married To," was written in response to Dorothy Parker's side of the story and published in the *Saturday Evening Post*. His weekly "The Diary of Our Own Samuel Pepys" is a goldmine for literary history sleuths.

In his lengthy writing career, **Robert Benchley** always managed to maintain the same light, humorous tone in anything he touched, whether it was theater criticism, satirical essays or radio scripts. The pieces in this collection are rare gems that showcase Benchley's trademark whimsicality. "Chaplin and Shakespeare, Eccentric Comedians" appeared in the New York *Tribune*, on January 21, 1917. However, the majority appeared in *Life*—a humor weekly around from 1883-1936—before Henry Luce bought the name and turned it into a picture magazine. When Benchley and many other Round Table members were *Life* contributors, it was the go-to publication of choice in the era before *The New Yorker* debuted. Benchley was the drama critic when Robert E. Sherwood was an editor. Later Benchley took his talents to radio broadcasts and movie studio back lots. After he attained great success and big paydays as a performer, his writing output dried up. There are a dozen fine collections of Benchley's best pieces that are haunting a used bookstore near you today.

Heywood Broun was a writing machine. He could pound out his column "It Seems To Me" in twenty minutes, whether at his desk or from bed. Broun joined the newspaper world straight out of Harvard (a credit short), in an era when reporters wore straw hats and suits on assignments. As a sportswriter he learned deadline writing, which he took with him to his position as a critic. The pieces in this book all come from his work on the *Tribune* and the *World*. Over time "It Seems To Me" matured from genial human nature studies to serious political analysis, but with a light touch. New York City Mayor Fiorello LaGuardia said, "No one during Heywood Broun's career ever questioned his sincerity or for a moment doubted that he wasn't speaking right from the heart." Although Broun's books are all out of print, his name lives on: the Newspaper Guild sponsors the annual Heywood Broun Award. It recognizes individual journalistic achievement by members of the working print media, particularly if it helps right a wrong or correct an injustice.

It was an easy transition for **Marc Connelly** to make from newspaper reporter to playwright: He just took what he learned as a journalist and applied it to the stage. The pieces in this collection are not from any of his hit plays—these are the articles and poems he wrote between the shows. He sold "A Little Later" to *Life*, as well as the parody "Calendar" that he and George S. Kaufman contributed. Perhaps they dreamed up these monthly doses of bad puns and topical jokes at the same time they were creating their next Broadway hit. In later years Connelly contributed pieces to *The New Yorker* in the same vein of light humor and satire.

Edna Ferber wrote so many short stories—more than 100—that they are collected in a dozen books. She also wrote 12 novels, scores of essays and several plays. This was all after she'd spent several years as a newspaper reporter and correspondent. The story in this collection, "Old Man Minick," appeared in *Woman's Home Companion* in the summer of 1922. The story has themes and devices common to many Ferber plots: a setting in Chicago, a widow coping alone, family squabbles and disarray, combined with a pessimistic outlook on life. Ferber said she was shocked that George S. Kaufman wanted to adapt "Minick" into a three-act play. Soon after she wrote this story, Ferber went back to Chicago for a long, hot summer while she worked on the book that would win her the Pulitzer Prize, "So Big." Although many of Ferber's novels are forgotten today, her legacy lives on each time "Showboat" and "Giant" are broadcast on television.

It can be said that **Ruth Hale** sacrificed her talents for her beliefs. She was a promising newspaper reporter, editor and critic when she overloaded herself with political causes and ceaseless work as a radical feminist partisan. Hale could write concise and thoughtful literary reviews and then change gears and compose bewildering essays on childrearing. Hale had to live in the large shadow cast by her husband, Heywood Broun, but the pair worked as a team. She may have ghostwritten some of his columns, which is ironic in that she spent so much of her time fighting the label "Mrs. Heywood Broun" and yet ultimately ended up writing *as* Heywood Broun. Their only child, Heywood Hale Broun, wrote the only account of her life and times in "Whose Little Boy Are You?"

James Thurber called **George S. Kaufman**, "The man who was comedy." Kaufman collaborated on more than 40 plays, half of them hits. For this collection, one of his essays for *The Saturday Review of Literature* dispels the myth of the Vicious Circle. His profile of Al Jolson caught the star at the cusp of superstardom and was written for the monthly *Everybodys Magazine*. Kaufman's reputation continues into the 21st Century as one of the most beloved comedic playwrights of the last

100 years. On a stage somewhere in America tonight, a George S. Kaufman show is being produced.

Harper's Magazine was once a prestigious short fiction publisher, and **Margaret Leech** found fame in its pages in October 1928 with her short story "Manicure." The beauty salon vignette was a sensation and included in "The Best Short Stories of 1929 and the Yearbook of the American Short Story." It was a finalist for the 1929 O. Henry Award (Leech was beaten by Dorothy Parker's "Big Blonde" for top honors). Leech did not have a great output of short fiction, concentrating instead on novels. She was a part-time journalist and wrote profiles for *The New Yorker* (all of them on women), before diving into non-fiction and serious historical research. Although the two books for which she won the Pulitzer Prize for History are easily available, none of her other work has ever been collected.

Dorothy Parker never thought highly of her talents as a writer, but she is the one Round Table member who has kept a book in print for 65 years. "The Portable Dorothy Parker" is a classic, but none of the pieces in this collection are in it. For Parker, the salad days of the twenties saw her writing for many popular magazines. For five straight years she wrote light verse and drama reviews on a weekly basis. "The New York Type" was written for *McCall's*; her groundbreaking review of Jewish Broadway star Jacob Ben-Ami for *Ainslee's*; "Men I'm Not Married To" for the *Saturday Evening Post*; and the verses for *Vanity Fair* and *Life*. In the last 10 years, Parker's short fiction, poems and essays have been collected in new editions. Almost 45 years after her death, Parker has more of her work in print today than when she was alive.

Today the name **Robert E. Sherwood** conjures up an esteemed author-playwright who wrote groundbreaking and memorable plays between the two world wars. However, this collection celebrates the life of someone who enjoyed silent movies, biting satire and poking fun at the world. Before he found fame in the theater, Sherwood was a wage slave at *Vanity Fair* and *Life*, which is where these pieces originated. He may have earned the Pulitzer Prize four times, but as a younger man,

Sherwood had a snappy writing style that bridged the gap between high art and low comedy. More than 50 years after his death, Sherwood's plays are still performed.

Laurence Stallings was a top magazine writer, newspaper columnist, playwright, screenwriter and author. His autobiographical debut novel "Plumes" went through 10 printings in one year. His Marine Corps experience never left him, and Stallings frequently wrote about patriotism, sacrifice and American policy. His *Saturday Evening Post* story "Turn Out the Guard" was typical Stallings: snappy military jargon, realistic scenarios, and an undercurrent of black humor. "Celluloid Psychology" was written for the *New Republic* when movies were still silent. Stallings wrote hundreds of columns that have never been unearthed. In 2006, "Plumes" was brought back into print, 82 years after it first came out.

It was **Donald Ogden Stewart's** early success at writing parodies that got him work at *Vanity Fair* and the other "smart" magazines in the twenties. Stewart wrote a series for *The Bookman*—in which "The Courtship of Myles Standish in the Manner of F. Scott Fitzgerald" appeared—that mocked icons such as Sinclair Lewis, Ring Lardner, Edith Wharton and Eugene O'Neill. Stewart's style can be called "crazy humor" for the wild non-sequiturs and nonsense subject matter— and it became a trap he fell into. In the Thirties, his style of comedy ceased to be popular. Just before World War II he became so politically active that G-men were watching his house, and Stewart's star fell from the sky. Stewarts's humor books have not been available since FDR was in the White House.

Frank Sullivan was beloved by his Round Table friends for his warmth and good humor, but also for his sharp wit and intelligence. Sullivan truly was a giant among giants. However, he took one big step that none of the others could ever bear to do: he quit on Manhattan when Manhattan quit on him. He was so shaken by the closing of his beloved New York *World* that he returned home to Saratoga Springs and the easy pace of the freelancer. It may have helped prolong his life, as he lived until 1976. The pieces in this collection are ones that Sullivan sold to *Life* and never collected again (or never gave to *The New Yorker*). His half-dozen books and a collection of his letters are no longer in print, but are well worth tracking down.

At one time **Deems Taylor** was so famous that his image was used in magazine advertisements as a high society pitchman. In the Twenties and Thirties when Taylor was not scoring music, he was writing about it. The *World* gave Taylor a platform to talk about American music and its place in culture. His newspaper and magazine articles—serious think pieces on symphonies, conductors and the business of music—were among the first in the genre to be written by a composer. His lone article in this collection, written after Taylor had attended the first public performance of "Rhapsody in Blue," is from the *World*. In 2003 James A. Pegolotti wrote a marvelous biography of Taylor; four years later Pegolotti published a fine collection of Taylor's light verse and criticism, plus selections from his books and radio scripts.

The unique talent of **John V. A. Weaver** was trumpeted by H. L. Mencken, who not only discovered Weaver, but also wrote a tribute to the poet after his tragic death. For a period that stretched into the Great Depression, Weaver was widely popular with the public. The earthy pieces in this book are from the *Smart Set* and *Harper's Magazine*; he wrote "Bootleg" for the collection "Nonsensorship" in 1922. After Weaver's death in 1938, his widow, Peggy Wood, followed "When I'm Through" to the letter: She quietly dispersed his ashes in four locations. Then she called the newspapers.

Harpo Marx compared **Alexander Woollcott** to a balloon in the Macy's Thanksgiving Day Parade. However—just like one of those giant creations—Woollcott was forgotten as soon as the life went out of him. His writing was so ephemeral that to read it today is like trying to hold on to wisps of smoke. Woollcott was one of the most powerful critics ever to cover Broadway (the brothers Shubert attempted to bar him from their theaters), he was chummy with stars and producers and he invented party guest journalism as "Shouts & Murmurs" in *The New*

Yorker. The ultimate gadfly, Woollcott cherished spending the night at the White House as the pet of the Roosevelts. The review pieces collected here are from his *Times* column "Second Thoughts on First Nights." Woollcott has been the subject of three biographies, but he went out of print within a year of his death.

For more information about the writers in this book, visit algonquinroundtable.org.

Appendix 3
For Further Reading

Franklin P. Adams, *The Diary of Our Own Samuel Pepys, 1911-1934* (New York: Simon & Schuster, 1935).

Franklin P. Adams, *The Melancholy Lute* (New York: Viking Press, 1936).

Franklin P. Adams, *Nods and Becks* (New York: McGraw-Hill, 1944).

Sally Ashley, *FPA: The Life and Times of Franklin Pierce Adams* (New York: Beaufort Books, 1986).

Nathaniel Benchley, ed., *The Benchley Roundup* (New York: Harper & Brothers, 1954).

Nathaniel Benchley, *Robert Benchley: A Biography* (New York: McGraw-Hill, 1955).

Robert Benchley, *My Ten Years in a Quandary and How They Grew* (New York: Harper & Brothers, 1936).

Robert Benchley, *Chips Off the Old Benchley* (New York: Harper & Brothers, 1949).

Heywood Broun, *Seeing Things At Night* (New York: Harcourt, Brace and Company, 1921).

Heywood Broun, *Pieces of Hate* (New York: George H. Doran Company, 1922).

Heywood Broun, *Sitting on the World* (New York: G.P. Putnam's Sons, 1924).

Joseph Bryan III, *Merry Gentlemen (and one Lady)* (New York: Atheneum, 1985).

Frank Case, *Tales of a Wayward Inn* (New York: Frederick A. Stokes Company, 1938).

Marc Connelly, *Voices Offstage* (New York: Holt, Rinehart and Winston, 1968).

Honoria Murphy Donnelly with Richard N. Billings, *Sara & Gerald: Villa America and After* (New York: Holt, Rinehart and Winston, 1982).

Ann Douglas, *Terrible Honesty: Mongrel Manhattan in the 1920s* (New York: Farrar, Straus and Giroux, 1996).

Robert E. Drennan, *The Algonquin Wits* (Secaucus, NJ: Citadel Press, 1968, 1985).

Gordon E. Ernst, *Robert Benchley: An Annotated Bibliography* (Westport, CT: Greenwood Press, 1995).

Edna Ferber, *So Big* (New York: Doubleday & Company, 1924; Perennial Classics, 2000).

Edna Ferber, *A Peculiar Treasure* (New York: Doubleday & Company, 1938, 1960).

Kevin C. Fitzpatrick, *A Journey into Dorothy Parker's New York* (Berkeley, CA: Roaring Forties Press, 2005).

Corey Ford, *The Time of Laughter* (New York: Little Brown, 1967).

James R. Gaines, *Wit's End: Days and Nights of the Algonquin Round Table* (New York: Harcourt, 1977).

Brian Gallagher, *Anything Goes: The Jazz Age Adventures of Neysa McMein and Her Extravagant Circle of Friends* (New York: Random House, 1987).

Charles Getchell, ed., *Benchley at the Theatre: Dramatic Criticism 1920-1940* (Ipswich, MA: Ipswich Press, 1985).

Jane Grant, *Ross, The New Yorker, and Me* (New York: Reynal, 1968).

Margaret Case Harriman, *The Vicious Circle* (New York: Rinehart, 1951).

S. L. Harrison, ed., *Robert Benchley's Wayward Press* (Miami: Wolf Den Books, 2008).

Beatrice Kaufman and Joseph Hennessey, eds., *The Letters of Alexander Woollcott* (New York: Viking Press, 1944).

Marilyn Kaytor, *"21": The Life and Times of New York's Favorite Club* (New York: Viking Adult, 1975).

Dale Kramer, *Heywood Broun* (New York: Current Books, 1949).

Thomas Kunkel, *Genius In Disguise: Harold Ross of The New Yorker* (New York: Random House, 1995).

Marion Meade, *Bobbed Hair and Bathtub Gin: Writers Running Wild in the Twenties* (New York: Nan A. Talese, 2004).

Marion Meade, *Dorothy Parker: What Fresh Hell Is This?* (New York: Villard, 1988)

Dorothy Parker, *Complete Stories* (New York: Penguin Books, 2005).

Dorothy Parker, *The Portable Dorothy Parker* (New York: Penguin Classics, 1944, 1973, 2006).

James A. Pegolotti, *Deems Taylor: A Biography* (Boston: Northeastern University Press, 2003).

George P. Putnam, ed., *Nonsensorship: Sundry Observations Concerning Prohibitions, Inhibitions and Illegalities* (New York: G. P. Putnam's Sons, 1922).

David Remnick, ed., *The Complete New Yorker* (New York: Random House, 2005).

Stuart Y. Silverstein, ed., *Not Much Fun: The Lost Poems of Dorothy Parker* (New York: Scribner, 1996).

Laurence Stallings, *Plumes* (New York: Harcourt, Brace and Company, 1924).

Donald Ogden Stewart, *By A Stroke Of Luck! An Autobiography* (London: Paddington Press, 1975).

Frank Sullivan, *A Pearl in Every Oyster* (New York: Little, Brown & Company, 1962).

Howard Teichmann, *George S. Kaufman: An Intimate Portrait* (New York: Atheneum, 1972).

Howard Teichmann, *Smart Aleck: The Wit, World and Life of Alexander Woollcott* (New York: William Morrow, 1976).

James Thurber, *The Years With Ross* (New York: Little, Brown, 1959).

Calvin Tompkins, *Living Well Is the Best Revenge* (New York: E. P. Dutton, 1982).

Amanda Vaill, *Everybody Was So Young: Gerald and Sara Murphy: A Lost Generation Love Story* (New York: Broadway Books, 1999).

John V. A. Weaver, *In American: The Collected Poems of John V. A. Weaver* (New York: Alfred A. Knopf, 1939).

E. B. White, *Here Is New York* (New York: Harper & Brothers, 1949; Little Bookroom, 1999).

Alexander Woollcott, *While Rome Burns* (New York: Grosset & Dunlap, 1934).

Ben Yagoda, *About Town: The New Yorker and the World It Made* (New York: Scribner, 2000).

Norris W. Yates, *Robert Benchley* (New York: Twayne Publishers, 1968).

SELECTED ARTICLES

Arnold W. Ehrlich, "The Algonquin at 75" (*The New York Times Sunday Magazine*, Oct. 16, 1977).

Christopher Hitchens, "Rebel in Evening Clothes" (*Vanity Fair*, October 1999).

Caryn James, "At Wit's End: Algonquinites in Hollywood" (*The New York Times*, Jan. 8, 1993).

Frederick Waterman, "The Raconteur Rats" (*Forbes*, FYI supplement, 1993).

For more books about the writers in this book, visit algonquinroundtable. org.

Appendix 4
Online Resources and Web Sites

Algonquin Round Table: algonquinroundtable.org
Robert Benchley Society: robertbenchley.org
Dorothy Parker Society: dorothyparker.com
George S. Kaufman: georgeskaufman.com
Edna Ferber: apl.org/history/Ferber/

Nat Benchley: natbenchley.com
Peter Benchley: peterbenchley.com

Algonquin Hotel: algonquinhotel.com
The New Yorker Between the Lines: Emdashes.com
Newyorkology: Newyorkology.com
The National Portrait Gallery: npg.si.edu/exh/caricatures/table.htm
New York Public Library: nypl.org
Gotlieb Archives at Boston University's Mugar Library:
bu.edu/archives
Internet Broadway Database: ibdb.com

About the Editors

NATHANIEL R. (Nat) BENCHLEY grew up in New York City under the aura of his recently-departed grandfather. His father, Nathaniel G. Benchley, was making a name for himself as a freelance writer. After college, Nat received a commission in the U.S. Navy and used his language skills to secure a billet with the Naval Security Group. For better or worse, this led to duty in Southeast Asia during the dust-up from 1969-1972. He returned to The World and worked as a producer/writer for a national drug abuse prevention campaign for a year. He followed this with four years at the Washington, D.C., public television station writing and producing program promotions and development. Since 1978, he has been a freelance actor and writer in New York, Los Angeles and Washington, DC. He has recorded two audio CDs of readings of his grandfather's short stories, aptly titled "Benchley on Benchley, Volumes 1 and 2." He works closely with the Howard Gotlieb Archives at the Mugar Memorial Library of Boston University to keep track of most Benchleyana. He lives in New York with his wife, Kathleen Peacock Benchley.

KEVIN C. FITZPATRICK was born in Baltimore in 1966 and raised in Bethlehem, Pennsylvania; Summit, New Jersey; Raleigh, North Carolina; and Webster Groves, Missouri. From 1984-1989 he served in the U.S. Marine Corps Reserve as a journalist-photographer, reaching the rank of lance corporal. He earned a B.A. from Northeast Missouri State University. In 1991 he moved to New York City. Fitzpatrick has worked for newspapers, magazines, TV networks, Web sites, ad agencies and publishing houses as a writer, editor and project manager. In 1998 Fitzpatrick launched dorothyparker.com and founded the Dorothy Parker Society. Today, the Society has more than 3,000 members worldwide. In 2005 Roaring Forties Press of Berkeley, California, published his first book, the literary travel guide *A Journey into Dorothy Parker's New York*. It will be followed by *The Algonquin Round Table's New York* in 2010. Fitzpatrick produces algonquinroundtable.org and leads literary walking tours of Manhattan. He and his wife, Christina Hensler Fitzpatrick, live on the Upper West Side and Shelter Island, New York.

About the Cover Artist

JACK ZIEGLER has had well over a thousand drawings published in *The New Yorker* magazine since 1974 and has published eight collections of his cartoons, the most recent of which are "How's the Squid?," "Olive or Twist?" and "You Had Me at Bow Wow." There's also a children's book, "Mr. Knocky," out there somewhere, plus a biographical compilation, "The Essential Jack Ziegler," written by his former editor at *The New Yorker*, Lee Lorenz. He and his wife reside in The United States of America.

Cover Design: Kevin C. Fitzpatrick
Back Cover Photo: Ruben Diaz